TRUE TO IRELAND

TRUE TO IRELAND

*Éire's 'conscientious objectors'
in New Zealand in World War II*

PETER BURKE

THE CUBA
PRESS

*To my mother, Mary Burke (née Warren), for carefully keeping so much
family history and memorabilia that made the writing of this book possible*

*and my father, Matt Burke, and his Irish friends,
who followed their consciences and were 'true to Ireland'.*

Cover design: Sarah Bolland.

A catalogue record for this book is available from
the National Library of New Zealand.

ISBN 978-0-9951107-8-6

Printed in Dublin by Digital Print Dynamics Ltd.

Images are from the author's collection unless otherwise credited.

THE CUBA PRESS
Box 9321 Wellington 6141, Aotearoa New Zealand
hello@thecubapress.nz

Contents

Acknowledgements

I would like to acknowledge the special contribution of Geraldene O'Reilly for the archival research; Fr Eamon Aylward for making available the Aylward collection and for peer review; Lynette Wharfe for editing the manuscript; Brad Patterson, Kathryn Patterson, Rory Sweetman and Peter Ryan for peer reviewing the manuscript; and all for their support throughout this project.

In particular I want to recognise:

Those in Ireland who have assisted: Eamon Ó Cuív, Tom Kenny, Walter McDonagh, Joe Loughrane, Marcus Thornton, Fr Neil Collins, Nessa Cronin, John Cunningham and Mary O'Shea.

Family members in Ireland: Geraldine and Mike O'Sullivan, Fidelma Burke, Marion O'Connor, Anne and Michael Kelly, Tim and Kathleen Griffin, Maria and Martin Barrett.

Families with connections to the Sons of Éire: John Knox, Pat Sheridan, Elizabeth Carr, Michael Carr, Josie Hogan, Kevin Bracken, Anne Furneaux (née Ongley) and Bernie Gardiner.

Those who have assisted with research: Archives New Zealand, Alexander Turnbull Library, Barry O'Kelly and Foynes Flying Boat and Maritime Museum, Galway Museum, National Archives of Ireland, Irish Bureau of Military History, David Grant, Peter Kuch, Jim McAloon, Jim Hartley and Max Lambert, Hugh Templeton, the *Press* of Christchurch, the *New Zealand Herald*, the *Evening Post*, Te Takaretanga o Kura-hau-pō (Levin Public Library), Louise McKenzie and Rosemary McLennan from St Patrick's College, Wellington.

Others who have contributed in numerous ways: Cathy Strong, Jenny Martin, Mary Kinnane, Deborah Burns, Lynley Goldsmith, Kevin Ikin, Mark Beatty, Denise Flanagan, Mary Galway, Archway Books, St Columbans Lower Hutt, Bronwyn Macfarlane, Paula Taylor, Colleen O'Donovan, Roger Steele, Jan Thomas, Tiziana Stoto, Dean Whiti and Shirley Hooper-Whiti.

And The Cuba Press for publishing this book.

Foreword

by Michael D. Higgins, President of Ireland

We Irish have, for long centuries, been a people formed by the experience of migration. Our culture was forged through the influence of successive waves of settlers, conquerors, and colonisers. Over the past three hundred years, generations of Irishmen and Irishwomen have left our island, fleeing famine, war, poverty and persecution, or simply seeking the opportunities denied to them at home. Some were banished, either for resisting oppression or for committing crimes of desperation.

Irish people first landed in New Zealand in the decades before the signing of the Treaty of Waitangi. They may have been escaped convicts fleeing the penal colonies across the Tasman Sea. For them, and for the tens of thousands of Irish people who followed, New Zealand would become a symbol of hope and opportunity, a great experiment in social progress in the southern oceans.

Those who left Ireland never forget their homeland, and the support and solidarity of the Irish abroad was to be vital in the great struggle for Irish national freedom. In the early decades of independence, the new Irish state and its people were sustained by the remittances of sons and daughters in foreign lands.

This year, we in Ireland and Irish people across the world are commemorating the commencement of our War of Independence and celebrating of the establishment of the legislative assembly of the revolutionary Irish republic, the First Dáil Éireann. All those who lived in Ireland during these foundational events could not but be caught up in the spirit of the age, or deeply affected by the great struggle underway in Ireland.

This volume, meticulously and lovingly researched and chronicled by Peter Burke, tells the story of six men – including his father Matt Burke – who lived through those years and who later emigrated to New Zealand in search of a better life. It is a tale of extraordinary moral courage demonstrated by Matt Burke and his comrades in following their principles during the Second World War. The very public stance that those Irishmen took was not popular, nor was it easy. Yet it was deeply admirable, and, as this wonderful book shows, understandable in light of the lives and ideals of those six Irishmen.

May I commend Peter Burke for not only recovering the memory of his father and his comrades, but for deepening our understanding of the shared history of Ireland and of New Zealand. Though we are separated by a vast distance, we are countries with a shared destiny, one founded on our common past and upon our commitment to the United Nations, to peace-keeping and to the great cause of world disarmament. The publication of *True to Ireland* will further our understanding of one another, and through that, expand our already deep and abiding friendship.

Michael D. Higgins
Uachtarán na hÉireann
President of Ireland

February 2019

Introduction

When Matthias Burke, commonly known as Matt, left Ireland just days before Christmas in 1929, little did he know that 12 years later he, along with many of his Irish-born friends, would find himself embroiled in a conflict on the other side of the world. His story is an important piece of New Zealand and Irish social history that until now hasn't been told, and which reflects the developing relationship between the two small but independent countries.

True to Ireland is about a battle of conscience by a group of Irishmen living in New Zealand, who opposed being conscripted into the armed forces during WWII. This stand was based on their citizenship of the Irish Free State, which was neutral during WWII, and because they had seen or experienced atrocities inflicted on their friends and relations during the Irish War of Independence, known as the Troubles. When called up they appealed as conscientious objectors, the only pathway available to them other than defaulting or leaving the country. The men declared they would fight for Ireland, if required, but could not in all conscience fight for New Zealand, and therefore Britain. They also said they would endure any hardship, including deportation or death, rather than fight for the Crown. And so began a long battle with the authorities while the Irishmen fought to be recognised as a 'special case'.

The men were in every sense of the words 'true to Ireland' – a phrase coined by Maurice Aylward, who was one of the leaders of the Éire National Association (ENA) that was formed to oppose conscription of Irishmen in New Zealand. Rather than requiring each of them to make their own appeal against conscription, the ENA arranged for six of their number to stand as a test case, with the outcome determining the fate of the other appellants. Matt Burke was one of the six, referred to in newspapers of the time as the 'Sons of Éire'.[1] There is a later list of 155 men, referred to as the 'Citizens of Éire', but it is believed that up to 500 Irishmen faced conscription into the New Zealand armed forces.

This story is deeply personal to me as Matt Burke was my father. I only found out about these events by chance in 2010 when going through my late mother's papers. Dad had died in October 1962 aged 53. My mother lived until

2005 to the ripe old age of 96, but she never told me about the treasure trove of information and photographs she had kept about my father. I remember hearing something about Dad refusing to fight for Britain, but this was never talked about. Imagine my surprise when I discovered an affidavit from some sort of court hearing, with his name on it. Upon further investigation the 'court' turned out to be the No.4 Armed Forces Appeal Board in Wellington.

In one sense this is a family history that hopefully will provide future generations with some insight into the lives of the Burke, Bohan, Milligan and Warren clans. It does contain what, as a journalist, I would regard as 'sidebars', or snippets of history, that will be of special interest to those families. However, what began as a family history, with the intention of telling the story about my rebellious father and a few of his Irish mates, developed into a broader study relevant to a wider audience in both New Zealand and Ireland. To understand what motivated these men and to show what helped form my father's strong views, I found myself examining the historical context of their lives in New Zealand and Ireland, in particular events in my father's village of Moycullen and around Galway.

There are many strands to this story and one that fascinated me was the friendship that grew between Éamon de Valera, Prime Minister of Ireland during WWII, and his New Zealand counterpart Prime Minister Peter Fraser, which I believe played a part in my father and his fellow Irishmen eventually winning their battle with the New Zealand authorities.

In writing this book I have reflected the strong republican views held by my father and his fellow Irishmen, so their voices are heard. They were unashamedly anti-British because of the way they and their families had been treated by various elements of the British armed forces in Ireland, but equally they loved New Zealand, which they saw as a haven from the Troubles in Ireland and a country that offered them a future they could never have had in their native Éire.

Matt Burke was a man I knew, but really didn't know. Since 2010 I have got to know more about him than when he was alive, partly because for so much of his life he was ill, suffering from a bad heart, and died when I was 16. As a young person I had little interest in learning about Ireland, but since my first visit in 1978 I have discovered the 'Irishness' in me, and I am now deeply proud of my strong links to my father's homeland and the extended family in Galway. Recently, I've been closely involved with Māori and have come to appreciate the richness of their culture and how they must have felt when they were dispossessed of their lands by the English, in much the same way as the Irish and Scots were. There are many cultural similarities and I now describe myself as 'Ngāti Irish', recognising the richness of the two languages and cultures that embrace me. I have made 12 trips to Ireland so far and will continue this love affair with the Emerald Isle until I breathe my last.

True to Ireland is the result of six years of detailed research, assisted by genealogist Geraldene O'Reilly and Fr Eamon Aylward, with one challenge being that all the key players are long dead. Even their sons and daughters are heading towards their seventies, so it has been difficult tracking down the histories of Dad's friends. Geraldene and I have gained access to as many government papers and files as possible, and talked to people of our generation who knew the six passionate Sons of Éire, who led the fight again Irish conscription in New Zealand. The Aylward collection and material supplied by many others has added to the richness of this narrative. I hope that over time others will want to delve deeper into the archives and build on what has been collected. To foster more research on this story and other aspects of the Irish diaspora to New Zealand, it is my intention to make my original material available to appropriate institutions in both countries.

In writing this book I have been conscious of the words of Maurice Aylward in his letter to the ENA members, where he exhorted them to be 'true to Ireland'. He also said:

> When the story of this war comes to be written and national and international rights are adjusted, the actions and attitude of each one of you and of all Éire citizens in calling for recognition of our national rights and status will have a very important bearing.[2]

This has been an inspiration to me. It was like Maurice saying, 'Get on with it, Pete – tell our story.' Well, mate, I have done my best!

Peter Burke
Wellington, New Zealand, 2019

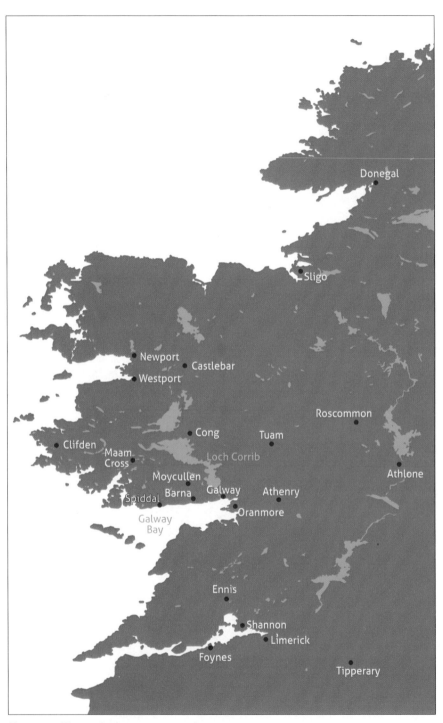

MAP OF THE WEST OF IRELAND

PART ONE

THE ROAD TO WAR

Matt Burke, mid-1930s.
Photographer S.P. Andrew

I

Ireland's risings

On Wednesday 30 July 1941, a shy but deeply passionate Irish republican, 32-year-old Matthias Burke from Ballydotia, Moycullen, County Galway, stepped into the witness box of the No.4 Armed Forces Appeal Board in Wellington, New Zealand, to state why he would not under any circumstances fight for Britain in WWII.

Matthias Burke was my father, and he, along with five others known as the Sons of Éire, was part of a test case representing about 500 Irishmen living in New Zealand who had been, or were likely to be, conscripted to fight in the New Zealand armed forces and by implication the British armed forces. They claimed to be conscientious objectors because, in their words, they 'could not in all conscience fight for Britain'. My father and his friends supported Ireland's neutrality in WWII and regarded themselves as citizens of Éire – not British subjects. From a young age they had been politicised into despising the centuries-long domination of Ireland by Britain, which came to a head with the brutality of the Crown forces in suppressing the Easter Rising in 1916 and the 1919–21 War of Independence, or the Troubles as it is commonly known. These young men either witnessed or heard about these events from those who had experienced it.

Like his fellow Irishmen, Matt didn't have to read history books to know what the Black and Tans, Auxiliaries and other British soldiers did in Ireland – they had seen it with their own eyes, and read about it in their local papers. The 'bush telegraph' played its role in spreading the message too. While Dad was just nine years old when the Troubles began, the absolute horror of what he saw was deeply ingrained in his mind. This prompted him to tell the armed forces appeal board:

> I do not base my claim of conscience on anything that has arisen since war broke out in September 1939, but on what I saw, felt and experienced in Éire between 1919 and 1921. It is only those who have been through that experience can realise how the memories of those frightful days have left something on one's mind that can never be blotted out.[1]

Matt saw family members and friends brutally assaulted and murdered by the Auxiliaries and the Black and Tans sent by Winston Churchill and his aristocratic cronies and generals to 'teach the Irish a lesson'. The gratuitous violence meted out by these often drunken thugs masquerading as soldiers was to have a profound effect on Dad and his friends when they were faced with being conscripted into one of Britain's armies at the outbreak of WWII.

My father and many like him supported Éamon de Valera, an avowed republican and one of the leaders of the 1916 Rising. De Valera's battle with Britain did not stop with the signing of the Anglo-Irish Treaty in 1921, but continued until full Irish independence was achieved in 1949. To understand the motives and passion of my father and the men who stood with him in Wellington, we must understand the history of Ireland, and in particular the west of Ireland, to get a sense of the physical, economic and political environment in which they lived before coming to New Zealand.

The Burke family grew up on a 20-acre family farm at Ballydotia that provided an income to support the family – father, Tom, and mother, Mary (née Bohan); Matt and his twin, Malachy; his two other brothers, John and Tom; and his sisters, Maria and Catherine. His parents were by all accounts hard workers and made the most of the land they had by raising cattle and growing potatoes and other vegetables.

Ballydotia is a delightful townland (the smallest division of land in Ireland). It is not far as the crow flies from the trout- and salmon-rich Loch Corrib. Dry stone walls separate the fields and the squeaky iron gates give a rustic look to the Burke farm today. At the turn of the 20th century, when Dad was born, it was typical of the small holdings in the area. Today a lot of them have been subdivided and there are some fancy houses tucked away behind the stone walls. My cousin Fidelma, who lives at Ballydotia, tells me that the old Burke barn, recently refurbished, is said to be about 300 years old.

A sketch of the house where Matt Burke was born in Ballydotia.
Drawn by Mary O'Shea, Moycullen

Cousin Fidelma Burke outside the family home at Ballydotia on the site of the original cottage.

The name Ballydotia or 'Baile Doite' means the 'boiled and burned village', relating, it would seem, to a fire there at some point in its history. In the 1911 census there were 38 people living in the townland, of which eight were at the Burke household, including Catherine Burke, my great-grandmother.

The farm at Ballydotia came into Burke ownership in 1869 when my great-grandfather John, born at Oranmore, Galway, on 15 February 1844, married Catherine Connor, the daughter of Matthias and Judith Connor (née McGouran), farmers of Ballydotia. They were married in the Parish of Moycullen. Catherine's father, it seems, handed the farm to the newlyweds, who were 23 and 19 respectively.

John Burke is listed on the marriage certificate as a farmer, and it appears that he worked on the Burke family farm at Oranmore before moving to Moycullen. John and Catherine had three sons – Matthias, Michael and Thomas (my grandfather) – and two daughters, Brigid and Julia. Michael joined the army, Matthias went to the United States and the two girls married into the Darcy clan. My grandfather Tom, who inherited the farm, married Mary Bohan on 20 February 1905.

The Bohans have strong Moycullen connections and are related to the Hanlys and Mulkerrins. These family connections are borne out by recurring Christian names such as Catherine, Malachy, Matthias, Thomas, John, Mary and Margaret.

My father and his siblings were all fluent Irish speakers and attended the Moycullen Parish School next to the Catholic Church. The original school buildings have long been replaced, as has the house where the family first

The Burke family in celebration mode at Ballydotia, Moycullen, c.1940. From left: Frank Faherty, Jim Hynes, Tom Burke (Dad's brother), John Darcy, Mary Burke (Dad's mother), Unknown, Maria Burke (Dad's sister), Unknown, John Burke, Malachy Burke, Mary Burke (John's wife), Kathleen Duggan. Unfortunately the person off-camera to the left holding the bottle and the reason for it to be there are unknown.
Courtesy of Marion O'Connor

lived. All that remains of the old house is a concrete slab which looks much smaller than the new house. The old house was damp, which contributed to my father contracting rheumatic fever. According to what he told my mother, he was near death and did not go to school for two years because of this. As he grew older, this illness was to haunt him and contributed to his death at just 53 years old.

The Parish of Maigh Cuilinn, as it is referred to in Irish, lies just 10 kilometres north-west of the city of Galway on the Clifden road and is in a Gaeltacht- or Irish-speaking area. The name Maigh Cuilinn means 'a plain of holly' and the sight of holly bushes around the village is still common.

Galway is a beautiful city immortalised in numerous wonderful songs. The sight of the houses at nearby Claddagh where the Corrib flows into Galway Bay is magical, as is the Spanish Arch that reminds us of this city's proud history in the province of Connacht. For more than a thousand years Galway city has been of significance to the hinterland it serves, and Ireland generally, especially as a prospering trading post with goods going to and from France and Spain. Claddagh gained fame in 1660 when Richard Joyce made a ring for his wife with a heart in the centre representing love, two hands for friendship and a crown to denote loyalty. The Claddagh ring has remained popular throughout the world.

Loch Corrib is a major feature in the area and is effectively the dividing line between good and bad land. The west, where Moycullen is situated, is less productive than the eastern side of the lake where the land is much flatter and the soil better for crops, cattle and lowland sheep. That is not to say there is no good land in the west, but there is less of it and more bog land where turf is cut and dried for use in home fires and stoves.

Heading out of Galway city and past Moycullen, you enter a surreal world of rugged beauty. It is a bit like the former coal-mining town of Denniston on the West Coast of New Zealand where my mother and grandmother were born. The big difference is that Denniston is all rock with no soil, and it would be impossible to even graze the rugged black mountain sheep that inhabit the rocky hillsides around Maam Cross and beyond in Connemara. My father used to talk romantically about the Twelve Bens (sometimes called Twelve Pins) – a mountain range with sharp peaks that dominate Connemara – and having seen them for myself they are just as he described. In the valleys the land is good, but the mountains of Maam are a challenge, even for the sheep.

Further north at the village of Cong there is exquisite beauty. It is where the 1950s classic movie *The Quiet Man* was filmed, starring Ireland's Maureen O'Hara and Hollywood hunk John Wayne. Nearby is Ashford Castle at the head of Loch Corrib, which is a sight that challenges the beauty of New Zealand's Milford Sound.

The ruggedness of the terrain in Connemara and Loch Corrib is important in the context of this story because it influenced the role that the men and

The picturesque Claddagh village in Galway.

Above: A vibrant Saturday in Galway city. Below: Fishing boats on the shore of Loch Corrib.

women of Moycullen were to play in the 1916 Rising and the Troubles. In a sense, Moycullen was somewhat isolated, with the Corrib a physical barrier to linking up with Galway East. Despite the apparent tranquillity in the west of Ireland, it had a reputation of expressing its discontent with English landlords and was the scene of much agrarian unrest.

Bigotry in Ireland was born in the cradle of British law and was the catalyst for ongoing unrest culminating in the 1916 Rising. Before that there were many unsuccessful uprisings and attempts to make minor adjustments to the law, but as far as Irish Catholics were concerned, the Protestant minority were favoured. In 1822 the great Daniel O'Connell had made an early bid for Irish independence, which ultimately failed.

Between 1845 and 1851 one of the most horrific and avoidable scourges to hit Ireland was the potato blight, which caused the Great Famine and resulted in the death of more than one million people over four years. The staple diet of the poor was the potato, but with the blight and lack of other food they died in appalling circumstances. Those who could fled to America and Canada on 'famine ships', while others were sent by British judges to penal colonies in Australia for stealing food to feed their starving families. Between the start of the famine in 1845 and 1911, the population of Ireland was cut in half, falling from eight million to four million.

Master of the mountains – an Irish sheep in Connemara.

The main street in Moycullen village.

County Galway was especially badly affected and starvation led to outbreaks of diseases such as dysentery and cholera. In *Famine: Galway's Darkest Years*, William Henry highlights some of the horrors endured while British and Irish landlords ignored the plight of thousands of Irish people and calmly exported food to England.[2] The British Secretary for the Treasury, Charles Edward Trevelyan, described the famine as 'punishment by God on an idle, ungrateful and rebellious country'.[3] His name is immortalised in one of Ireland's great anthems, 'The Fields of Athenry':

> For you stole Trevelyan's corn
> So the young might see the morn.

Henry tells of an instance of 140 people dying of starvation on the roadside as they tried to reach Galway city from Clifden.[4] Reusable coffins were common and places called 'workhouses' were set up to provide basic refuge for the destitute. Ships taking people to America and Canada were, for good reason, referred to as 'coffin ships'. To add to this misery British landlords evicted Irish tenants off the land if they couldn't pay their rents, and demolished their homes so they were forced to leave the area. The landlords also banned the Irish from catching fish and wild game on their lands – it seemed starvation was effectively condoned in Ireland.

The Irish famine ended only 60 years before my father was born, so to him this was modern history.

While Ireland was going through dreadful pain and suffering, 18,000 kilometres away New Zealand was in the process of colonisation that led to the signing of the Treaty of Waitangi in 1840, which secured New Zealand as a British colony. The British were busy buying, or in numerous cases confiscating, land from the indigenous Māori. Their first brief contact with Europeans was in 1642 when the Dutch explorer Abel Tasman sailed into New Zealand waters. But it wasn't until 1769 when Britain's Captain James Cook made his first visit to New Zealand that the pathway to colonisation began in earnest. The Māori tribes clamoured to get muskets from merchants, and even missionaries. In fact, some Māori made provision of muskets a precondition of conversion to Christianity.

Theft of land seems to have been a feature of British colonisation, and in that the Māori and Irish share a common grievance. It's perhaps interesting to note that there has been a long history of Māori/Irish intermarriage in New Zealand, including many celebrated Māori, most notable being Sir Tipene O'Regan, the former leader of the South Island's Ngāi Tahu. The colloquial term 'Ngāti Irish' has some real validity. The Irish and Māori share similar values, especially around the sacredness of land and respect for their ancestors and the dead. The relationship with Britain was central to the place of both Ireland and New Zealand in the world, with the two nations sharing plenty of common ground.

Meanwhile in Ireland, resentment against Britain was like a smouldering fire that had never been extinguished and it erupted into a fully fledged blaze with the 1916 Rising and the War of Independence. There were also tensions within Ireland as to how the matter should be resolved, as there were some who supported Home Rule and others who wanted an independent state, with various strands within those groups that didn't necessarily work together.

Since the mid-1880s various attempts had been made at Westminster to introduce Home Rule for Ireland, with a Bill finally passed in September 1914. But as WWI had broken out on 28 July 1914, the implementation of the legislation was put on hold until after the war. Interestingly, when the Bill was passed, individual Irishmen in New Zealand sent congratulations to the British Prime Minister H.H. Asquith. The New Zealand Hibernian Society cabled its sponsor John Redmond: 'Redmond, House of Commons London. Heartiest congratulations Hibernians Wellington on magnificent achievement.'[5]

While Britain was at war, the Irish Republican Brotherhood (IRB) saw an opportunity to make a bid for independence, and in January 1916 the

Special Edition.

CONNACHT TRIBUNE

GALWAY, WEDNESDAY MORNING, APRIL 25, 1916. [PRICE 1d.

IS IT INSURRECTION ?

ALLEGED GENERAL "RISING" IN IRELAND.

The Irish Volunteers

WILD RUMOURS FROM DUBLIN.

REPORTED SEIZURE OF GOVERNMENT OFFICES.

GALWAY ISOLATED.

POSTAL AND TELEGRAPHIC COMMUNICATION CUT OFF AND RAILWAY LINE TORN UP.

TWO LOCAL ENGAGEMENTS

AT ORANMORE AND CARNMORE.

POLICE CASUALTIES.

Incidents at Oranmore

How the news of the 1916 Rising was heralded in Galway.
Connacht Tribune, 25 April 1916

Military Council of the IRB, which included Éamonn Ceannt of Galway, agreed to plan an insurrection.

When Patrick Pearse famously read the proclamation of the Irish Republic from outside the General Post Office in Dublin on Monday 24 April 1916, my father was only seven years old. The battle in Dublin between the rebels and British forces lasted only six days and resulted in 485 deaths (260 civilian, 82 rebels and 143 Crown forces) and more than 2600 wounded (around 2200 civilian and rebels, and 399 Crown forces).[6]

There were interesting Kiwi connections to the Rising. Some New Zealand servicemen were in Ireland on leave from the Western Front and were called in to assist Crown forces, and a prominent Irishman with links to New Zealand was one of the victims. Dr (Fr) Felix Watters was the founding rector of St Patrick's College, a boys school in Wellington, from 1885 until 1898, after which he returned to his native Ireland. At the time of his death during the Rising, aged 66, Watters was rector of University College Dublin. He was shot in the thigh while visiting a wounded fellow priest and underwent surgery, but peritonitis set in and he died on 8 May 1916. Watters was a well-known Home Rule supporter. At his instigation, a gold

The Anzac effect

The Easter Rising occurred the day before the first anniversary of Anzac Day, which commemorates the landing of Allied troops on the Gallipoli Peninsula in Turkey. Anzac is seen as New Zealand's blood sacrifice for the British Empire in that an estimated 2700 New Zealanders were killed and a further 5000 wounded. Irish casualties are harder to pinpoint because they were mixed up with British casualties, and potentially Australian as well, with estimates of between 2000 and 4000. Different countries and regiments claimed various battles in WWI. Gallipoli is regarded as the 'Anzac's battle', but reality suggests otherwise, as more British lives were lost than Australian and New Zealand. Gallipoli was one of several ill-conceived military campaigns by Winston Churchill, who was First Lord of the Admiralty.

harp on a green background were the first colours of St Patrick's College Rugby Football Club. It is understood that Watters also played a role in the foundation of Victoria University of Wellington.[7]

County Galway was one of the few areas outside Dublin where there was a significant action in support of the Rising. It took place in Galway East, but not in the west around Moycullen where my father lived. Galway had always been the scene of agrarian unrest and was badly hit by the famine. It has been described as being the most troublesome and violent county in the country from 1878 until the turn of the 20th century.[8]

In the east of the county, Liam Mellows led about 100 Volunteers in an attack on the Royal Irish Constabulary (RIC) barracks in Clarenbridge, about 17 kilometres from Galway city. Later they attacked the RIC barracks at Oranmore. They also barricaded roads, cut telephone lines, and damaged railway tracks, and there was a shoot-out at Carnmore Cross Roads in the Parish of Claregalway. The reaction of British forces to the

Dr Felix Watters – first rector of St Patrick's College, Wellington.
Courtesy of St Patrick's College Archives

Mellows-led attacks included shelling areas around Galway city. Mellows and the Volunteers, men and women, retreated to the agricultural training farm at Athenry, which still operates today under the Agriculture and Food Development Authority, Teagasc. The rebels made a stand at nearby Moyode Castle but, facing overwhelming opposition, they quietly gave up the fight with many going on the run until they were caught and imprisoned. One of the young people who fought in these actions was Paddy Feeney, who emigrated to New Zealand in January 1926 and later played a major role in the Éire National Association, the organisation set up to prevent Irishmen being conscripted into the British army in WWII.

There was no rebellion in the west around Moycullen for various reasons, including confusing orders, lack of arms and organisation.[9] In his paper 'Military Activity in the Peripheral Region of Moycullen from 1916 to 1923', Darren McDonagh refers to an article in the *Galway Express* on 4 March 1916, which stated that Mark McDonagh of Ballyquirk, Moycullen, was arrested and sentenced to three months imprisonment for leading a group of about 60 Irish Volunteers to disrupt a (British) recruiting meeting in Moycullen, at which the band of the local Connaught Rangers was playing. The paper reported that a Volunteer spat on some recruiting pamphlets and that some Volunteers jostled a man attending the meeting. There was also a report that someone drove a car into the group of Volunteers.[10] Local historians say Mark McDonagh was a 'bit of a local leader' and his imprisonment may have contributed to the lack of a rebellion in Galway West,[11] but it was the arrest of Mícheál Ó Droighneáin that probably sealed it.

Ó Droighneáin was captain of the Spiddal Company of Irish Volunteers in 1916, and was well connected to the leaders of the Rising including Éamonn Ceannt and Patrick Pearse. He described events in the west leading up to the Rising itself in his witness statement to the Bureau of Military History.[12] He had been told by Ceannt that the Rising was coming and a coded message about exactly when it would happen would be sent to him. This happened on Good Friday when Mrs Martin Conlon from Dublin came to see him and took a letter out of her stocking, which included the code words that the Rising was to take place on Easter Sunday. Ó Droighneáin saw a fleet of British warships in Galway Bay and began to have misgivings. On Easter Monday morning he received another message from Dublin to say that the Rising had been called off, but it did actually occur that day. Later that morning he cycled into Galway city but within minutes was arrested by the RIC and immediately imprisoned, ending any hope of the Rising taking place in Galway West.

The full story about how Galway participated in the Rising is told in brilliant detail by William Henry in *Pathway to Rebellion: Galway 1916*, where he sums up the situation: 'While Galway did not demonstrate the same blood sacrifice as Dublin, its people were not lacking in courage.' [13]

My father and his friends, who in 1940 were to take on the might of the Crown in New Zealand, were probably innocent bystanders to all this activity in 1916. But as they grew older they grasped the significance of what had happened. When the War of Independence began in January 1919, Dad was nearly ten years old and clearly aware of the role of the IRA forces during that event, if not involved in some way. The terrible incidents in Moycullen and Galway, which Dad witnessed from that time, are detailed in his and other testimonies to the No.4 Armed Forces Appeal Board. Suffice to say the events made a lasting impression on him.

Meanwhile in New Zealand, while the Rising and the disastrous Gallipoli campaign were making major headlines in 1915/16, another important event was taking place. This was the establishment of the Labour Party, which had its genesis in the trade union movement. One of the founding members was Peter Fraser, a Scot and Presbyterian who was to become one of the foremost political figures in 20th-century New Zealand politics, in much the same way the staunch Catholic Éamon de Valera did in Ireland. (Fraser and de Valera would later form a strong and crucial friendship that would help broker a deal for Irishmen in New Zealand opposed to conscription in WWII.) In December 1916 Peter Fraser was arrested and jailed for 12 months for speaking out against conscription and the 'imperialist war'. He was not a conscientious objector as he did enlist, but was rejected on medical grounds because of his poor eyesight. In 1918 Fraser won the parliamentary seat of Wellington Central and held it until his death in 1950. [14]

The War of Independence was a ferocious guerrilla war waged by the Irish against the British occupying forces and the Black and Tans and Auxiliaries between 1919 and 1921. It culminated in the December 1921 Anglo-Irish Treaty, negotiated by Michael Collins, which granted dominion, but not republican status to the 26 counties. When de Valera rejected the Treaty there was much confusion, and finally a bitter and tragic civil war broke out in June 1922 which pitted neighbour against neighbour and brother against brother. This saw two great Irish leaders, pro-Treaty Michael Collins and anti-Treaty de Valera, who had worked closely together during the War of Independence setting up their own armies, and a fierce struggle ensued. One of the huge tragedies of the Civil War was the assassination of Collins. The pro-Treaty forces won what was a bloody pyrrhic victory.

The Nazi propagandist

While my father was growing up in Moycullen, a young man who was
to play a bizarre role in WWII was being educated at St Ignatius Loyola
College in Galway city. William Joyce was three years older than my father,
but even as a six-year-old was displaying traits that would blossom as
he reached adulthood. J.A. Cole, in *Lord Haw-Haw*, quotes one of Joyce's
teachers as saying: 'That boy will end up doing something very great in
the world, or he will finish on the end of a rope.'[15] His English mother
was Protestant and his father Catholic but their loyalty clearly lay with
Britain, with his father owning the property occupied by the Royal Irish
Constabulary (RIC) in Galway city. The young Joyce proudly claimed to
have worked as a spy or informer for Crown forces, which didn't fit well
with the locals. The family moved to Britain in 1921. Joyce became a rabid
fascist and defected to Germany just days before the start of WWII, quickly
finding fame as an English speaking propagandist on German radio with
the nickname 'Lord Haw-Haw'. After the war he was arrested, convicted of
treason and hanged. He was buried at Wandsworth Prison in Britain but in
1976, at the request of his daughter, was reburied at Galway's Bohermore
Cemetery.[16]

During Joyce's trial at the Old Bailey in London, a crowd gathered
outside the court calling for him to hanged because he was a traitor to
Britain. A lone Irishman also called for his blood, shouting he should be
executed because he supported the Black and Tans in Ireland during the
Troubles.

I have not been able to find any specific documents relating to Dad and
his family's role or position in the Civil War. My assumption is that given
distant family links to de Valera, and the positive relationship that the Éire
National Association in New Zealand enjoyed with de Valera before, during
and after WWII, the Burke family would have been anti-Treaty.

These events set the scene for what would later be played out in a
courtroom in New Zealand in 1941.

2

A future in New Zealand

Following the end of the Civil War in Ireland in 1923, the country faced building a new political entity without many of its leaders, who had been killed during the conflicts of 1916, 1919–21 and 1922–23. A new assembly was formed with William T. Cosgrave as head of the Irish Free State. He led the pro-Treaty political party Fine Gael which commanded the majority of seats in Dáil Éireann (Parliament). Éamon de Valera, who led the anti-Treaty faction, was elected to the Dáil in 1923, but it wasn't until 1932 when Fianna Fáil gained the majority that de Valera was able to introduce reforms that were to set Ireland on the path to full independence from Britain. By that time my father, Matt Burke, was living in New Zealand.

While the fighting was taking place, and later when an uneasy peace descended on Ireland, Matt continued his schooling in Moycullen. According to the school records he probably began his education in 1916, but there are gaps in his attendance – evidence that he missed a lot of school through illness. In January 1925 he is listed on the roll by his Irish name Maitias De Búrca, but appears to have left school in March that year, when he was 16. While his schooling may have been limited, Matt was clearly an intelligent and articulate man – something borne out by the evidence he would give to the No.4 Armed Forces Appeal Board, stating his reasons for refusing to be conscripted in 1941.

Matt Burke aged 21, April 1930.

After leaving school he helped his father on the farm as well as getting a job as a roadman, and probably started planning his long-term move, which so many Irish men and women did and still do, to emigrate. In his case the options were limited. He wanted to go to America but his rheumatic heart condition made him ineligible for immigration to that country. Why he chose New Zealand instead of, say, Australia we'll never know, but it's likely he had friends there. His twin brother, Malachy, stayed in County Galway and later owned a successful construction company. Matt's move to New Zealand would not earn him a fortune and would take him away from his family forever, except for one brief visit in 1957, by which time both his parents were dead.

Before he left Matt obtained a reference from the County Surveyor of the County of Galway, Western Division, M.J. Kennedy. This was his passport to work in New Zealand:

> To all whom it may concern. The bearer – Matthew Burke of Ballydotia, Moycullen, was employed on road work for the Galway County Council from time to time during the past four years under my supervision.[1] I have always found him an honest and capable workman, and have pleasure in recommending him for employment.
>
> Signed M.J. Kennedy, 7 December 1929.

Two weeks before Christmas 1929 Matt Burke boarded a train from Galway and then caught a ferry to Britain. He travelled to Southampton, where the sleek new 17,000-tonne New Zealand Shipping Company liner *Rangitane* was waiting for him. It left for New Zealand on 20 December 1929, under the command of Captain A.W. McKeller, with 201 passengers and a crew of 194. I must admit being somewhat perplexed as to why he left so close to Christmas and why he didn't stay a few extra weeks before departing. There were probably reasons, but these are unknown.

Matt was just 20 years old when he began his epic 18,000 kilometre journey to one of the most isolated countries in the world – New Zealand. Sadly neither I, nor my relations, have any records of that journey or what farewells may have taken place. Perhaps the Irish took leaving their homeland less hard than others, given that emigration from Ireland was a way of life. Also unclear is how Matt funded his passage that cost about £40, although I vaguely recall Malachy telling me that their father, Tom, helped with the fare, perhaps as some compensation for Matt not inheriting the family farm.

Until I carried out this research I had always been under the impression that my father travelled to New Zealand with a close friend, John Clancy

The *Rangitane*, which Matt Burke came to New Zealand on,
berthed at the Wellington wharves in the 1930s.
Alexander Turnbull Library, G-15819-1/1

from Knockaunranny, Moycullen. However the passenger list of the *Rangitane*
makes no mention of John. The shipping records show there were at least
four Irishmen and one Irishwoman on this voyage, but there appears to be
no mention of other people my father may have known.

Wellington newspaper, the *Evening Post,* carried a lengthy story about the
maiden voyage of the *Rangitane.* After leaving Southampton, it encountered
strong north-westerly winds and heavy seas for the first two days and stopped
for a few hours at Madeira, an island south-west of Portugal in the North
Atlantic. It then resumed its journey to Colón and on through the Panama
Canal, before crossing the Pacific Ocean to New Zealand. It berthed at
Wellington's Pipitea Wharf on 5 February 1930, taking 42 days for the journey.[2]
For a young man it would have been an adventure, and no doubt Matt was
full of hope for what the future would hold, but he would never lose his love
for and loyalty to his native Ireland.

Like most Irishmen arriving in a new land, he would have had names of
people who could help him find accommodation and work. The key contacts
and meeting places would have been the well-established Irish club, the

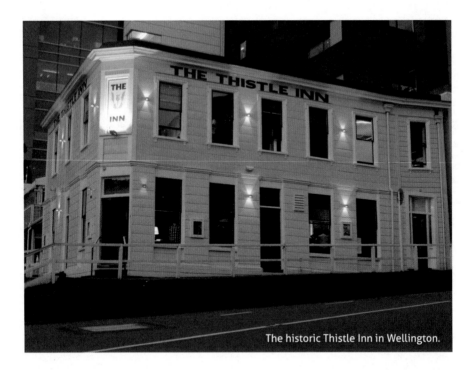

The historic Thistle Inn in Wellington.

Catholic Church, and probably the names of boarding houses and potential employers. I know he found the hotel called the Thistle Inn, which still stands close to the Catholic Cathedral in the Wellington suburb of Thorndon.

One place he probably went to at some stage was 11 Guildford Terrace, right opposite the Cathedral. My mother's aunts and one of their families, the Kellys, lived there and it was an open house for priests and the Irish. My great-uncle Fr Dan Milligan was a Marist priest. The family had moved from Denniston on the West Coast, buying a pub in Wellington called The White Swan, which was universally known as the 'Dirty Duck' for its apparent lack of cleanliness – no wonder they didn't last in that business.

Soon after his arrival in New Zealand, Matt headed north to Whanganui where he found employment as a road worker. References that he kept from employers show that he had casual work there in February 1930, and obtained a full-time position for the Waitōtara County Council as a roadman in April 1930, and later as a quarry worker. According to a reference by the county engineer, he sadly lost this job at the height of the Depression in February 1933 because they had to give the position to a married man. The reference stated:

> I have no hesitation in recommending him (Matthias Burke) for a position where hard work is required. He is sober, industrious and of good character.[3]

Matt later worked for another Whanganui contractor before relocating to Wellington. Hurling was a sport that he enjoyed, but while in Whanganui he took up hockey and played it with some success.

Matt got a job as a farmhand and lorry driver for St Thomas's Boys School in Naenae (sometimes spelt 'Nai Nai'), Lower Hutt. St Thomas's was a home for disadvantaged boys run by the Sisters of Mercy. They held regular fundraisers, and among the guests at the school's annual garden party in April 1937 was Peter Fraser, Minister of Education, eventually to become New Zealand's wartime prime minister. Fraser was highly regarded and he in turn had huge respect for the Catholic Church. The head of the Catholic Church in New Zealand, Archbishop Thomas O'Shea, was also present at this function.[4]

My father joined the Irish club, where he met up with his mate John Clancy from Moycullen. The club in Wellington was active during the 1930s and 1940s, and throughout the war years provided something of a haven from public criticism of Ireland's neutrality. Miss Mary Warren, my mother, is mentioned in a newspaper report in June 1934 on an Irish club function at St Francis Hall next to the Catholic Cathedral in Hill Street.[5] It is almost certain that she and my father met at the Irish club, but I never asked them when and how the romance began and blossomed.

Matt Burke (left front) with his hockey team, c.1930s.

Matt Burke (in foreground) with the St Thomas's Boys School truck, c.1935.

Irish club function in Wellington, c.late 1940s.

So while Matt Burke, like millions of others worldwide, was eking out a living during the Depression in the 1930s, major political events and interactions were taking place both in Ireland and in New Zealand that would shape the outcome of his later bid to avoid being conscripted into the armed forces. While the two countries are at opposite ends of the world there are some amazing similarities in how they both developed in the 1930s – politically, socially and economically.

Éamon de Valera gained power in Ireland in 1932, having severed his ties with Sinn Féin in 1926 and formed his own party, Fianna Fáil. He immediately began the process of dismantling those parts of the Anglo-Irish Treaty that tied Ireland to England. Specific examples of this included swearing allegiance to the King of England, and paying land annuities owed to Britain for loans provided under the Irish Land Acts. Britain reacted angrily and imposed 20 per cent tariffs on Irish primary exports to Britain, and de Valera responded in kind by imposing levies on UK imports. This economic war lasted until 1938. Britain could do little except complain, while Ireland had to endure the economic consequences of the sanctions. The Irish cattle farmers were badly affected – Britain was, and still is, their major market. Independence was to prove expensive for Ireland, but de Valera's unequivocal goal was to cut the shackles that had held Ireland prisoner to Britain for centuries, regardless of the cost, and to establish it as an independent entity on the international political stage.

What de Valera had lost on the battlefield during the Irish Civil War he recaptured in his role as prime minister of the Irish Free State. A major piece of his legislation was the Irish Nationality and Citizenship Act, which made everyone living in Ireland an Irish citizen, rather than being a British citizen as they had been classified under the 1921 Treaty. Amazingly in the days of Brexit this legislation has renewed significance. The Act applied to all of Ireland, not just Éire, and today the people of Northern Ireland have, under this legislation, the right to become citizens of Éire and therefore citizens of the European Union.

This decision on citizenship status was to be raised later in New Zealand at the No.4 Armed Forces Appeal Board hearing when Matt Burke and five fellow Irishmen presented their reasons for refusing to be conscripted. Technically they were British subjects, but with the passing of the Irish Nationality and Citizenship Act in 1935 they argued they were Irish citizens, not British. Their status was a contentious and controversial issue.

On 7 February 1934 de Valera, acting in his capacity as the Irish Minister of External Affairs, sent Despatch No.1 to New Zealand Prime Minister

George Forbes, alerting him that the Irish Free State Citizenship Bill was to be introduced and outlined the essence of it.[6] Forbes diplomatically responded:

I have the honour to acknowledge receipt of your Despatch No.1 of the 7th of February and to thank you for the information forwarded therewith in reference to Irish nationality. I have the honour to be your obedient servant Geo W. Forbes (signed).[7]

The British Government also received this despatch from de Valera, and a flurry of cables followed as the British tried to come to terms with what the Irish leader was doing. On 27 August 1934 Éamon de Valera sent another despatch (No.5) to Forbes stating the Citizenship Bill had been introduced into the Dáil on 27 June 1934, and attached a copy of it for his information.[8] The British Government kept the New Zealand Government informed on the passage of the Bill through Governor-General Lord Bledisloe, and directly from 10 Downing Street to Forbes. Inevitably they put their own spin on the implications of the Bill.

Meanwhile in New Zealand the First Labour Government, in which Peter Fraser became Education Minister, was elected to office in late 1935 on the back of a campaign to improve the lot of the working class. Its election led to the birth of what is known as the welfare state, where social policies were put in place to help the disadvantaged. Many of these, including universal superannuation (a pension) for those over 65, still exist. Prime Minister Michael Joseph Savage was to become one of the most revered politicians in New Zealand history. Savage was born in Australia, immigrated to New Zealand in October 1907, and immediately became involved in the trade union movement. He was a Catholic, but very pro-British, supported conscription and signed up to serve in the armed forces of New Zealand in 1918. He was a founder of the Labour Party and held the Auckland West seat from 1919 until his death in 1940.

In May 1935, before the Labour Party had been elected to Government, Peter Fraser was sent to represent New Zealand at the Empire Parliamentary Association in London. After the conference he went to the British Trade Union Congress at the seaside town of Margate in Kent. This was his first time back in the UK since leaving for New Zealand in 1910. Before Fraser and his wife, Janet, left on this trip the Labour Party hosted a special farewell function at which he was presented with an attaché case and Janet a travelling bag.[9]

In terms of what happened at both conferences, it appears that they were relatively uneventful. In their book *Tomorrow Comes the Song*, Michael Bassett and Michael King note that, as there are no entries in Fraser's surviving diary, he simply attended the sessions and listened to the speakers, who included

Peter Fraser leaving on one of his wartime overseas trips.
Alexander Turnbull Library, F-36332-1/1

Chancellor of the Exchequer Neville Chamberlain. At the Trade Union Congress, where Fraser was welcomed as a 'fraternal delegate', he found himself in the midst of a discussion on Mussolini's invasion of Abyssinia (Ethiopia).[10]

After the congress Fraser flew to Dublin, along with a party colleague Mark Fagan, where he met Éamon de Valera for the first time. While they discussed current events and there were the general niceties expressed on the trade, social and economic issues, it is clear that the pair got on very well on a personal level. In his book about Peter Fraser, James Thorn recounts that when Fraser got home from his trip he said:

> ... that the Irish leader was not the harum-scarum, impulsive person he had been painted. On the contrary, de Valera was 'a soft-voiced and quiet gentleman who went calmly about his actions and always seemed to have the responsibility of his position in the forefront of his mind.'[11]

The positive impression that Fraser gained of de Valera was probably contrary to what he had heard at the Empire Parliamentary Association, which reflected the scorn widely heaped upon de Valera for setting Ireland on the pathway to being a republic and cutting political ties with Britain. This was the first of four known meetings between the pair and helped forge a life-long friendship. In some ways they were an odd couple. De Valera was the academic, mathematician, soldier, politician, committed Catholic, and Irish patriot, who had escaped the firing squad in 1916 by virtue of his American birth. Fraser was Presbyterian, self-educated, a fighter for workers' rights, a man whose ancestors' land in Scotland had been confiscated by the British, and who stood for the independence of New Zealand. As a consequence Fraser was able to empathise with both the Irish and Māori, and establish a special rapport with them. He was universally popular with both throughout his long and successful political career.

Ireland and New Zealand were, and still are, essentially large farms with some major cities. Until the advent of the European Union (EU), both relied almost entirely on Britain as a market for their primary produce. While both are geographically small, they have never let themselves be subsumed by larger nations. From 1932 onwards Ireland, under de Valera, set its own foreign policy agenda.

De Valera spoke out against the Italian invasion of Abyssinia and the failure of nations such as Britain to oppose this in a speech to the League of Nations, in Geneva in July 1936:

> Perhaps as the representative of a small nation that has itself experience of aggression and dismemberment, the members of the Irish delegation may be more sensitive than others to the plight of Ethiopia. But is there any small nation represented here which does not feel the truth of the warning that what is Ethiopia's fate today may well be its own fate tomorrow, should the greed of some powerful neighbour prompt its destruction? [12]

The New Zealand Labour Government sided with Ireland on this issue, and Britain, the so-called 'mother country', stood aside while Italy invaded the small nation. Interestingly, Prime Minister Michael Joseph Savage received a cablegram from the Abyssinia Association in London dated 13 October 1938, saying it admired the attitude of New Zealand as a member of the League of Nations for its opposition to the Italian annexation of their country. [13] While in England for the coronation of King George VI and the Imperial Conference in 1937, Savage openly criticised Britain for weakening the League by not condemning Italy, and also condemned German rearmament and Japanese expansion in China. The prime ministers of Britain, Canada and Australia criticised the stance by Savage.

New Zealand, like Ireland, was inextricably socially, politically and

What if ...

According to de Valera's grandson Éamon Ó Cuív, his grandfather told him that if Mussolini had been stopped by the League, Hitler may have curbed his policy of invasion and WWII may have been averted.

economically tied to Britain, but it is clear in this instance that New Zealand was starting to chart its own foreign policy and the two small countries were showing they would not be bullied by the superpowers of the day. This was arguably the beginning of a special political relationship of mutual respect between Ireland and New Zealand that would carry on well into the future and potentially influence the outcome of the fight by the Sons of Éire to win their battle with Britain.

The final act for Ireland in terminating political links with Britain was the passing of the Irish Constitution by the Dáil, followed by a national plebiscite which saw it enacted on 29 December 1937. Some key points in the constitution included the abolition of the post of governor-general, as the King's representative, who was replaced by a president defined as the 'Guardian of the Constitution', whose role was largely ceremonial. However, there was a minor role for the King in that he could be called upon to assist with diplomatic issues. This was de Valera's way of allowing Britain a toe in the Irish tent – but no more. The constitution designated Irish as the nation's first language and English as its second. It also, controversially, gave all peoples of Ireland, including Northern Ireland, the opportunity to be part of the nation, and gave women full voting rights. It allowed for religious freedom and while it was being drafted all the major religions were consulted, but it did recognise the 'special position' of the Catholic Church. To counter the impression that Ireland was a 'confessional state', de Valera and W.T. Cosgrave, leader of Fine Gael, supported the election of Douglas Hyde, a Gaelic scholar and member of the Church of Ireland (Anglican) as the first president of Ireland in 1938.

Britain protested the change, but realised the inevitability of a Republic of Ireland so the protest was somewhat muted.

Ireland's rise from a subservient colony of Britain to international statehood in just 21 years (1916–37) was a remarkable achievement, though the effect of three military revolutions followed by a massive political upheaval to legitimise the battles in the field was huge. The administrative task alone was impressive.

New Zealand also began to assert itself as an independent nation during the 1930s, both in foreign and domestic policy. The advent of the Labour Government in 1935 saw the country go through a transformational change. New Zealand was moving to a more egalitarian state where 'Jack was as good as his master', and Labour politicians felt uncomfortable with some British politicians, whom they regarded as patronising. Despite this, many New Zealanders of European descent still regarded Britain as home, and some still do. The apron strings have never been completely cut, although they are now pretty thin and well worn.

The political events playing out on the other side of the world, especially the developing relationship between Ireland and New Zealand at a ministerial level, were to be pivotal later as the Sons of Éire battled during WWII to be recognised as Irish rather than British citizens. They would have greeted de Valera's moves with joy and a huge sense of pride. This would have given great heart to my father and his friends.

3

Calm before the war

In 1938 Europe was on the verge of war after Mussolini's invasion of Abyssinia (Ethiopia) and the failure of the League of Nations, including Britain, to do anything. Hitler skilfully grabbed Austria and then the Sudetenland, and planned the invasion of Poland which started WWII in September 1939.

The rise of Hitler and Mussolini in Europe and Japan's ambitions in Asia and the Pacific were clear signs to all, including the Irish living in New Zealand, that war was inevitable. There would have been talk in the Wellington Irish club about what would happen if war broke out, given that they were classed as British subjects. In New Zealand preparations were being made for war, with the Royal New Zealand Air Force (RNZAF) officially coming into being in 1937.

Carl Berendsen, Head of the Prime Minister's Department, foresaw the inevitability of war when the League of Nations failed to act on the invasion of Abyssinia, saying:

> The League's cynical abandonment of all principles in the face of deter-mined evil was a low point in the history of civilisation and Britain – though we were to fall lower in the foul abandonment of Czechoslovakia.[1]

He also noted that: 'the League would do nothing effective to prevent the colossal conflict that was looming'.[2] After attending a session of the League in Geneva, Berendsen and his wife, Nellie, travelled via Germany and were depressed at what they saw and experienced, in what he described as 'a police state'.

On his return, Berendsen told the government and the public that another world conflict was imminent.[3] During 1936 he got Prime Minister Michael Joseph Savage and his cabinet to prepare a War Book, which was a strategic plan on how New Zealand would deal with a war. It covered a whole range of contingencies including defence, trade, the national economy and censorship. The cabinet contained some men who were pacifists and had opposed WWI, but they recognised the signs and threats that lay ahead, and supported the production of the War Book.

In *Tomorrow Comes the Song*, Bassett and King also refer to the War Book and the formation in May 1937, at Peter Fraser's instigation, of a Council of Defence which was located within the Prime Minister's Department.[4] Within this council was the Organisation for National Security, which began systematically planning for any military and civil aspects of war that might arise. Special regulations were drafted and controls determined that could be implemented when war was declared. In 1937 New Zealand increased its defence budget by 37 per cent, with most of the money being allocated to the newly created RNZAF. Preparations continued after the Labour Government was re-elected in October 1938 – winning 53 seats to the National Party's 25.

Matt Burke and his fellow Irishmen also saw the inevitability of war. Faced with the prospect of being conscripted into the New Zealand armed forces, they decided to form a separate organisation to deal with this and other issues of status that they thought likely to arise. They couldn't work through the Irish club because its rules did not allow the social club to advocate for members on 'political or religious' issues. The new organisation was to be nationwide and voluntary, and would sit outside the rules and objectives of Irish societies and clubs that existed around the country. In a sense they were working on their own 'war book'.

Even with the ominous signs of war, St Patrick's Day was celebrated in style in Wellington in 1938. The *Evening Post* reported that a concert would be held in the city that night and that St Patrick's College, Silverstream, in Upper Hutt, and St Patrick's College, Wellington, would hold their annual picnics as all Roman Catholic schools in the province were observing a holiday.[5] With the influence of Irish nuns and priests, St Patrick's Day was a highlight of the school year, even in my days in the 1950s. Each parish arranged its own concert and the schools played a big part in this. We all wore green ribbons and often precious shamrock sent from relatives in Ireland.

Meanwhile in Ireland, British control of key ports was still an issue. The ports of Queenstown (now Cobh), Berehaven in Bantry Bay in the south-east, and Lough Swilly in the far north near Derry represented the last vestiges of the Anglo-Irish Treaty. In WWI the ports had been important to Britain to protect shipping lanes from German U-boats, but by the 1930s modern aircraft could range further over parts of the Atlantic Ocean, which potentially reduced their importance. They were handed back to Ireland as part of an agreement signed on 25 April 1938 by de Valera and British Prime Minister Neville Chamberlain.

Dressing down in London

While preparations for war progressed in New Zealand, there were some lighter moments played out with the New Zealand Prime Minister and his top officials in London. All were invited to attend the coronation of George VI and most were decidedly unhappy about having to dress up in what some would consider 'fancy dress', with frock coats and the like. They left hiring these clothes until the last minute and ended up with ill-fitting garments. In one embarrassing episode, Carl Berendsen discovered to his horror that the so-called fitting room at the suit hire shop was in fact the front window of the establishment and that he had an audience as he tried on his fancy pants. They also realised that the coronation would be a long day with no possibility of any sustenance. The enterprising Berendsen packed some chicken sandwiches and put them in his top hat, sharing them with the New Zealand Prime Minister and others during the long service at Westminster Abbey. For once the fancy hats and outfits were put to practical use by the irreverent Kiwis.[6]

On 26 April 1938 Éamon de Valera sent Despatch No.3 to New Zealand Prime Minister Savage containing a copy of this agreement.[7] The port and Royal Navy facilities at Spike Island near Cobh were returned to Ireland on 11 July, Berehaven on 29 September and Lough Swilly on 3 October. The Irish Free State was on target to declaring itself a Republic in 1949.

The day after Berehaven was handed back to Ireland, Neville Chamberlain returned from a meeting with Adolf Hitler in Munich to declare 'peace in our time', having signed over the Sudetenland. War with Germany was just a year away. Britain was concerned that Ireland would favour the Axis forces, but de Valera was intent on charting a course of neutrality. In the end Britain could see some value in a 'friendly neutral' Ireland, rather than an antagonistic one.

Throughout Europe and the British Commonwealth preparations for war proceeded at speed and every day gave Britain and New Zealand more time to train service people and to produce the necessary military equipment. On 1 September 1939 Hitler invaded Poland. Peter Fraser, standing in for the gravely ill Prime Minister Savage (who was suffering from colon cancer), broadcast this news to the nation. Hours later a state of emergency was declared.

On 2 September de Valera advised the Dáil that neutrality was the best policy for Ireland in any world conflict. A day later, the much anticipated news came through that Hitler had refused Britain's ultimatum to withdraw German forces from Poland, and on 3 September at 11.30pm, Acting Prime Minister Peter Fraser announced that New Zealand had followed Britain and declared war on Germany.

Savage was a devoted Catholic and at times critical of Britain, but he was first and foremost loyal to the Crown. His immortal words were broadcast on radio in New Zealand on 5 September:

> We range ourselves without fear beside Britain. Where she goes, we go. Where she stands, we stand.[8]

With war declared the Labour cabinet, with Berendsen and a retinue of government officials, gathered at Parliament buildings in Wellington to implement the War Book, and approve the vast array of regulations that would officially put New Zealand on a war footing. It took all night and Berendsen aptly summed it up:

> That night neither Peter Fraser nor I got any sleep. He then took me to Bellamy's,[9] the first and last time I ate there. I had been working for 36 hours without rest and went home sadly, knowing that our world would never be the same again, that millions would die and millions more would mourn.[10]

Parliament buildings in Wellington where Prime Minister Peter Fraser and his officials met to implement the War Book.

Peter Fraser.
Alexander Turnbull Library, F-37488 1/2

Britain and her allies declared war but the Irish euphemistically declared it 'the Emergency'. Ireland, like New Zealand, passed a whole raft of emergency regulations ranging from freezing wages to restrictions on the possession and use of pigeons, the latter presumably to prevent spying.[11]

Despite its neutrality during WWII, significant numbers of citizens from the Irish Free State still served in the British armed forces. It seems that no one can agree on exact numbers. Robert Fisk's *In Time of War* points to the numbers being around 42,000, but then says there have been claims that the number could have been as high as 165,000.[12] The *Scotsman* newspaper on 12 June 2009 stated that 'more than 3600 citizens from the Republic were killed in WWII'.[13] Nearly 5000 members of the Irish Defence Forces deserted to fight for Britain and her Allies, and after the war they were discriminated against, losing their rights to pensions and barred from holding government jobs. They were finally pardoned in 2013.[14] In WWII the Victoria Cross was awarded to eight Irishmen, and one was also awarded the George Cross. Canada, with a million people in its armed forces, only won ten such awards.[15] New Zealand had 154,000 people in arms in WWII with eight New Zealanders awarded the Victoria Cross, and Charles Upham winning a bar to his.

And while Ireland was officially neutral, it was clear they favoured the Allies. When Allied airmen landed in Ireland they were quickly taken across the border to Northern Ireland, while German aircrew languished in Curragh Prison for the duration of the war.

Robert Fisk recounts incidents where Allied air crew were well treated by the Irish. This included Commanding General Jacob Devers of the United States Armored Force, who got completely lost on a flight from the Middle East to Portugal and, somewhat amazingly, finally made land near Athenry, just outside Galway. The story goes that the local Irish Army commander took the general to a nearby hotel and gave him an impromptu banquet before making arrangements for him to travel to Northern Ireland. An American pilot whose Flying Fortress aircraft crash-landed near Clonakilty in County Cork somehow managed to get £200 out of a local bank and bought drinks for just about everyone in the town. The crews of some aircraft that landed in Ireland in a damaged state were often allowed to stay until their aircraft were repaired and to then fly to Northern Ireland.[16]

Another example of friendly neutrality was that British and American servicemen and politicians regularly travelled in flying boats via Foynes, a village near Limerick on the Shannon Estuary. New Zealand Prime Minister Peter Fraser left from Foynes en route to the United States and it is speculated, but not proven, that even Winston Churchill did likewise.

There are some interesting stories in relation to Ireland's neutrality at the border between north and south. During the war, houses in Northern Ireland were required to comply with the blackout so lights were out at night, while those in Éire had their lights on as the blackout didn't apply to them. Half of the village of Pettigo in County Fermanagh is in the Republic of Ireland, with the other half in Northern Ireland, which meant only half the town was in darkness.[17]

As part of its neutrality policy, Ireland banned the wearing of all military uniforms in the country for the duration of WWII, except for Ireland's own military forces. This created something of a problem for Irishmen serving in the British armed forces. Under military law they were required to wear uniforms when on leave, and unless they got an exemption from their unit, they had problems visiting their families in the Irish Free State.

While Churchill grumped about Ireland's neutrality, others high up in the British Government referred to the land across the Irish Sea as their 'neutral state'.[18] It seemed that Irish neutrality suited both Britain and Germany, and despite Churchill, in one of his irrational moments, threatening to invade Ireland and take over the Treaty ports, saner minds within his government and armed forces prevailed. Sadly Churchill's contempt of the Irish led him to make gratuitous insults that soured his historical legacy for some. For example, he's alleged to have said: 'Invading Ireland was not worth it … we left the de Valera government to frolic with the Germans and later the Japanese' and that … 'legally I believe they are at war but skulking'.[19]

Such outbursts were not uncommon. Churchill's top military advisor, General 'Pug' Ismay, described his leader to a colleague thus: 'He is not the least like anyone you and I have ever met. He is a mass of contradictions. He is either on the crest of a wave or in a trough; either highly laudable or bitterly condemnatory; either in an angelic temper or a hell of a rage; when he isn't fast asleep, he's a volcano.'[20] David Lloyd George summed up the British leader quite well when he said: 'Churchill always needed someone to apply the brakes to save him from himself and from his own impetuosity, unlimited ideas and violent energies.'[21]

Churchill's reported comments on Ireland's neutrality helped fuel the hysterical cries of the Returned and Services Association (RSA) and other pro-British, anti-Irish organisations in New Zealand that condemned Ireland's wartime policy. Anti-Irish sentiment, both during and after the war, ran high. It wasn't helped that the friendly neutral policy which Ireland adopted was pretty much kept under wraps by both Ireland and the UK governments for fear of German retaliation. However the words from Westminster would fuel anti-Catholic bigotry in New Zealand and haunt the Sons of Éire.

4

The beginning of the battle with Britain

With war declared against Germany, New Zealand was looking at how best to defeat the German and Italian forces, while keeping an eye on the potential threat from the Imperial Japanese forces. The Irishmen in Wellington were also quickly forming their own much smaller army to oppose any attempt by the Crown to conscript them into the largely British-controlled armed forces. Probably over a pint or two, a group of men from the Wellington Irish Society got together to form a single-purpose organisation to prevent their call-up into the armed forces. They called themselves the Éire National Association (ENA). I have been unable to find records of exactly what date or how it was formed, but I know they elected an executive of ten, which included my father, Matt Burke.

The ENA records show that subscriptions started in 1940, and most of the members each contributed £27 over five years to cover its running expenses. Some made smaller contributions, a few slightly larger. Two Catholic priests, Fr Hanrahan and Fr McGlynn, also made minor contributions to the ENA, which by 1945 had a paid-up membership of 284.[1]

Three people played a pivotal role in the formation of the organisation: Paddy Feeney, Maurice Leo Aylward and Fred Ongley.

Paddy Feeney was one of seven children born to Peter and Bridget Feeney in Waterdale, Claregalway. In the 1911 census he is listed as being able to read and write both English and Irish. Leaving Ireland in October 1925, he arrived in Wellington from Sydney on the SS *Maheno* on 4 January 1926.

Feeney had fought with Liam Mellows in the 1916 Rising at the age of 18. He served as a Volunteer in the Claregalway Company of the Galway Brigade and fought at Carnmore Cross, Athenry Agricultural Station, Moyode and Limepark. His commanding officers were Mellows, Nicholas Kyne and Alfred Monahan. In 1916 he was arrested and held in Richmond Barracks in Dublin, but released in August of that year. He later served as a battalion officer with the IRA in the War of Independence and took part in attacks on RIC barracks at Loughgeorge, Bookeen, Kilroe and Headford. In the Troubles he held the rank of battalion commander of the 1st and 3rd Battalions of the Galway and North Galway Brigades respectively. He was also a member of

Paddy Feeney (2nd from right) at the handover of the Renmore Barracks, Galway 1922.
Courtesy of Tom Kenny

a flying column in 1920 and features in a photograph with colleagues in a book about Castlegar Parish.[2] During the Civil War, Feeney fought on the anti-Treaty side and attacked Free State troops at Mount Talbot, Lissnally, Tuam and Ballyglinin.[3]

Feeney's military involvement indicates a relationship with Fianna Fáil, and hence with de Valera. He was one of the few Irishmen living in New Zealand who received a military pension from the Irish Government for his role in the 1916 Rising and the 1919–21 Troubles.

When Feeney arrived in Wellington, he worked on the waterfront and became involved in the Irish Republican Association which was largely controlled by Gerald Griffin, a well-known socialist, republican and supporter of de Valera. Griffin was born in Cork in 1903 and arrived in New Zealand in 1913, where his father set up a bookshop in Wellington. Initially Feeney got on well with Griffin, but later the pair fell out over the purchase of some hurling sticks. Griffin was once described as a 'personality wrapped up in barbed wire' because of his apparently abrasive style. He went on to have a successful career in the trade union movement.[4]

Following his spat with Griffin, Feeney left the association and became involved in waterfront union politics and a prominent member of the

A wandering Paddy

While working on the wharves, Paddy Feeney would have come into contact with one of the great characters who inhabited the Wellington waterfront in the 1920s and '30s – a dog known as Paddy the Wanderer. His original mistress was a young girl, the daughter of a seaman. When she died, Paddy the dog made the waterfront his home and was looked after by 'wharfies' and seamen alike. His death on 17 July 1939 at the age of 19 saw a notice appear in the local paper. A procession of 12 taxis led by a traffic officer and followed by a cortège of 60 men made the short journey from Queens Wharf to the incinerator for his cremation. Today a special drinking fountain for dogs at the wharf is a constant reminder of this well-loved local identity.

Wellington Irish Society. In January 1930 he married Bess Sherlock and the pair were frequently mentioned in newspaper reports on the society's functions. On 7 October 1936 Bess Feeney is reported by the *Evening Post* as being a hostess at the National Irish Dance at St Francis Hall in Thorndon. She is said to have worn pink with white fur trimmings. All the tables were draped in the green and yellow colours of the club and one of the guests of honour was Monsignor Connolly.[5] St Francis Hall was next to the Basilica of the Sacred Heart – now the Cathedral – and also next door to the house where members of my extended family lived for many years. The chances are that my mother and father were at the function, but they were not mentioned in the newspaper report.

As Paddy Feeney was active in trade union matters on the waterfront, there is reason to believe that he would have had contact with Peter Fraser, who was the member of parliament for Wellington Central and the future wartime prime minister. Feeney therefore had early contact with the future leaders of both Ireland and New Zealand who were to play an important role for the Sons of Éire, and with his strong IRA background, organising ability, political connections in Ireland and mana, he was the logical choice as president of the ENA.

His able deputy was Maurice Leo Aylward, who was born in Knockmoylan, Ballyhale, County Kilkenny, on 14 May 1909.[6] Like my father, Maurice was too young to have actively participated in either the 1916 Rising or the War of Independence. According to his nephew and family historian, Fr Eamon Aylward, Maurice's brother Patrick was a local commander of the IRA, and his brother William was an active member of his unit in South Kilkenny. Patrick

Maurice Aylward, c.1923.
Aylward collection

was a commander in the 1916 Rising, as well as being involved in the 1919–21 Troubles. William lost an eye in an abortive attempt to blow up a railway bridge at Knockwilliam. Because of Patrick's involvement in the IRA, the Aylward family was targeted by the British forces and Maurice would have experienced raids on the family home.[7]

Maurice Aylward was elected secretary of the ENA and later assumed an additional role as the official emissary of the organisation, representing it at meetings with the New Zealand Government and ultimately taking the group's case to de Valera in Ireland. His genial nature combined with his deep abiding passion for Ireland equipped him well for a negotiating role.

In his early years Maurice was seen as a scholarly type. At one stage he was identified as a future priest and was funded by the Coonan family to attend St Joseph's Secondary School in Roscrea with this intent. But the priestly life was not for Maurice and on 8 August 1929 he boarded the liner *Orsova* in London, bound for Melbourne, Australia, where he initially stayed with his uncle Dick Raftis. He worked in Australia before arriving in New Zealand on 2 June 1939. Like other leaders of the ENA, Maurice also retained strong links with the Wellington Irish Society and became president in 1946.

While the Irishmen in the ENA felt they had right on their side, they were well aware that they would need legal representation. In particular they needed someone capable of dealing with the armed forces appeal boards set up to hear cases of conscientious objection. Some of the members of the boards were magistrates chosen for their hard-line approach to conscientious objectors (also called 'conchies' or 'COs').

The ENA chose F.W. Ongley as their lawyer. He would have been known to them, in particular to Paddy Feeney, because of his connections with the waterfront workers.

Ongley's mother had emigrated to New Zealand from County Tyrone and came from a large Catholic family with many relations who were priests and nuns.[8] Fred Ongley's father, Frederick senior, was a professional gardener from England and the family settled in the North Otago town of Ōamaru. Frederick senior had an adventurous trip to New Zealand when the ship he boarded sank in the Bay of Biscay and he was rescued after two days, clinging to the ship's mast.[9] He later resumed his voyage on the *Edwin Fox*.[10]

In Wellington, Fred Ongley represented watersiders and seamen in numerous cases, ranging from receiving goods and theft to taking part in an alleged illegal strike. He represented a seaman charged with bigamy, a seaman charged with breaching the Censorship and Publicity Emergency Regulations, a soldier charged with desertion, and even a man charged with fortune-telling.[11] In some of these cases Ongley represented clients who appeared before magistrate W.F. Stilwell. This is significant because Stilwell later became Chair of the No.4 Armed Forces Appeal Board that would hear the case of the Sons of Éire.

Ongley won a scholarship to St Patrick's College and then studied law and practiced in Ōamaru before moving back to Wellington, where he became a partner in the firm Ongley, O'Donovan and Arndt. One of Ongley's brothers was killed in WWI, while another was imprisoned as a conscientious objector. Fred was pro-Irish and widely known for saying, 'No Irishman could be conscripted to fight an Englishman's war.'[12]

As the Irishmen started to mobilise, New Zealand continued to make

preparations for war. While it was generally recognised as far back as the mid-1930s that New Zealanders would end up going to war, there was always a question of where they'd fight. This was because of the twin threats posed by the Japanese in the Pacific and the Axis forces in the Northern Hemisphere. Understandably, with a small population, New Zealand's resources were at best meagre. But on 9 September 1939 the New Zealand Government informed the British Government that the first echelon of a New Zealand

Fred Ongley, detail taken from the ENA executive 1945 photo.

Division for service in any theatre of the war would commence training on 3 October. Four days later an Emergency Regulations Bill was passed that allowed the government to control prices, prevent profiteering and secure public safety. It was also made clear that there would be equality of sacrifice, meaning wealthy people would not be exempt from serving.[13]

The starting point for establishing the New Zealand Division was finding an officer to command the army, and to that end Fraser was sent to London in 1939 to find a suitable person. But it was more than just a recruiting trip, as he also represented New Zealand at the Conference of Dominion Prime Ministers, and met First Lord of the Admiralty Winston Churchill. Fraser went because Prime Minister Savage was seriously ill with cancer and unable to make the arduous journey by flying boat. The journey took him via Australia, the East Indies, Singapore, Bangkok, India, Iran, Israel, Egypt, Crete, Greece, Italy, Marseilles in France, and then on to London. Later Fraser visited the Western Front with an Australian government representative, and both came back dissatisfied with the preparations being made to hold the inevitable German attack.[14]

While in London Fraser spoke on the BBC, making comments which no doubt would have warmed the heart of Éamon de Valera: 'We must this time make a most earnest effort to build a new world in which the rights of smaller nations will be as secure as those of larger nations, and in which men and women everywhere will be assured of access to all the good things of life.'[15] This was a line which Fraser was to echo after the war at the San Francisco Peace Conference, and similar to what de Valera had said at the League of Nations in 1936.

The preferred candidate to head the 2nd New Zealand Expeditionary Force (2NZEF) was Major General Bernard (Tiny) Freyberg, who, although born in Britain, came to New Zealand when he was two. He qualified as a dentist and worked briefly in Levin, about 100 kilometres north of Wellington. He had joined the armed forces in WWI and served at Gallipoli and the Western Front, and was awarded the Victoria Cross among other military decorations. Fraser and Freyberg met in England and got on well. On 23 November 1939 Freyberg was appointed to head the 2NZEF, a post he held until the end of WWII. Interestingly, Freyberg joined Massey's Cossacks to help break the waterfront strike in 1913, which would have seen him and Fraser, the trade unionist, on opposing sides. However they formed a solid bond during the war, putting aside possible enmities from the past.

The pair arrived in New Zealand on Christmas Day 1939, and Freyberg immediately started the task of selecting officers and training his troops.

As this began so did the debate over conscription, and in New Zealand the jingoism of the opposition National Party came to the fore. The party had grown out of the Farmers' Union, whose members were part of Massey's Cossacks. The National Party largely represented wealthier New Zealanders and farmers, who were strong supporters of conscription.

The Labour Party on the other hand was traditionally opposed to this. Tim Armstrong, James Thorn, Bob Semple and Peter Fraser had all been imprisoned in 1917 for sedition after speaking out against conscription. Paddy Webb was jailed for two years for refusing to serve in the armed forces in WWI.[16] At one stage half the executive of the party were in jail. Walter Nash, who would become Deputy Prime Minister to Fraser when Savage died in early 1940, was also a former pacifist.[17]

Paddy Webb and fellow Labour MP Jim O'Brien were both Catholics and trade unionists with strong New Zealand West Coast connections, and had led the charge opposing conscription. An interesting factor that may have helped inflame this debate during WWI on the West Coast was the strong opposition to conscription in Australia by the controversial Archbishop of Melbourne, Dr Daniel Mannix. Many gold miners on the Coast came from the goldfields of Victoria, hence the strong connection between the two regions, particularly in the township of Hokitika.

The appalling and brutal treatment of conscientious objectors in WWI was uppermost in Fraser's mind. He'd been in prison with Mark Briggs, whose cruel treatment, along with that of Archibald Baxter, is recounted by David Grant in *Field Punishment No.1*.[18] The other problem for Labour was that many of its constituents were known pacifists. In essence, the Sons of Éire found themselves in a somewhat unholy (or was it holy?) alliance that included members and ministers of the Methodist Church. There were protests in Wellington against the war, but most were short-lived as the police quickly hauled speakers off their soapboxes, took them to jail and a date with a generally unsympathetic magistrate.

The year 1940 was special for New Zealand as it marked 100 years since the signing of the Treaty of Waitangi, the founding document of the dominion. On 22 January de Valera sent Prime Minister Savage a cable on behalf of the people of Ireland offering 'cordial congratulations and sincere good wishes for the ever increasing prosperity and happiness of the people of New Zealand.'[19] A day later Savage thanked de Valera and expressed 'warm appreciation of the good wishes you have been good enough to extend.'[20] This exchange of messages could only reinforce the bond between the two small nations.

With Savage battling cancer, Peter Fraser carried much of his boss's workload. Finally on 27 March 1940, New Zealand's Prime Minister died at the age of 68 and the country went into mourning. Michael Joseph Savage had been the architect of the welfare state as it is today, and his picture still adorns the offices and living rooms of Labour supporters. His state funeral included a Requiem Mass at the Basilica of the Sacred Heart in Hill Street, which overlooks Parliament buildings. His body was then taken by special train to Auckland where he had been the MP for West Auckland. He was buried at Bastion Point, a stunning site overlooking Auckland's Waitematā Harbour.

Peter Fraser was destined to take on the role of prime minister and on 4 April he was duly elected with an overwhelming majority. The party later elected Walter Nash as Deputy Prime Minister.[21] Carl Berendsen, a man who clearly did not tolerate fools or poorly performing politicians, offered high praise for Fraser, describing him thus:

> Fraser was surprisingly well equipped for his role as a wartime leader. Fraser was above all a consummate politician … He had an uncanny sense of anticipation and could, and did, prepare for difficulties before they arose.[22]

While the politics within the government and especially the Labour Party were playing out, the ENA had officially formed itself and elected an executive with Paddy Feeney (Galway) as president, Maurice Leo Aylward (Kilkenny) as secretary, Tom Cahill (Galway) as treasurer, Edward Walsh (Cork) as vice president, Michael Lafferty (Roscommon), Patrick Hickey (Kildare), Tim McCarthy (Limerick), Con Horan and Denis Roche from Kerry, and Joe Nally and Matt Burke from Galway. Fred Ongley was appointed as 'consul of law'.

It is interesting that four members of the executive were from Galway, but there is no evidence to suggest why. Maybe they were just a rebellious lot prepared to speak their mind and with no love for Britain. A subscription was determined, and from the final set of accounts it appears that most members who joined at the start contributed just over £5 a year for the five years the ENA was in existence.

With Ongley appointed as their lawyer, a man well connected in Wellington, they began lobbying the Labour Government. Fraser, who was also the MP for Wellington Central, had many Catholic friends and there is little doubt that the ENA briefed these people to get their message across to him. With his waterfront union affiliations, Feeney is likely to have been advising a man known to have influence with Fraser, Fintan Patrick Walsh. One of the most colourful characters in the New Zealand trade union

Éire National Association (ENA) executive, 1940–45. Front row, from left: Tom Cahill, Edward Walsh, Paddy Feeney, Maurice Leo Aylward, Michael Lafferty, Fred Ongley. Back row: Patrick Hickey, Tim McCarthy, Con Horan, Joe Nally, Denis Roche, Matt Burke.

movement, he was born Patrick Tuohy in the Bay of Plenty, New Zealand, but after visiting Ireland where his mother was born, changed his name to Walsh in 1919. He would probably have met Feeney and other ENA members in his role as president of the Seamen's Union. It is also known that Walsh and Ongley did not get on, so there is conjecture as to the part Walsh may have actually played.

Following the invasion of Poland by Germany there was a lull in the war before the Germans attacked the Netherlands, Belgium and France. Known as the Phoney War from late 1939 into 1940, this time was used by the Allies to build up their forces and hone the legislation (including conscription), which would be needed to prosecute the war. Likewise the ENA used this time to organise themselves and lobby the government, including Prime Minister Fraser, with the objective of excluding Irishmen in New Zealand from those eligible for conscription.

Just a matter of days after Fraser's war cabinet was formed on 30 April 1940, Hitler made his move.[23] On 10 May German forces invaded France and the Low Countries of Europe, and Winston Churchill took over from Neville Chamberlain as Prime Minister of Britain. It was now game on.

While historically the Labour Government was anti-war and anti-conscription, they were now faced with a situation where the future of New Zealand and the dominions was under threat. Fraser, after consultation with colleagues and the trade union movement, followed the plan in the War Book, and on Tuesday 18 June the National Service Emergency Regulations 1940 were promulgated.[24] In an ironic twist it was Lord Galway, the Governor-General, who signed them into law. These regulations gave the government virtually unlimited power to direct people and resources in the way that they considered necessary to fight the war.

A key regulation was conscription, which required all men between the ages of 19 and 45 to register. The regulations also covered the setting up of appeal boards and the hearing procedure, as well as medical examinations and how these should be conducted.

A week later, the *New Zealand Gazette* carried the announcement of the appointment of the Minister of Public Works as Minister of National Service. That man was Bob Semple. It seems bizarre that a man who had been imprisoned in WWI for speaking out against conscription was now in charge of conscription and manpowering New Zealanders into essential industries, and was to take a hard line against those who refused to fight.

The 2000 names from the first ballot appeared in the *New Zealand Gazette* of Wednesday 2 October 1940. These men were called up for service with the Territorial Force and among them was no. 376301 Matthias Burke, Lorry Driver, 12 Ngaio Gorge Rd, Kaiwharawhara, Wellington. Also in that ballot were 236837 Maurice Leo Aylward, 281826 Brian Kennedy, and 235375 Patrick Sullivan, whose appeals were to be included in the test case of six men later called the Sons of Éire. The other two, Jeremiah Allen and John James Moriarty, were not in that first ballot. Two members of the ENA executive, 235453 Con Horan and 141558 Thomas Cahill, were also selected in this first ballot.[25]

Given Semple's hard line, it is not surprising that the armed forces appeal boards, to which conscientious objectors had to put their case, had sweeping powers. In *Out in the Cold*, David Grant states that the personnel chosen to hear the appeals were hardly CO-friendly.[26] Six boards were established nationally, consisting of a chairman who was either a magistrate or lawyer, plus two advocates – one representing employers and the other employees. There was also a Crown representative, who was a lawyer to assist in legal matters. No women were ever appointed to these boards. The criteria for appointment was that they were 'men of standing in the community, they had to be over military age and without sons eligible for service'.[27]

Minister of National Service Bob Semple draws the first marble for conscription into the Territorial Service, in Wellington on 24 September 1940. From left: Adjutant-General Col O.H. Mead, Unknown, Minister of Defence F. Jones, Unknown, divisional clerk J.B. Black, W.F. Stilwell (supervising the ballot), Bob Semple, Director of National Service J.S. Hunter, Assistant Director of National Service H.L. Bockett.
Evening Post collection, Alexander Turnbull Library, N-P-2038-5/1

Lower Hutt.

249304 Bullen, George Charles, grocer, 36 Cudby St., Lower Hutt.
131401 Bullock, Maitland Alfred, stevedoring timekeeper, 26 Waitoa Rd., Hataitai, Wellington.
128358 Bundy, William Henry Kay, fisherman, 10 Milne Tce., Island Bay, Wellington.
376349 Burd, Charles Frederick, joiner, 38 Bolton St., Petone.
163032 Burdan, Eric James, farm labourer, Wainui-o-mata, Lower Hutt.
270141 Burke, Daniel Joseph, porter, care of Post Office Hotel, Grey St., Wellington.
395944 Burke, Harold Wilfred, farm hand, Porirua Rd., Glenside, Johnsonville.
376301 Burke, Matthias, lorry-driver, 12 Ngaio Gorge Rd, Kaiwarra.
395932 Burley, Albert Cornelius, bushman, care of Hazelwoods Store, Upper Hutt.
378219 Burnette, Athol Cyril Bernard, grocer's assistant, 39 Motueka St., Ngaio, Wellington N. 4.
290214 Burnette, Reginald Clarence, clerk, 39 Motueka St., Ngaio, Wellington.
227121 Burns, George, apprentice turner and fitter, 6 McDonald Cres., Wellington.
253245 Burns, Martin David, brass-finisher, 90 Melbourne Rd., Island Bay, Wellington, S. 2.
126002 Burr, Leslie Alfred, boot-machinist, 65 Rintoul St., Newtown.
lorry driver, 10 Waitui Cres., Lower Hutt.

Matt Burke's call-up.
New Zealand Gazette, 2 October 1940

On 16 January 1941 the government gazetted the names of the men who would serve on the appeal boards. In the case of Wellington the appointments were Wilfred Fosberry Stilwell as Chair, with James Walisham Godkin Brodie and Andrew Parlane as advocates.[28]

A day later the Director of National Service J.S. Hunter issued a 26-page directive to the Boards setting out their roles and responsibilities.[29] It also set out the grounds for appeal, which included 'status' and the words: 'has ceased to be a British subject'.[30] This was extrapolated later in the circular where it noted that appeals on this ground would be uncommon.[31] It also defined conscientious objection as 'conscientiously objects to serving with the armed forces'.[32]

The circular went on to state how appeals were to be heard and noted that while lawyers could be used by appellants, 'other persons' (presumably friends or advocates) should be allowed 'sparingly'.[33] The rules stated that hearings by the appeal boards should be public, no doubt to name and shame those refusing to fight. There was an interesting provision relating to evidence stating that 'the appeal board may admit and accept such evidence as it sees fit, whether admissible in a court of law or not.'[34] A clause that would affect the Sons of Éire referred to 'public interest' and noted that the 'Dominion must produce the maximum output possible of all forms of primary production required for the armed forces'.[35] Manpower needed to run essential industries was to become a problem for New Zealand as the war progressed, especially as many farmers and others in the primary sector joined the armed forces. There were suggestions that the Americans wanted New Zealand butter and other produce more than they wanted New Zealand soldiers.

The other key point about the regulations was that any appeal had to be lodged with the Director of National Service within ten days of a person's name being published in the *Gazette*, so the appellants had to act quickly.[36] The regulations also allowed for 'two or more persons to appeal in respect of any one man called up', which legitimised the test case taken by the Sons of Éire.[37] From both parties' point of view it represented a saving in time and money. The directive called for clergy and doctors to be exempt and set guidelines on the issue of undue hardship. It also warned boards not to pre-judge a case or give 'any substantial suspicion of pre-determination which would render the proceedings illegal'.[38] In essence, it was telling the boards to keep their thoughts to themselves, and for some that was difficult.

In a final gesture of generosity to those appealing their call-up, the rules allowed for an appellant or witness attending an appeal board hearing to be reimbursed for 'second-class travelling accommodation and reasonable out-of-pocket expenses'.

With the rules defined it was up to appellants, such as the Sons of Éire and their lawyer, Fred Ongley, to frame their case around the prescribed regulations. It was not a case of a simple appeal. Rather, it was a matter of seeing how a panel of men and a lawyer paid for by the government would legally interpret their case.

5

Paper war

By January 1941 WWII was in full swing. The British Army had been defeated in Europe and only a military miracle at Dunkirk, due to the efforts of a flotilla of small boats and ships, saved thousands of soldiers from captivity. The British military were seasoned professionals when it came to making defeats seem like victories, such as the withdrawal from Gallipoli in WWI.

In the Battle of Britain the RAF thwarted German aspirations to invade the UK, in a large part due to the efforts of New Zealander Keith Park who headed 11 Group of Fighter Command. This group made up of Spitfires and Hurricanes was tasked with defending London and south-east England. Churchill waxed lyrical about the victory but Park was unpopular and criticised by some British RAF leaders, so he was unceremoniously relieved of his command and sent to Training Command. Park deeply resented this and only in relatively recent times has his contribution been recognised – most spectacularly by a statue erected in London in 2010. The war of the Atlantic was also in full swing as German U-boats attacked convoys from the United States bound for Britain with vital supplies. New Zealand farm produce was also sent to help feed Britain.

Being neutral did not save Ireland from being bombed by the Germans, which was put down to incompetence by Luftwaffe pilots. In August 1940 the Shelbourne Creamery in Wexford was hit and three people killed. Several more raids followed over the next nine months, with the most deadly on 31 May 1941 when bombs fell in the North Strand of Dublin killing 28 people. This was nothing compared to what happened in Belfast in April and May 1941 when 900 people were killed in a concerted blitz. Such was the extent of the fires caused by one of the raids that firemen from Dublin drove north to help put out the blaze, another example of the friendly neutral stance of de Valera's administration.

Back in New Zealand the events of the war in Europe further fuelled the need for the ENA to prepare to take on the issue of conscription. I assume that Feeney and Aylward, in particular, were lobbying Fraser and his government. They probably did not bother with government officials as they were not seen

The South British building in Wellington where ENA lawyer Fred Ongley had his office. It was only 100 metres from the AMP building where the No.4 Armed Forces Appeal Board was based.

as particularly friendly to the Irish cause. More than a little truth was contained in the claim from Ted Whitehead: 'Under the English legal system you are innocent until you are shown to be Irish.'[1]

Before the ENA made public their intentions to become an official organisation to represent Irishmen opposed to conscription, they consulted both the New Zealand and Irish governments. This included letters sent by Fred Ongley on the official letterhead of Ongley, O'Donovan and Arndt, from their offices in the South British Building, Lambton Quay, Wellington, to the New Zealand Government, and one with similar wording to Irish Prime Minister Éamon de Valera, on 19 February 1941:

> We have been consulted by Éire Nationals at present residing in the Dominion of New Zealand. These men are all over 16 years of age and they are concerned to know whether they are liable to be called up for war service by the Government of the Dominion of New Zealand. For your information we forward herewith:
>
> 1. The Emergency Regulations Act 1939
>
> 2. The National Service Regulations 1940
>
> 3. The General Reserve Classification Order 1940
>
> 4. The National Service Emergency Regulations 1940 Amendment No.2
>
> 5. The National Service Emergency Regulations 1940 Amendment No.2
>
> Regulation No.5 of the National Service Emergency Regulations 1940 establishes a 'General Reserve' and includes 'every person resident in New Zealand'.
>
> Regulation No.8 makes these persons liable for National Service outside the armed forces.

Regulation 13 provides for male reservists being called up for service with the armed forces.

These Éire Nationals have all attained 19 years of age, they are unmarried and are under the age of 46 years. Thus they become First Division Reservists under Regulation 3 of the General Classification Order 1940 if they are natural-born British subjects.

The view put forward is that these men are natural-born British subjects, they having been born in Ireland. Regulation 14 makes provision for the selection by Lot of Reservists as required for service with the armed forces.

A number of your Nationals have already been selected by lot for service 'Outside the Armed Forces' and others have been selected by lot for 'Service with the Armed Forces' in pursuance of these provisions.

These men wish to know their position and their liability and as to what their attitude should be and what they should do in view of the neutrality of Éire.

They desire to have the guidance of the Government of Éire on the matter as they do not wish to take any action that will in any way be prejudicial to Éire or the Government of Éire or the neutrality of Éire.

This letter has been submitted to the New Zealand Government before being sent to you and is sent with the permission of that Government.

We have the honour to be, Sir, your obedient servants.[2]

I have been unable to find a response from de Valera to this letter, but it is probably safe to assume that as the ENA went ahead with its appeals, their actions were either sanctioned or deemed to cause no embarrassment to Éire.

A week later on 26 February 1941 another letter was sent to Prime Minister Fraser by Fred Ongley on behalf of the ENA:

Referring to the memorandum sent you by or on behalf of persons born in Éire and claiming to be citizens of Éire and to their interview with you.

We are acting for these men. In their memorandum to you they state that they are prepared to do any work other than combatant work being given them. They realise that residing in New Zealand entails obligations on them notwithstanding the neutrality of Éire. They wish to fulfil that obligation by doing work of a noncombatant character that may be given them so that they can assist in maintaining the resources and development of the country.

Please advise us whether anything can be done to meet the position.

We have the honour to be, Sir, your obedient servants,
Ongley, O'Donovan and Arndt.[3]

This letter to Fraser confirms that ENA representatives, most likely Feeney and Aylward, had met with him. Who else did we don't know. It would seem that Ongley's letter was designed to provide a paper trail of the contact. It is, in essence, an early affirmation of the ENA's position that it would support the New Zealand war effort in any way, except in a military role that would involve its members wearing a 'British' uniform.

On 28 February 1941 Fraser responded by acknowledging the letter and saying:

> I have to inform you that I shall be pleased to arrange for the matter to receive early and careful consideration of Government.[4]

This is arguably the typical form letter response, but the way it was worded suggests that the plight of the Irishmen was weighing on Fraser's mind and that he was looking for a solution which might be acceptable to a multitude of political positions, both within and outside of government. It was apparent that the Sons of Éire case did not exactly fit into the normal conscientious objection definition. In his statement to the appeal board later on, John James Moriarty claimed the government ignored this approach by the ENA.[5] This was probably not surprising because to have intervened may have drawn a negative public response and appear that Fraser was usurping the authority of the appeal boards.

The contents of the letter to both governments indicate that the ENA was politically astute, being careful not to embarrass or offend either the Irish or New Zealand governments, or cause trouble by their stance. They were not looking for a fight, but rather a compromise that would be acceptable to all parties.

The letters and their tone also suggest that the ENA felt it had support and friends within the New Zealand Labour Party. That they were prepared to clear de Valera's letter with the government, and that Fraser was prepared to sanction the sending of the letter, suggests that there was some sympathy at the top political level for the Irishmen's cause. At the lower levels and in the bureaucracy this was not the case. I assume Aylward with the silver tongue and Fianna Fáil connection, and Fred Ongley with his legal expertise and New Zealand connections and networks, were behind these letters, especially given that the copy of this correspondence came from Aylward's personal collection of documents. They were building relationships and starting to position the ENA as some sort of interim, semi-political representative body of the Irish in New Zealand. In his testimony to the No.4 Armed Forces Appeal Board, Maurice Aylward stated that Éire had planned to appoint a consul to New Zealand but this had been postponed.[6]

Bob Semple and his cat, Fluff.
Alexander Turnbull Library, F-29111 1/2

Membership of the ENA grew, presumably as the Irish network in Wellington and other parts of the country realised that a collective voice was much stronger than an individual. Although a few did take individual action, in some cases before the much publicised Sons of Éire test case.

New Zealand introduced conscription for overseas service in June 1940 after it was clear that insufficient numbers of men were volunteering.

In November 1915 the *Maoriland Worker* had quoted Bob Semple as saying: 'Conscription is the negation of human liberty. It means the destruction of every principle that is held sacred to the working class. It means the destruction of the democracy at home. It is the blackest industrial hell.'[7] Twenty-five years later Semple was singing a very different song. He scorned pacifists in much the same way as he did communists, and was a defender of the detention camps that were set up to incarcerate conscientious objectors in WWII.[8] He proudly drew the first ballot and was later quoted as saying:

> We do not want wholesale exemptions. By 1943 every young man at present of military age will be out of the country or in a camp. If we are too liberal and too sympathetic with the fellow who wants to dodge we will have trouble.[9]

In fairness to the Labour Government, they had little choice but to introduce conscription in WWII and, while it may have been against their principles, pragmatism prevailed. Though the likes of Fraser and Semple had been jailed for sedition opposing conscription in WWI, they saw the two world wars as completely different. In their eyes WWI was a 'capitalist brawl' whereas WWII was a fight for freedom and unionism.[10]

Liberally minded people were hoping that conscientious objectors might receive sympathetic treatment from the government, while the RSA and Labour's opponents expected Fraser to be 'soft' on the pacifists.[11] Fraser's relationship with the RSA was far from harmonious. When the RSA demanded that conscientious objectors remain in detention after the war and lose their civil rights for ten years after it ended, he is reputed to have given them a tongue lashing, saying their arguments lacked credibility.[12]

Fraser seemingly left the handling of conscription issues to Bob (Bulldozer) Semple, as he never publicly embraced conscription in the same way as his colleague did. This was clever politics because it allowed Fraser to have some wriggle room in negotiating with Britain and Ireland over the outcome of the Sons of Éire case later on in 1942. The Labour Government surprised everyone and proved to be a fine prosecutor of the war effort.

On Tuesday 4 March 1941 the first two of the six later referred to as the Sons of Éire, Jeremiah Allen, cellar man, and Brian Kennedy, freezing worker, were called up for overseas service and their names published in the *Gazette*. Two months later, on Wednesday 7 May 1941, the *Gazette* published the names of the others: Maurice Leo Aylward, freezing worker; Matthias Burke, battery process worker; John James Moriarty, labourer; and Patrick Sullivan, freezing worker.[13] Their fate, along with 56 other ENA members also called up, which would eventually climb to 155 (the Citizens of Éire), was to hinge on the outcome of the Sons of Éire case.

Within ten days of their names appearing in the *Gazette*, the men appealed their call-up. At that point it would seem that the six Sons of Éire were chosen or volunteered to be the 'test case'.

The other 56 men were listed as: Patrick Boyle, labourer; Denis Brosnan, fire brigade man; Jeremiah Brosnan, gold miner; Martin Brosnan, railway worker; Thomas Cahill, barman and porter; Michael Carr, labourer; Tim Carr, council employee; John Clancy, barman; Michael Collins, farm labourer; Michael Connell, labourer; Michael Connolly, cleaner; Peter Connolly, Martin Conor, Hubert Conway, labourers; Patrick J. Coughlan, porter; Thomas Crowley, freezing hand; Daniel Culloty, labourer; Terence Curtin, James Curtin, factory workers; Richard J. Dunne, carpenter; Edward Faherty, barman; John Fleming, Stephen Forde, Charles V. Giles,[14] Thomas Grealish, John Grogan, Patrick Grogan, Peter Heffernan, labourers; Patrick J. Hickey, barman; Con Horan, barman porter; Anthony Kearney, labourer; Dennis Kelliher, blacksmith; Frank Kelly, bricklayer; Dermot Anthony Kennedy, male nurse; Joseph Loughrey, freezing-chamber hand; Thomas McCabe, solderer; Thomas A. McCarthy, barman; Edward Mahoney, freezing hand; Michael J. Mannion, labourer; Thomas Meehan, clerk; Peter J. Melvin, bushworker; Michael Mongan, carpenter; Michael J. Moore, casual labourer; John Moriarty, hotel worker; Neil Murray, freezing works employee; Denis O'Connor, Richard Power, labourers; Jeremiah Riordan, striker; Denis F. Roche, freezing works employee; Thomas Scully, John

Some of the Citizens of Éire, c.1941. Back row from left: Con Horan, Eddie Shanahan, Mick Carr, Joe Nally, Eddie Faherty, Tom Crowley, Mick Connell. 4th row: Dan Crowley, Barney Mulholland, Con Collins, Jack Sheehan, Charlie Giles, Ned Mahoney, Tim McCarthy, Paddy Coughlan, Denis Roche, Joe Nihile, Bob Giles, Pat Hickey, Jack Fleming. 3rd row: Jack Farrell, Martin Brosnan, Bill Sullivan, Peter Sullivan, Dave O'Connell, Lew O'Regan, Matt Burke, Joe Whooley, Jack Dolan, Mick O'Connor, Tim Tangney, Tim Carr, Peter Melvin. 2nd Row: Tom Cahill, Peter Boyle, Eddie Walsh, Maurice Aylward, Paddy Feeney, Fred Ongley, Dick Fitzgerald, Sean Traynor. Front row: John Clancy, Dick Knox, John Grogan, Hugh Trainor, Mick Lafferty, John James Moriarty, Denis Kelliher.

Sheehan, Michael Sheridan, labourers; Patrick Joseph Sullivan, freezing works employee; Timothy Tangney, labourer; and Sean Traynor, carpenter.[15]

These men were all from Military Area No.5 – Wellington (the region), so their appeals were to be heard by the No.4 Armed Forces Appeal Board based in Wellington city. It is evident that other appeals took place elsewhere, mainly in Auckland, but it appears that the authorities held back making any decision on these appeals until the Sons of Éire test case was concluded in October 1941, as it was seen as setting a precedent. All other appeals by Irishmen from then on were seen as pointless unless there were extenuating circumstances.

With their appeals lodged, the six Sons of Éire worked with Fred Ongley to prepare their individual cases. It's likely that the affidavit which was presented by my father was a template devised by Ongley to be used by the appellants, as it was carefully formatted while allowing room for the men to add their own insights into what they saw during the War of Independence.

Just days before Maurice Aylward, Matthias Burke, John James Moriarty and Patrick Sullivan were balloted to serve overseas, Prime Minister Fraser began the long and torturous journey to London to meet with Churchill and the New Zealand forces overseas. He, along with Private Secretary C.A. Jeffery and Head of the Prime Minister's Department Carl Berendsen, travelled by flying boat, which had a limited range by today's standards. All told it took two weeks just to get to Cairo.[16] Fraser spent considerable time in the Middle East meeting troops and top military commanders before going on to London. Later he would meet with de Valera in Dublin.

May 1941 was not a good month for the New Zealand armed forces. On the 20th the Battle of Crete began, and ended twelve days later with 671 New Zealanders killed in action and more than 2000 taken prisoner, out of a total

Fraser with Carl Berendsen, Head of the Prime Minister's Department, and Private Secretary C.A. Jeffery.
Alexander Turnbull Library, PAColl-5547-051

force of 7000. Two men, Charles Upham and Alfred Hume, won the Victoria Cross for their actions in Crete.[17] The campaign, seen by many as one of New Zealand's greatest military disasters, had been advocated by Churchill, and arguably not well executed by Freyberg. More New Zealanders would have lost their lives or been taken prisoner but for the intervention of Fraser, who was in the Middle East and successfully pressured the British commanders to evacuate more New Zealand troops when it was clear the battle was lost. Fraser was known to have fears about the success of the campaigns of Greece and Crete long before they began. His firmness in dealing with the British military hierarchy was seen as another example of his loyalty to the New Zealand forces.

With Fraser overseas, it was left to his able deputy, Walter Nash, to deal with the issue of the Sons of Éire as their day with the No.4 Armed Forces Appeal Board drew closer. Fred Ongley and the ENA had been busy analysing the rules under which a person could object to being conscripted into the armed forces. It was evident that despite the ENA having a good case, the regulations as written did not take special circumstances into account, and focused entirely on the premise that a conscientious objector was a person opposed to war and therefore refused to fight in any conflict.

Ongley wrote to Nash on 9 June 1941, the day before the appeals of some Irishmen were to be heard in Auckland, formally bringing their special case to his attention.

> We wish to bring this matter under your notice. There are, as you know, a number of men in New Zealand who were born in Ireland who have appealed against being called up for service under the National Service Emergency Regulations 1940. Their appeals are on two grounds:
>
> 1. They are Éire Nationals and not properly liable to conscription by this Dominion for Military Service.
>
> 2. Conscientious grounds.
>
> For your information we enclose a copy of the statement lodged by them in support of their appeal.
>
> In view of the neutrality of Éire and with the permission of the Attorney-General we wrote some time ago to the Prime Minister of Éire for information for the guidance of these appellants (copy of our letter herewith). So far we have not had a reply and whether or not the letter reached its destination we do not know. Appeals have been adjourned from time to time but a number of appeals will come before the No.1 Armed Forces Appeal Board tomorrow. In the press the Chairman (of that board) is reported as follows:

'All the board would have to do is decide was whether such men were British subjects or not, and the Attorney-General has ruled that as they are natural-born Britishers they are liable for service.'

So far as the conscientious objection is concerned these appellants sincerely and conscientiously object because of what they and their relatives saw and/or suffered during the unfortunate Black and Tan Troubles in Ireland. Their cases were probably not in contemplation when the regulations governing conscientious objectors were drawn up. As you know the grounds are 'a genuine belief that it is wrong to engage in warfare under any circumstances' or a 'genuine belief that it is wrong to perform combat services in the armed forces'.

We are instructed to ask that something be done to meet these cases. The appellants have already offered to do any work other than combat work. If their appeals are dealt with it seems they must be dismissed as the Regulations as they now stand and these appellants will automatically become liable for service with the armed forces. The appellants concerned could then avoid compromising their position only by refusing to comply with the order calling them up. It is desired to avoid that position.

Ongley, O'Donovan and Arndt.[18]

It seems from this letter that Ongley was admitting that the appeals would fail even before they took place, unless the government took steps to amend the regulations. He was alerting Nash that the Sons of Éire's case was quite different to that of other conscientious objectors, and confirmed that the men were willing to do what they could to help New Zealand's war effort as long as it didn't involve taking up arms.

It is also worth remembering that Peter Fraser and Walter Nash were not only colleagues but close lifelong friends, and a conversation with Nash was as good as a conversation with Fraser.

The message from the chairman of the Auckland appeal board was obviously not going to be contradicted by the Wellington appeal board. This and other letters all pointed to the anomalies in the regulations, and it's hard to see that there would have been willingness for any change, especially considering some of the anti-Irish sentiment in the New Zealand bureaucracy.

Despite the logic of Ongley's last-ditch appeal for the government to intervene it would seem that Nash, himself a pacifist, was not prepared to take the step that would separate out the Irishmen from other conscientious objectors. There were undoubted pressures at the time, not the least of which would have been the fallout from the Crete campaign and a mood across the country that everyone should 'do their bit' and fight. Standing up for Irish neutrality was not a vote-winning cause.

With no apparent positive response, the ENA went on preparing their case to the appeal board, probably knowing that the chance of success was not high. But it was not in the nature of any Irishmen, least of all these, to capitulate to British law. It was to be in every sense of the word a test case.

No doubt the men were anxious knowing they would be facing a largely hostile panel and the Crown lawyer, Mr C.O. Bell, who was known for his pro-conscription views, and had served on the RSA committee that twice led deputations to Prime Minister Peter Fraser requesting harsher treatment for conscientious objectors.[19] According to David Grant, Bell took a 'prosecutory role' at hearings and was known to wear his RSA badge to intimidate appellants. He was described by one conscientious objector as 'a nasty piece of work'.[20] My father was to come face to face with Bell in his appeal and, from the transcript of his case, it seems he got the better of this snarly, sarcastic man. Dad was not in the least bit intimidated by him or Stilwell.

Members of other boards around the country were also openly hostile to appellants, with some resorting to racist slurs. One appellant was told that if he did not accept his responsibility to fight, he should go down to the pipi bank and live like a Māori.[21] The two members on each board representing the interests of employers and employees tended to be more like bystanders with the chairman controlling the proceedings.

Interestingly, even at government level where there was sympathy for the 'conchies', Bob Semple became quite shamelessly pro-conscription and followed the hard line of the bureaucracy. Fraser and Nash were more circumspect and presumably had to bite their tongues on hearing some of the rhetoric. It would seem that the political risk of appearing to be soft on conscientious objectors was too great.

Against this backdrop, the Sons of Éire in their hearts would also have known that the chance of their appeals succeeding was negligible, but they were intent on at least showing the injustice of a system that took no account of their unique position. To fight to the last was being 'true to Ireland' and honouring the blood sacrifice of the 1916 martyrs.

PART TWO

THE ACTION BEGINS
IN EARNEST

6

Appeal day

'I do not base my claim of conscience on anything that has arisen since war broke out in September 1939, but on what I saw, felt and experienced in Éire between 1919 and 1921. It is only those who have been through that experience can realise how the memories of those frightful days have left something in one's mind that can never be blotted out.'[1]

These words were spoken by my father, Matt Burke, as he gave evidence to the No.4 Armed Forces Appeal Board in Wellington on the morning of Thursday 31 July 1941.

Not long before, he and his fellow Sons of Éire, Maurice Aylward, Jeremiah Allen, Brian Kennedy, John James Moriarty and Paddy Sullivan, accompanied by Fred Ongley and some supporters, had left Ongley's office in the South British Building at 326 Lambton Quay, for their date with the appeal board. The hearing was held on the 5th floor in the AMP building at

The AMP building in Wellington where the Sons of Éire appeal was held.

SONS OF EIRE
MILITARY SERVICE
—
WILL NOT ASSIST BRITAIN
QUESTION OF STATUS

"To ask me to wear the uniform of a British soldier is not only cruelty, but it is something against which my conscience rebels," declared Maurice Leo Aylward, a freezing worker, who, with five other "Sons of Eire,"

Evening Post, 31 July 1941, p.10

86–90 Customhouse Quay, a walk of about 100 metres. The weather that day was said to be fair to fine, but cold.[2]

I don't know for certain who their supporters were, but it is possible my mother was there, since she later had a copy of the transcript of Dad's interaction with the appeal board. However the notes may have been taken in shorthand by a legal associate or someone else, because they give a precise account and are neatly typed up.

The Sons of Éire case would have been one of many appeals heard that day and it appears from the newspaper report that theirs was one of the first. Waiting for them was the No.4 Armed Forces Appeal Board, chaired by Wilfred Fosberry Stilwell, a well-known magistrate seconded to the job. He had fought at Gallipoli and in France in WWI, attaining the rank of captain and awarded the Military Cross. He was originally a lawyer in Auckland, where he served a term as mayor of the borough of Mount Albert from 1931 to 1933.[3] He was a keen golfer and played at the prestigious Miramar Golf Club in Wellington with other city elite.

Dad read his affidavit to the appeal board. He started off by saying that he was born in Éire and claimed to be a citizen of that state, and then pointed out that it was a neutral state just like Sweden, Yugoslavia and America, and that he expected to be treated in the same way as citizens of those countries.

He went on to make it clear that even as a person from a neutral country currently residing in New Zealand, he was prepared to do any work other than combatant work, and fully realised that the work must be done and the country's resources maintained and developed.

In paragraph 4 of his affidavit he set out his other reasons for not wanting to fight for the British, based on his experiences in Moycullen, County Galway, and statied that these were why he would only undertake noncombatant duties and not serve as a soldier, sailor or airman. Extracts from his statement show the deep and raw emotion that he felt about what he'd seen in Ireland during the War of Independence, and in particular the brutal reprisals meted out by Black and Tans.

'I saw them and experienced the brutalities committed in the name of British law and in conscience I could not take part in the war [WWII].'

'My home was actually broken up by the Black and Tan soldiers in the name of British law and order.'

'The very thought of association with war work revives in my mind the most unhappy memories of my whole life and I cannot in conscience take any such part.'

'I have actually witnessed the funerals of victims of the Black and Tan devilry in Éire.'

'I desire to assure you that it is not cowardice that is the cause of this, but the fact that my people and myself went through suppression and outrage at the hands of the Black and Tan soldiers and how could I in conscience take part in this war.'

'I feel strongly that Éire is cut in two and partitioned while the war is being waged to keep Poland intact.'

'I have no attachment to Germany or any country on the continent of Europe. My devotion lies first to the country of my birth [Éire] and to the country of my adoption [New Zealand].'

'I am prepared to do any kind of work in New Zealand apart from combatant service.'

'I say that I am a conscientious objector in the full sense of the word. I wish to be allowed to work in any class of work other than combatant work.'

'I do not base my claim of conscience on anything that has arisen since war broke out in September 1939, but on what I saw, felt and experienced in 1919–21 in Éire. It is only those who have been through that can realise how the memories of those frightful days have left something on one's mind that can never be blotted out. To ask me to now wear the uniform of a British soldier would not only be a cruelty but one against which my conscience rebels.'

'I therefore ask that I be exempted from military service on the following grounds:

1. I am a citizen of Éire, a neutral state;

2. That I be allowed to do any useful work in New Zealand during the war; or

3. That I be permitted to return to Ireland,

4. On well-founded and really conscientious grounds which have been set forth in paragraph 4.'

From left: Paddy Sullivan, Unknown and Matt Burke, mid-1930s.
Photographer S.P. Andrew

Having read his affidavit, my father was then questioned by the lawyer for the Crown, C.O. Bell, who asked him which part of Ireland he came from.

'Moycullen, County Galway,' he replied.

Before Bell could continue Stilwell interjected and, according to the transcript I have of the trial, smiled sarcastically and asked Dad to keep in mind that the Irish brogue, when spoken quickly, was hard for the Board to understand.

'With all due respect to the Board, I am quite certain if I said anything detrimental, I am sure this would be quickly understood and undoubtedly received with open arms if I expressed the slightest disloyalty to this country [New Zealand],' said Dad.

This drew laughter from those present at the hearing, but probably not from Stilwell. Quick Irish wit made a mockery of the anti-Irish judge.

Bell went on, asking my father when he left Ireland and when he arrived in New Zealand, to which he replied that he left Éire in 1929 and arrived in New Zealand on 5 February 1930.

'But you never intended to return to Éire, Mr Burke?' asked Bell.

'I have never stated my intentions. So there is nothing on record to prove that,' responded Dad.

'Oh! No,' said Bell.

'Why put that question then?' asked my father.

It is clear that far from being intimidated by Bell, Matt Burke, lorry driver from County Galway, was getting the better of the old soldier. I imagine, as a member of the so-called 'ruling class', Bell was not used to being openly challenged and mocked in this way. I believe the other Sons of Éire would have been smiling with glee as Bell got flustered and continued to bluster on.

He had only one game plan and it wasn't working and there appeared to be no Plan B.

'Now would you fight for Éire?' asked Bell, trying to provoke a reaction.

'Most decidedly! I would die for Éire tomorrow if the necessity arose,' Dad said.

'But you would not fight for Britain?'

'No.'

Bell then came up with a question that Dad was probably expecting and one that was designed to smear the Sons of Éire.

'But you have been in New Zealand and have enjoyed all the privileges of a British subject during the past eleven years.'

'Well, if you call work a privilege,' retorted my father. 'I have given my best to this country. In fact, 100 per cent service, as can be proved in my record of service to New Zealand. In truth this country owes me more than I owe it.'

Turning to Stilwell he continued, 'What is more, this is the first time I have been before a magistrate and I can tell you I never expected that I would have to stand before a magistrate in a democratic country, such as New Zealand professes to be, to prove that I am a citizen of Éire.'

I imagine both Bell and Stilwell were getting more riled by the minute with Dad's response. But my father did not stop there. 'I did not leave home with the intention of living in New Zealand all my life and what is more I don't intend to become a British subject in any British dominion while British laws are responsible for the partition of my country.'[4]

Bell again asked Dad to confirm that he objected to fighting for the British Empire and got the obvious answer of 'Yes!' Bell then asked him to expand

The man who clashed with Matt Burke and other Irishmen at their appeal against conscription in 1941, W.F. Stilwell enjoys a round of golf with legal colleagues at the Miramar Golf Club at Wellington in November 1938. From left: S.A. Wiren, A.M. Golding, W.F. Stilwell, J.W. Ward.

Evening Post collection, Alexander Turnbull Library, N-P-2037-14

on his reasons for doing so. This question gave Dad the opportunity to go into some of the detailed reasons for objecting to fight for Britain and New Zealand. He carefully turned the question around and said to Bell that he and other appellants would be classed as traitors in Ireland if they fought for Britain.[5] He then had this to say: 'Supposing that Éire was instrumental in partitioning New Zealand and by force of arms and foul and brutal laws domineering the New Zealand people down through the ages. From what we have seen and know of New Zealanders we are convinced that they have a better and more honourable principle than to pronounce that they would fight for Éire and betray their own country.'

That was probably not the answer Bell or Stilwell were expecting and, despite the Irish brogue, they no doubt heard it loud and clear which probably made the pair wish the sooner the appeal was over the better. After all, the media were reporting the event, and the transcript of the hearing could potentially be provided to Prime Minister Peter Fraser.

At this point my father, like the other appellants, gave his account of what he had witnessed of the Black and Tan thuggery in his village of Moycullen in 1919–21.

'I myself was in Éire during this time and it may be of interest to this court[6] to hear of one or two incidents which took place in my own part of the country and for which the Black and Tans were responsible. I can even now see the mortal remains of John Geoghegan who had been tortured to death by the Black and Tans after being dragged from his mother's arms to the front gate of their little garden where 25 bullets were discharged into his body by these same Black and Tan soldiers.[7] I also saw eight Irishmen, three of whom were relations, stripped to the waist and publicly flogged by these same Black and Tan soldiers who were working in conjunction with the British forces.'[8]

He then spoke of one of the most appalling and horrific murders committed by British Forces during the War of Independence – the murder in Galway of a Catholic priest, Fr Michael Griffin.

'I viewed the bog hole where the Rev Father Griffin's body was disposed of after he had been tortured and shot.'[9]

'There is one memory I hate to recall,' he continued as a silence came over the room, 'and that is the thought of the brutal and inhumanely cowardly torturing of Margaret Burke, my cousin. Her hair was shorn with a sharp knife, her body bruised from kicks and rough handling and added to that she was imprisoned for nine months with hard labour because she would not tell of the whereabouts of her brother and his companions who, through fear,

This photo of my father, Matt Burke, was taken shortly before he appeared in front of the appeal board.

could not sleep in their own homes during the Black and Tan regime in Éire.' Turning to Stilwell and politely referring to him as 'your honour', Dad said that two of his friends at the hearing, Paddy Sullivan and John Clancy, both from Moycullen, could verify these statements.

In his evidence my father chose to single out the few events that he had witnessed, but he would have been aware of other incidents in Galway that followed the arrival of the Black and Tans in 1920. In *Blood for Blood*, William Henry describes in graphic detail the horrors that the men, women and children endured under the uncontrolled reign of the Black and Tans and Auxiliaries. Young women were terrorised, and on 27 September 1920 the people of Moycullen were threatened with violence if they attempted to stop the agent of a former landlord of the village returning to that person's farm.[10] In another incident a young woman sitting in front of her house holding her nine-month-old baby was shot dead by a group of Black and Tans for no apparent reason.[11] Men were regularly arrested, some shot, allegedly for trying to escape – others tied to the back of a truck and hauled along the road until they were dead. Two others had their heads blown off when gelignite was put in their mouths and the fuse was lit.[12]

The Black and Tans' driving force was hatred of the Irish and they unleashed this with the support of the British Government, who at every opportunity covered up the war crimes of these savages in uniform. It was little wonder that Dad and his colleagues saw the British army uniform as a symbol of oppression and murder of their people.

It would seem that all six had similar experiences of the violence in Ireland which they related to the appeal board, but only one of these, Maurice Aylward, was reported in the newspapers.[13]

Responding to further questioning by Bell about whether he would fight for New Zealand if it was directly attacked, Dad said he would if an aggressive power did this, but went on to point out that as he saw it, this war was Britain's war and that he, as an Irishman, would not fight for it. He also stated that this was not a fair question to ask any Irishman.

He went on further to state that in the 1916 Rising no force was used against the hundreds of Englishmen living in Ireland, and reiterated that he and his fellow Irishmen would not in any way hinder New Zealand in her present war effort for Britain.

Dad's final impassioned speech to the appeal board drew heavily on what he as a young lad in Moycullen and Galway had seen and heard of the atrocities committed by the Black and Tans. It was a deeply fearless, patriotic and passionate oration that could have been delivered by any Irish rebel in history. I can almost visualise him now – standing tall, tense and determined, and looking Stilwell in the eye, his voice quivering with emotion: 'Now, could any sane man ask and expect me to put on a British uniform and go and fight for that same country which has been quietly persecuting, shooting, publicly flogging and hanging, without trial, hundreds of our people down through the ages? And on top of that, divided my country in two parts, while this present war rages. No, your honour, I will not put on a British uniform. Nor will I fight for Britain even to the point of the bayonet, the revolver or the machine gun, and I am prepared to stand by those sentiments until death. And I can assure you that holds good for every Irishman in this appeal.'

Finally my father turned to Stilwell and said: 'If the appeal board is in any doubt as to the correctness of the foregoing statements, I can call on Mr Clancy and Mr Sullivan, both here present, to substantiate my remarks.'

I imagine you could have heard a pin drop after that. It would have been interesting to see the reaction of Stilwell and Bell and possibly the other members of the Board, Parlane and Brodie. This was fighting talk, and a direct challenge to the New Zealand authorities who seemed to be trying to be 'more British than the British'.

It would appear that my father was one of the last of the six to give evidence to the Board, but there is unfortunately no official record of what happened that morning. There is a reference to the hearing in an article in the *Portland Guardian* in Australia, which states that John James Moriarty related his account in which he said his group had sought an opportunity to put their special case to the New Zealand Government but this was ignored.[14] He also claimed that he asked to leave New Zealand in 1940 but was refused permission to do so.

The coverage of the Sons of Éire appeal in the *Evening Post* on the day of the hearing would suggest that Maurice Leo Aylward was the first to take the stand, as he was the only one of the group included in the report that appeared on page 10. It was one of the most prominent articles on a page devoted to war news. There was a major piece on the air struggle in Europe and petrol rationing in New Zealand; an article reporting that 400 American technicians had arrived in Northern Ireland as part of the 'lend-lease' agreement and were being paid £12 per week; and an account of Prime Minister Peter Fraser's visit to Edinburgh in his native Scotland where he met twelve New Zealanders and also thanked workers at a local shipyard who were building a ship for New Zealand.

While Dad's evidence was detailed and compelling, it was the evidence of Maurice Leo Aylward, from Kilkenny, which made the headlines, both in New Zealand and overseas. Like my father, Aylward had the same key message for the appeal board:

'To ask me to wear the uniform of a British soldier is not only cruelty, but it is something against which my conscience rebels. I think the people of Ireland would disown me if I took up arms for Britain.'

Like the other five, Aylward told the appeal board he was not a conscientious objector within the meaning of the regulations, but that he considered himself a conscientious objector in the true sense of the word. He went on to outline his experiences during the War of Independence, stating that these were some of his main reasons for refusing to fight for Britain.

'I saw young men taken to their graves in the prime of their life. I saw my home broken up, my mother suffering and my eldest brother hunted in the hills of Ireland. My second brother went through life with one eye. He too had to take to the hills. The mere thought revives in my mind the most unhappy memories of my own life and I cannot in conscience take part in this war,' he said.

Aylward went on to state the view common to all six Sons of Éire, that he had no attachment for Germany or any other country in Europe and that his devotion was first to Éire and after that New Zealand, where he was now residing. Like Matt Burke, he said he was prepared to do any work other than combatant work and realised that it was necessary for New Zealand's resources to be developed.

Aylward pointed out to Stilwell that the ENA had a meeting with Peter Fraser before they were called up in which they asked to be allowed to leave New Zealand or do noncombatant service.

'We were asked to put it in writing and the Prime Minister was in sympathy with our views,' said Aylward.[15]

'I am only concerned with the result of the interview,' retorted Stilwell.

'He (Fraser) told us to put the case in writing and he would discuss it with his colleagues. In February we wrote to the Prime Minister and asked what could be done to meet the position. He replied that the matter would receive the early and careful consideration of the government, but since then nothing has been heard,' responded Maurice Aylward.

At this point Bell and Stilwell combined, as they did with my father, to go on the offensive with a line of questioning that appeared designed to intimidate and besmirch Aylward and the Irish generally.

'If you were allowed to return to Ireland and if Ireland were attacked, you would fight for Ireland?' asked Bell.

Stilwell could not help himself and caustically interjected: 'Like an Irishman, you want to choose your fight, is that it?'

The smooth talking and highly intelligent Aylward was not put off by this put-down and jokingly said: 'An Irishman has always been in a fight.'

'So you are prepared to fight for Ireland?' noted Stilwell, to which Aylward replied, 'Yes, it would be an honour to fight for Ireland.'

Bell said that the way the regulations were framed meant that any appeal by the Sons of Éire could not stand, and Aylward agreed with him. Bell went on to say that to be judged a conscientious objector under the regulations, a person had to prove that they were not prepared to take part in any war and that by Aylward's, and others' admission, they were prepared to engage in war, namely fighting for Ireland.

John James Moriarty, according to the report in the *Evening Post*, was the next appellant to take the witness stand and his evidence followed a similar pattern to that of Maurice Aylward's.

Moriarty stated that as a citizen of Éire he was in the same position as any other subject of a neutral country. He added that the ENA had tried to put their special case to the government but had been ignored. Moriarty claimed that he'd only arrived in New Zealand in 1939 and had applied to leave the following year, but had been refused permission to do so.[16]

The ENA lawyer, Fred Ongley, as he did with the other Sons of Éire, put a question to Moriarty about how long he had held his views on his homeland.

'Ever since I was a kid. Like the others here today my family suffered at the hands of Black and Tan reprisals from 1919 to 1922,' he said.

There is no record of what Paddy Sullivan, Brian Kennedy or Jeremiah Allen said to the appeal board, but the similarity of the evidence given by my father and Maurice Aylward suggests that their statements would have followed the same pattern, but with some specific accounts of their own experiences with the Black and Tans. The stamp of Fred Ongley ensured consistency and avoided any ambiguity that could be seized upon by Bell or Stilwell. The Sons of Éire appeal was carefully choreographed to get across key messages, not only to the appeal board, but also to the Government of New Zealand, as well as those of the other dominions, and of course Éire. It was arguably a futile appeal, based on the earlier interpretation of the regulations, but the ENA saw it as a battle worth having. It was a metaphorical blood sacrifice.

At the end of the proceedings Stilwell made the observation that he had no option but to dismiss the appeals on the grounds of conscientious objection, as all six men had stated their willingness to fight for Ireland.

'You have been candid enough to say that you would fight for Ireland but will not help the British Empire,' he mused.

Fred Ongley at that point addressed Stilwell, noting that the Chair of the Auckland appeal board had made the observation that it would be useless to ask such men to do military service. Stilwell responded that he was not prepared to associate himself with such views because the ENA had already made representations to the Prime Minister and his cabinet. In one last dig at the Irishmen he did offer to 'express his views to the government'.

Aylward spoke up, pointing out that one of the problems he and the others faced was the lack of diplomatic representation in New Zealand: 'Prior to the war Éire was about to appoint a consul in New Zealand, but this was postponed,' he said. He again raised the issue that the Sons of Éire should be treated no differently to the citizens of any other neutral country.

'Irishmen in England are exempt from military service because they claim Éire citizenship and we Irishmen in New Zealand are being denied that right. We Irishmen deserve better treatment than to be forced to fight for Britain. We will never wear a British uniform. It was a few weeks ago when the British Government was about to impose conscription on part of my country [like many Irish he regarded Northern Ireland as part of Ireland] that Mr de Valera, Prime Minister of Éire, and the Éire Government took action and through representations made to the British Government, conscription was immediately dropped. My people have been fighting for hundreds of years against aggression and for the right to work out their own destiny. My people would disown me if I took up arms in the present conflict,' proclaimed Aylward defiantly.

Finally, Maurice Aylward quoted de Valera as saying there could not be a more grievous attack on any fundamental human right than to compel an individual to fight for a country to which he objected to belong. Legal argument with Ongley, Stilwell and Bell continued on the issue of status – as to whether the Irishmen were citizens of Éire or British subjects.

The proceedings were adjourned and it's likely the Sons of Éire went to one of their favourite watering holes to have a beer or two and discuss the events of the day. One can imagine Aylward being the leader of the talk. He had a strong personality and, while Paddy Feeney was the president of the ENA, Aylward had become the real driver of the ENA's actions. He was the one who had met Fraser and other officials and later went to Ireland as the representative of the ENA. No doubt much talking, singing and drinking took place that night as the men and their supporters gave their take on how the day had gone.

It would seem that the issue of status was not resolved on the day of the hearing, because five days later on 5 August it was raised again at the appeal board. The *Evening Post* reported that Ongley, on behalf of the Sons of Éire, and Bell, on behalf of the Crown, made submissions to Stilwell, the appeal board chair.[17] Ongley submitted: 'In view of the constitution of Éire it was a question of whether the appellants were British subjects at all and even if they were, there was the further question whether they could be conscripted in New Zealand having regard to Éire's constitution. It is no satisfaction to the appellants to be told that those matters had been left undetermined and that they could not be informed whether they would be called upon to serve or not.'[18]

Bell again stated that the issue was whether the appellants were natural-born British subjects or not. Stilwell agreed and said the Board would reserve its decision.

I assume that the reason for discussing the issue on a separate day was due to the appeal board having other cases on the first day, or that the Sons of Éire appeal took all day and they simply had to make extra time available to debate the contentious and highly important issue of status. The appellants claim of conscientious objection was lost, but the issue of status was somewhat blurred, at least in the eyes of the ENA.

It was now just a matter of waiting for an answer from Stilwell, who may or may not have had discussions with the government. It is likely he had discussions with the Department of National Service and possibly some of the chairmen of other appeal boards.

This was in some ways the 'phoney war' for the Sons of Éire.

In this period the men would have been heartened by the *Portland Guardian* report on Monday 15 September 1941. The small weekly newspaper in the seaside town of Portland in Victoria ran the story of the Sons of Éire under the headline 'Irishmen in New Zealand – May Not Have to Fight'.[19]

The report stated that the New Zealand military appeal boards had recently been confronted with 'their thorniest and most embarrassing problem: Has a British dominion the right to conscript citizens of neutral Éire for overseas service?' The report goes on:

> The Irishmen say 'no'. The Boards say they are not quite sure and have so far side-stepped the issue by shelving appeals or vaguely referring them to the government. The only government pronouncement given to a group of petitioning Irishmen is a statement that 'the matter will receive early and careful consideration'.
>
> Indications are that the [New Zealand] Government will exempt these citizens of Éire from compulsory military service if they can fairly establish their citizenship. If Britain found it too much trouble to conscript Northern Irelanders, New Zealand will certainly think twice before applying the sweeping conscription laws to men from south of the border. While these points exercise officials of state departments, Irishmen have been vehemently fighting their case before appeal boards.

Then the report reproduced the essence of the story in the *Evening Post* about the appeals, mentioning the names of all the men, quoting the evidence of Aylward and Moriarty, and that the appeals had been referred to the government.

Under the main heading of the New Zealand case is a subheading that refers to a similar court case heard in the Richmond court in Melbourne. It says a 28-year-old Irishman pleaded exemption from military service on the same grounds as the Irishmen in New Zealand.[20] But his claim was rejected, with the court saying that 'according to English and Australian law, Éire, like Australia and Canada, were regarded for the purposes of the British Army Act as a colony and that anyone born there was a British subject'. He was fined £1 for having refused to take the oath of service.

How the articles appeared in such a small-town newspaper is a mystery, but it might be that a copy of the *Evening Post* article about the trial was sent by an Irishman in New Zealand to a relative or friend in Portland, and they passed it on to the editor of the local paper. Many of the Irishmen, including Maurice Aylward, had strong connections in Australia and it is possible that information was traded, but there is no evidence to support this.

For the Sons of Éire there was little they could do except wait for the No.4 Armed Forces Appeal Board to decide their fate. There wasn't much point in lobbying the government as it had indicated that it was up to the authorities to decide the outcome.

7

The Troubles in Moycullen

While I have no doubt that my father's testimony to the No.4 Armed Forces Appeal Board was valid, the journalist instinct in me wanted to check the authenticity of his statements and find out more about what happened in and around Moycullen between 1916–21. I was already aware of the activities of Tom Barry, Dan Breen and the great Michael Collins, but from a family history perspective I hoped to gain a deeper understanding of what drove my father to play such a pivotal role in opposing the conscription of Irishmen in New Zealand into the 'British' army.

The circumstances of the murders of John Geoghegan and Fr Michael Griffin in Moycullen form the backdrop to the world my father had grown up in. The role of Mícheál Ó Droighneáin, a much revered man in Galway for his IRA affiliations, was central to both events. He had joined the Irish Republican Brotherhood (IRB) in late 1910 while teaching in Dublin and

Discovering Moycullen's secrets

In 2011, and again in 2016, I spent time in Galway and Moycullen talking to my cousins and wider family, their friends and local historians to find out what happened in this small, and now much sought-after, village. On that first visit, my cousin Marion O'Connor took me to see the memorials to Fr Michael Griffin and John Geoghegan, and also the stained glass window memorial to Geoghegan in the Moycullen Catholic Church. Another cousin, Fidelma Burke, who has a great interest in local history, gave me a book about Fr Griffin written by Fr Pádraic Ó Laoi, which describes in considerable detail the barbaric murder of this dedicated and innocent priest by the Crown forces. A display and booklet produced by the Galway Museum also provided valuable and authentic insights.[1] Finally the witness statements from the Irish Bureau of Military History revealed some amazing material from Mícheál Ó Droighneáin, who was the Commandant of the East Connemara Brigade of the IRA and whose eyewitness accounts fully support my father's testimony.[2]

Mícheál Ó Droighneáin.
Courtesy of Tom Kenny.

later took part in the 1916 Rising, for which he spent time in Frongoch Prison Camp in Wales. He was released from there just two days before Christmas 1916 and reached home on Christmas morning.[3]

In 1918 Ó Droighneáin was one of the leaders of a group of Volunteers who disrupted a British recruiting meeting in the town hall of Galway. Ó Droighneáin and his men cut the power to the town hall at a crucial time and then set off a series of foul-smelling stink bombs, all of which caused pandemonium and forced the meeting to be abandoned.[4] The policy of disrupting meetings of pro-British supporters continued and added credibility to the Volunteers.

The East Connemara Brigade, according to Ó Droighneáin, continued to undertake various operations, including an abortive attempt to attack the police barracks at Rosmuc for arms. Later, a successful raid on the house of Lord Killanin yielded two shotguns and some ammunition. They burnt the vacated police barracks in Moycullen, Barna and Tully. They forced shops to close in the area for a day as a protest at the treatment of political prisoners and organised a hurling match in defiance of the authorities. There was also a major shoot-out with the Black and Tans when Ó Droighneáin was bringing a box of explosives, revolvers and ammunition from Dublin. This saw one 'Tan', a man named Crumm, shot dead along with two Volunteers.[5] In the greater scheme of things all these were minor incidents, but they had the effect of tying down Crown forces and took some pressure off the more active counties.

The murder of Fr Griffin was the incident that was etched on the minds of the people of Galway. The reason for his murder was the execution of a British spy by Mícheál Ó Droighneáin and his group of Volunteers. It started, according to Ó Droighneáin's witness statement, when Joe Togher and another man, whose name he could not recall, were working for the Galway Postal Service. They intercepted letters addressed to various British officials in Ireland reporting on the activities of Ó Droighneáin and his men, and included the names of Fr Griffin and Fr O'Meehan. The letters were unsigned.

When seeking to identify the letter writer, suspicion fell on the principal teacher of Barna National School, Patrick Joyce. To get proof Ó Droighneáin claimed to have entered the school at night and obtained a sample of Joyce's handwriting. There was also a suggestion someone sold Joyce a raffle ticket that he had to sign his name for, and the handwriting proved the letter writer was Joyce. The East Connemara Brigade leaders sought advice from the IRA leaders in Dublin, and Ó Droighneáin sent John Geoghegan of Moycullen to Dublin with the letters and samples of handwriting to ask for instructions. Geoghegan met Dick Mulcahy, the IRA chief of staff, who examined the documents and advised that it was up to the local brigade to take what action they deemed necessary.

Ó Droighneáin noted that this worried him greatly, and even more so when he received three more letters via Fr Griffin from Joe Togher, which were addressed to the officer in charge at the Renmore Barracks in Galway, the officer in charge of the Lancers at Earl's Ireland and, finally, to Sir Hamar Greenwood, Chief Secretary of Ireland, at Dublin Castle.[6] The letter to Greenwood complained that no action had been taken in respect of the earlier letters. After reading these letters Ó Droighneáin decided that immediate action was required.

According to Pádraic Ó Laoi, the Volunteers were deeply upset and surprised that Patrick Joyce would stoop so low as to betray them as he was trusted in the community, so they delayed taking action to consider the situation and to consult again with their superiors in Dublin.[7]

Permission to carry out a court martial of Joyce was given orally by General Mulcahy, with the understanding that the paperwork would follow within a week.[8] Because Joyce was a Catholic it was decided that a priest should be present to give the last rites in the event of him being executed. However, to avoid suspicion falling on Fr Griffin, who was a known associate of the Volunteers, another priest from the other side of Loch Corrib was sent for. It was John Geoghegan who rowed across the lake and brought the priest to the disused cabin where the court martial of Joyce was to take place.

At 11 pm on Friday 15 October 1920, seven Volunteers knocked on the Joyce family's door, and when his son answered a canvas bag was thrown over his head. The boy's father was taken from the bedroom and the house was searched, but no further evidence was found, so Joyce was taken by sidecar to an unused house on the Barna–Moycullen road. While he was being arrested by the Volunteers, Joyce's daughter had appeared and, unsure about what was happening, clung to her father. The Volunteers were apparently kind to her and had assured her that everything would be all right. They told Joyce's family not to leave the house until morning.[9]

The atmosphere of the court martial was surreal – a disused house lit by candles, and four highly ranked IRA officers as the court. The judges were Morgan Davoren, Tim Kyne, Ned Walsh and Ó Droighneáin, with Michael Thornton prosecuting, who produced the incriminating letters and the copy of Joyce's handwriting.[10] One of the letters appealed to the officer in charge of the Galway Black and Tans to 'send a dozen or so men to confiscate the Colgan house'. Mrs Colgan was the principal of the girls school and Joyce was the principal of the boys school, both at Barna. Mrs Colgan's husband had resigned from the Royal Irish Constabulary and become an active IRA Volunteer.

Joyce feebly denied the accusations but the court convicted him of spying and handed down the death sentence. Other accounts say Joyce pleaded for mercy, even to the last minute saying, 'Let me go home to my family … on my word of honour I will do you no harm.' But Ó Droighneáin didn't think they could trust him so his pleas were rejected. He was blindfolded and the firing squad took up their positions.[11] The reality was that Joyce would have known who his accusers were and, despite promises of never doing it again, the East Connemara Brigade leader was not willing to take the risk. The priest from Shrule, Fr Tommy Burke, heard Joyce's confession and he was shot at 2.30am.[12] The name of the person, or persons, who shot Joyce have never been revealed. His body was buried in a simple coffin in a nearby bog.[13]

In his witness statement to the Bureau of Military History, Joe Togher recalled the lead up to the execution of Joyce and the subsequent murder of Fr Michael Griffin.[14] Togher was the intelligence officer for the Galway Brigade and worked in the Galway Post Office. That gave him access to mail being sent to the RIC by alleged informers. He noted that one letter he opened specifically recorded the movement of IRA companies and mentioned Brigade Commandant Michael Thornton and others. It was signed 'a friend'. Togher noted that the handwriting was not terribly good and after several more letters the handwriting was recognised as that of Joyce, the teacher at Barna. Togher also noted that Fr Griffin and Joyce were not on the friendliest of terms because of 'parish trouble'.

Any pretence of innocence by Joyce was quickly dispelled by the immediate response from the Crown forces and, not unexpectedly, the Black and Tans. They retaliated with all the brutality my father and other Sons of Éire spoke of in their statements to the appeal board. Joyce's execution took place within a few kilometres of Dad's home, and not far from those of his mates Paddy Sullivan and John Clancy.

Mícheál Ó Droighneáin went into hiding, staying close to his house, and watched the lorry loads of Black and Tans searching for him and other suspects. They beat up one of his friends, Pádraic Connelly, hitting him with rifle butts and knocking out his teeth as they demanded, 'Where is he,' referring to Ó Droighneáin. Beatings and wild shootings continued unabated, all of which would have come to the attention of the villagers of Moycullen, including my father. Absolute chaos reigned as the British forces, notably the Black and Tans, raged around Galway beating up innocent people as well as capturing some Volunteers. 'Where is Joyce?' they screamed. Initially they thought he was being held hostage.[15]

They called at Ó Droighneáin's home and threatened his wife, who was looking after their two young children. Joyce's son Joe was on one of the lorries that turned up. They moved on to Cappagh, near Joyce's residence, interrogating and beating people up, and later shot a horse belonging to a villager. At Spiddal they beat up a man and fired a shotgun over his shoulder, slightly wounding him.[16]

While Ó Droighneáin remained on the run through bog fields and mountains, the rampages of the Black and Tans continued with more indiscriminate killings, including that of a Paddy O'Flaherty, a local garage owner. The Tans wrongly assumed that it was his rubber-tyred sidecar that had taken Joyce to his court-martial and later execution.[17]

The violence unleashed on the people of Galway by the Crown forces, and in particular the Black and Tans, was nothing compared with what was then to happen. Word had got out that Joyce was dead, and that being a Catholic, he had been administered the last rites by a priest. The Tans shifted their attention to the local clergy, and in particular to Fr Michael Griffin, a young curate in the Rahoon Parish of Galway city.

Fr Griffin was born on 18 September 1892 and was ordained a priest in June 1917. A year later he was appointed to the Parish of Rahoon which included the church at Bushy Park on the Moycullen Road, where

Fr Michael Griffin, 1913.
Courtesy of Tom Kenny

some of my relatives are buried. Fr Griffin was a well-known ardent nationalist who believed that Ireland's future rested in achieving self-government. He kept these feelings quiet in public but was open about his sympathies with close friends.[18] Conversely his fellow curate Fr O'Meehan was more public about his republican views and the Black and Tans had warned him that he was 'a marked man'.[19] On a visit to the Barna and Furbo schools Fr Griffin was warned by assistant teacher Michael Thornton that he too was 'a marked man' and to be careful.[20] It was said that Fr Griffin had a great love of the Irish language and an interest in the IRA.[21] In Fr Pádraic Ó Laoi's book there is a picture of him in an IRA military uniform.[22]

Knowing Fr Griffin's association with the Volunteers, it was not surprising that the Black and Tans suspected, wrongly of course, that Fr Griffin was the priest who had administered the last rites to Joyce. On Saturday 13 November 1920, Ó Droighneáin's wife met with Fr Griffin.[23] That same night men with blackened faces raided three homes in Joyce's village of Cappagh, breaking windows, doors and furniture and setting them on fire.[24] Terror reigned in this and other villages as the Crown forces and their agents, including the Black and Tans, took revenge on innocent citizens.

Sunday 14 November was a cold winter day, and Fr Griffin said Mass at two villages and asked the congregation to pray for the safe return of Patrick Joyce. His sermon was in Irish.[25] That evening he returned to his presbytery to play cards with two priest friends. Fr Griffin talked about the disappearance of Joyce and the Black and Tan response. At 10.30pm the card game finished and Fr Griffin went to bed at 11.00pm.[26]

What happened next is unclear, except that around midnight Fr Griffin was woken by knocking on the door and his housekeeper heard him say, 'All right, I'll be down in a minute.' Her initial assumption was he was needed to visit a sick parishioner, but it transpired that the priest didn't take with him the holy oils used for anointing the sick. Three men allegedly led Fr Griffin away. There was speculation as to who they were. Mícheál Ó Droighneáin claimed they were known to Fr Griffin,[27] while Joe Togher speculated that one of the people was William Joyce, later to become infamous as Lord Haw-Haw. Togher believed that William Joyce (no relation to Patrick Joyce) had access to RIC cyphers and strong links to the Crown forces.[28] Joyce later joined the 4th Worcester Regiment in England and, by his own account, claimed to have been a spy for the British. That tends to suggest that there may have been merit in Togher's theory.

The next day, when Fr Griffin was reported missing, many feared that he had been tortured and shot by the Black and Tans. Search parties were organised while the clergy asked the RIC for help. The Divisional Commander, Richard Cruise, a Catholic, promised to get his men to search for Fr Griffin and assured them no member of the Crown forces would be guilty of abducting a priest.[29] But the rumours persisted, with a 'Tan' being overheard saying to one of his colleagues: 'There was a bloody parson shot last night.'[30] The issue was raised in the House of Commons, with Chief Secretary for Ireland, Sir Hamar Greenwood, denying that Crown forces were in any way implicated. He said that 'it is obviously such a stupid thing that no member of the forces of the Crown would do it'.[31] But as the days passed such words were seen as completely implausible.

Finally, on Saturday 20 November Fr Griffin's body was found by a farmer moving his cows in a paddock at Cloughscoiltia, close to the Barna–Moycullen Road. The discovery of his body triggered new outrage and anger at the British, and deep sorrow throughout Galway and Ireland. Fr Griffin had been shot in the head and his body unceremoniously dumped in a bog hole. In the House of Commons there were further futile denials that Crown forces were in any way implicated. One priest in Ireland, Fr Dempsey from Cork, described Fr Griffin's death as 'a sacrilegious murder'.[32] Clergy from other denominations joined in the chorus condemning the murder. A huge funeral followed, with Galway brought to a standstill.

In his witness statement Mícheál Ó Droighneáin notes that his two eldest sons, Piaras and Sean, were baptised by Fr Griffin and that he had much to do with the young curate. The murder of innocent Fr Griffin did little to quell the unrest. Rather, like the executions of the leaders of the 1916 Rising,

A group of Black and Tans lining Mill Street in Galway city at the time of Fr Griffin's funeral.
Courtesy of Tom Kenny

Above: Fr Griffin's funeral procession through the streets of Galway city.
Courtesy of Tom Kenny

Left: The memorial for Fr Griffin near Moycullen, where his body was dumped by the Black and Tans.

it incited even greater hatred of the British presence. As was so often the case, the killer, or killers, of Fr Griffin were never identified or bought to trial. Fr Griffin was just 28 when he was murdered. My father would have been aware of this whole barbaric episode and it is easy to understand how he and his friends in Moycullen came to openly despise the British.

The next significant event my father bore witness to was the murder of Commandant John Geoghegan, Mícheál Ó Droighneáin's quartermaster in Moycullen, on 20 February 1921. Geoghegan, who was 26, was a farmer and lived with his widowed mother and siblings at the settlement of Ogoole, Moycullen, a townland about five kilometres from Ballydotia. Dad said in his statement to the appeal board that he had seen the body of John Geoghegan after he had been shot. That in itself would have been a traumatic moment for him.

There are numerous accounts of what happened the night that John Geoghegan was killed, all of which point to another brutal murder by elements of the Crown forces – likely the Black and Tans, to whom justice appeared a complete anathema and gratuitous murder and violence a badge of honour. In his witness statement, Ó Droighneáin vividly outlined the events of that night.[33] He stated that he'd sent Geoghegan to Galway to meet a dispatch courier from Dublin bringing an important message. The plan was for Ó Droighneáin to meet Geoghegan in Moycullen at 1 o'clock on the Sunday morning. Ó Droighneáin stated that he left Spiddal late that night and cycled towards Moycullen, on the Spiddal–Moycullen Road.

> About half a mile from the village I saw in front of me at the priest's gate the light of a cigarette in a person's mouth. I came off my bicycle immediately and moved into the side of the road where there was a little boreen or pathway. I heard people talking and I at once took them to be the enemy. I got the fright of my life when I felt they were coming towards me and horrified to find them turning into the boreen where I was standing with my bicycle hidden. I had a .45 revolver and levelling it I shouted at the top of my voice 'hands up'. 'Oh my God,' said one of the persons and put his hands up as did the other two persons who were with him. It was Fr Cunnane, then in charge of the Moycullen Parish and he was accompanied by Tim O'Connor and Eddie Geoghegan, brother of John. Then I recognised them and heard from them the sad story of John.

In his paper 'Military Activity in the Peripheral Region of Moycullen from 1916 to 1923', Darren McDonagh quotes an article in the *Freemans Journal* which reported that the first indication the Geoghegan family got that their house was being raided was the crashing of glass in the kitchen window and a man shouting: 'We want John Geoghegan.' The door was opened and two

One of Moycullen's heros of the Troubles, Commandant John Geoghegan, who was dragged out of bed and executed by the Black and Tans outside his house on the Killagola Road, Ogoole in February 1921. He is shown here on the far left with Watt Regan, an unidentified man, Pádraic Thornton, and a man believed to be called O'Toole.
Courtesy of Marcus Thornton

men entered. The article describes the men, with one wearing a military uniform and the other in a black coat carrying a revolver. The two had Irish accents.[34]

In *The Black & Tans* David Leeson quotes Geoghegan's brother Michael saying the man with the overcoat asked where John Geoghegan was, and John spoke up and said, 'I am here.' The two men then told him to get up at once and dress. They accused him of being a friend of Michael Collins, with the man in the black coat accusing him of being a traitor to Ireland saying he was now going to suffer. Once dressed he was taken outside and shot. Five rifle and six revolver cartridges were found near his body.[35]

It is also claimed that a note was attached to his coat saying, 'Yours faithfully, M. Collins', implying that the Minister of Finance was a friend of Geoghegan's.[36] These accounts back up the statement in my father's evidence that he saw the mortal remains of John Geoghegan, who had been tortured by the Black and Tans and riddled with bullets.

According to Ó Droighneáin, in the course of getting dressed just prior to being shot, John told his brother Michael that a dispatch he had collected from the courier from Dublin was in a 'cock of hay in the haggard', which was later found and passed to Ó Droighneáin. He also mentioned that when he

My cousin Marion O'Connor beside the memorial to John Geoghegan on the site where he was killed by the Black and Tans.

arrived at the Geoghegan's house, John's body was stretchered on the kitchen floor and while his trousers and coat were on, he had no shoes. Fr Cunnane had anointed him.[37]

Ó Droighneáin in his witness statement describes Geoghegan:

> He was a wonderful man, the most unselfish I have ever come across. It was he I sent to Dublin in connection with the Joyce letters. It was he that I sent across the Corrib for a priest [for Joyce]. I had given him orders not to sleep at home, but his answer was: 'If they come looking for me and I am not there, they will shoot one of my brothers and I cannot allow that to happen.'[38]

As was the case with almost all the murders by the Tans, the culprits were never found or held to justice by the British forces, which further angered the local Irish population.

The Black and Tans showed no mercy in their efforts to suppress the Irish in Galway and other parts of Ireland. There were attacks on innocent people in Moycullen and surrounding villages, which no doubt my father was also aware of. My relations in Moycullen have their own accounts of the brutality inflicted on their folks. One of them, Patrick Kelly, was shot three times and left for dead by a group of drunken Tans. Others were forced to watch family members beaten to death. There are lots of examples of savagery, such as men being tied to the back of trucks and dragged along until they were dead. Horrific public floggings were commonplace. Family members were jailed and tortured in the hope they would reveal the names of IRA

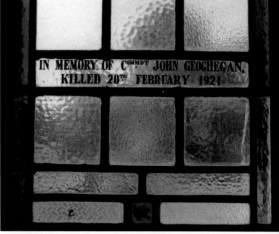

John Geoghegan is commemorated in a stained glass window in the Moycullen Catholic Church.

colleagues, but they remained staunch. The violence was not confined to men – cousin Margaret Burke was one of those brutally tortured by these 'men of violence'. My aunt, Mary Burke (née Connelly), and her brothers were all IRA supporters. As a young child Mary acted as a messenger for the IRA. From a family perspective, it would seem that the Burkes of Ballydotia were passive rather than active IRA supporters, but they still hated the atrocities perpetrated by the Crown forces.

Moycullen Catholic Church.

Of the other statements made to the No.4 Armed Forces Appeal Board, further supporting evidence comes from Fr Eamon Aylward, nephew of Maurice Aylward. He said he could imagine his uncle as a leader, given the family involvement in politics, but that he was a bit young in 1916 to be involved, and it wasn't until the Black and Tan war that he became active.

> He witnessed the Black and Tans coming into his parents' home and looking for one of his brothers ... and that would have had a strong influence on him that would have formed his attitude towards wearing a British uniform because here were these people violating his home, abusing his mother and in New Zealand he's being asked to wear the same uniform of that same man – that was obviously an influence.[39]

What Maurice Aylward and Matt Burke saw as young men was likely mirrored by the other four Sons of Éire and their friends, who were part of the opposition to fighting for Britain and wearing a uniform of the Crown. The incidents they witnessed in Éire must have been horrific and life-changing. But for me, a novice to Irish history, they have helped me gain a better understanding of my late father – the man I thought I knew in the 1950s.

8

Watching and waiting

While the No.4 Armed Forces Appeal Board was making its decision on the Sons of Éire case in late 1941, my father and other members of the ENA executive had time to reflect on the likely outcome. They had presented a strong case but were under no illusion about their chance of success. As they waited for the decision, and later when the decision was made, the men were well aware that publicly at least they had few friends.

As far as the war was concerned, the British battleship *Hood* had been sunk, the Germans had invaded Russia, and the Japanese had invaded Indo-China. In New Zealand at the end of July 1941 all married men in unreserved occupations were called up for military service to cover the losses suffered in Crete. Dad and his fellow Irishmen would have been wondering how such developments would affect the outcome of their case.

In Ireland the price of de Valera's neutrality started to bite with the announcement from shipping companies in London that a shortage of ships meant fuel supplies to Ireland would be drastically reduced. This was presumably due to the attrition rate in the Battle of the Atlantic. In January 1941 the petrol ration in Ireland was about eight to ten gallons, and the next month it was cut altogether for private motorists, with exceptions made for doctors and clergy. The bicycle and the horse became the transport of necessity. While petrol restrictions affected relatively few people, rationing of paraffin used for cooking and lighting did affect the general populace. Wheat was also in short supply and so was tea. Ireland suffered little disruption at first, but as the year wore on this changed. Winston Churchill saw no sense in Irish neutrality:

> The separation from Great Britain is absolutely impossible. The interests and the affairs of the two islands are eternally interwoven … the economic dependency of Ireland on England is so absolute and quite apart from moral, military and constitutional arguments … the two nations are bound together till the end of time by the national force of circumstances.[1]

Churchill may have publicly scorned Ireland for its stance, but other members of the government were more muted in their criticism, and despite animosity at times, trade went on. For example: in June 1940 Britain agreed to purchase all of Éire's wool exports at a price to be negotiated.[2] Then there were ongoing kerfuffles about butter exports from Ireland to the UK. Britain's Ministry of Food contracted to take all of Ireland's surplus butter in 1940, but there were claims that Ireland was holding back supplies for its own people, and that it was more expensive than New Zealand butter. Others claimed Ireland was not holding back at all but rather Britain was trying to buy more of the cheaper Kiwi butter.[3] In England, Irish butter became a black market item and buying it directly from Ireland was illegal. Lt Col A. Maude was fined three guineas for obtaining butter from his daughter in Ireland, as was Mrs Eleanor Hollis who received butter from her son living in Waterford.[4]

While the people of Britain were being prosecuted for having a few extra ounces of butter, little was mentioned about the lavish lifestyle that Winston Churchill and other privileged Britons continued to live throughout the war, finding a way around the rationing restrictions. 'It's the rich that get the pleasure and the poor that gets the blame', so one version of the song goes, which is absolutely true! Churchill never missed out on his champagne or plover eggs.[5]

If Dad and his Irish mates thought life was going to be easier 18,000 kilometres from Ireland, far from the war, they were mistaken. Petrol rationing followed a similar pattern to Ireland and for most people living in New Zealand, the bicycle, the horse and 'Shanks's pony' were the main form of transport. Sugar and tea, and eventually butter and meat, were rationed during the war as the country needed to send produce overseas to feed the armies of its allies. With the war in 1941 not going well and New Zealand casualties mounting, anger grew towards those men who wouldn't fight.

During WWII in New Zealand there were 3000 appeals against conscription and 600 were allowed. Most of those who lost their appeals relented and served in some capacity in the armed forces. However, 800 refused to comply, making them defaulters, and so they were sentenced along with conscientious objectors to detention in camps, mostly in isolated places around the country, making it hard for friends and relations to visit. The camps were said to be uncomfortable, and inmates remained there until the war ended.[6] At that time there were still 200 men in the camps, and the RSA wanted the government to keep the detained men in camps for a further 12 months and to disenfranchise them for 10 years. This proposal was rejected, but it should be noted that the last conscientious objectors were not released until a year after VE Day.[7]

The appeal boards had the final say on whether a person should be detained, and the government rejected any notion of appeals against these decisions. Prime Minister Peter Fraser was quoted in the *Evening Post* saying:

> The appeal boards are fully competent to determine appeals fairly and impartially on the evidence submitted ... it has been found neither desirable nor practical to make any such provision.[8]

New Zealand's treatment of conscientious objectors was punitive compared with other countries. In Australia conscientious objectors were directed into civilian work not connected with the war, while in Canada only 300 of 11,000 conscientious objectors were held in camps, with the rest being directed to work in industry. Even in Britain, half of those who lost their appeals were exempted to do non-military work, and those imprisoned were paroled to do civilian work after serving a sentence of about three months.[9]

It is interesting to note that even in Britain, New Zealand was seen as taking a tough stance against those who refused to fight. In the House of Lords in March 1942, the Duke of Bedford commented that 'the position was even harsher in New

WAR OBJECTORS

MOTION IN LORDS

Alleged "Harsh" Conditions In

New Zealand

Auckland Star, 3 March 1943, p.3

Zealand where about 700 conscientious objectors were imprisoned or placed under detention for periods of two years.'[10] He said that since the outbreak of war, 1600 of them had been imprisoned in Britain but only 305 were still detained.

John Cookson, Emeritus Professor of History at New Zealand's Canterbury University, published a paper on the formation of government policy on conscientious objection, in which he highlighted New Zealand's harshness towards objectors:

> In no other Commonwealth country – we might add the United States as well – was a proportionate number of conscientious objectors imprisoned or detained, much less indeterminate sentences imposed. New Zealand was also exceptional in the total severity of its policy.[11]

Cookson draws an interesting comparison with Britain, pointing out that the New Zealand armed forces appeal boards, in comparison to the British tribunals that performed the same function, were 'too formal, too ignorant and too busy', which led to conscientious objection in New Zealand becoming a controversial topic, which was not the case in Britain.

While the Sons of Éire were waiting to hear the outcome of their appeals, an issue which was to later affect them was being worked out in Wellington. In August 1941 a special tribunal was set up with the objective of determining 'alternative service and sacrifice'.[12] It was this tribunal that set a rate of pay of £4 per week for men classed as conscientious objectors who were prepared to be manpowered into essential work. This was known as 'soldiers' rates' but the COs did not get some of the other financial benefits associated with this rate, such as allowances for families that serving soldiers received when posted overseas.

Arguably New Zealand's system of imprisoning its defaulters and conscientious objectors was a waste of money and manpower. The men in the camps were assigned to somewhat meaningless work instead of productive work on the land or industry where there was a chronic shortage of labour. It also put stress on families, and this must have been a dilemma for the Fraser Government because they would have known that many of the people in the camps were Labour supporters.

This sentiment was reflected in a letter to the *Evening Post* on 17 October 1941 when 'Fair Play' noted that:

> I am glad to see that you mentioned in 'The Post' that it was time something was done to determine what sacrifice should be made by conscientious objectors. While there are some enjoying the privileges and profits of civilians, others are dismissed from their work and subject to penalties including imprisonment. Surely it would be better if all objectors, irrespective of their appeals being allowed or dismissed, were made to do useful work at little or no pay.[13]

Another letter writer to the *Evening Post* suggested that 'conscientious objectors working in shops ... should be got out of soft jobs and put into heavier industrial industries, leaving the easy jobs for returning soldiers.'[14]

It is interesting to note that some employers planned to dismiss staff who were proclaimed conscientious objectors. The Wanganui Education Board reportedly passed a resolution that:

> The Board dismiss from their service any teacher who is known to have conscientious objection regarding his duty under the National Service Regulations.

Chair E.F. Hemingway said:

> If such teachers were allowed to teach children, there would grow up a nation of conscientious objectors.

The Board apparently held back from implementing that decision until the government announced its plans for dealing with conscientious objectors.[15]

The Wellington Hospital Board also adopted a motion against employing any active pacifist, with one member saying the 'hospital service should not be used as a funk hole by people with distorted ideas'.[16] The Wellington City Council decided not to employ any objector who would give no community service at all, but stated it would treat every case on its merits.[17] The momentum against conscientious objectors increased, with the RSA no

THE "CONCHIES"
OLD SOLDIERS' ATTITUDE
(P.A.)
DUNEDIN, This Day
At a special meeting of the R.S.A. some criticism of the Government took place. One member said: "If the conscientious objectors get away with it we know what will happen. It will be the same as last time, and the objectors of that time are running the country today."
A voice: Put them out!
Another voice: Who put them in?

Evening Post, 23 September 1941, p.8

doubt having some influence. For example, the Hawke's Bay Education Board took a stand: 'If a man is not prepared to defend the British Empire he is not fit to teach British children'. The Nelson Education Board promptly congratulated their colleagues in Hawke's Bay.[18]

But not everyone followed that line. An attempt by the Hastings Rugby Union to bar men who refused to wear the uniform of the King was rejected, with one man reported as saying: 'There are worse people than conscientious objectors.' A similar move was also rejected by the Wellington Rugby Union.[19]

However, by and large the public mood was against those who refused to fight, with the RSA saying it would bring to the notice of the authorities instances of disloyalty. It is worth remembering that Bell, the Crown Prosecutor in the Sons of Éire case, was a staunch RSA man.

While my father and his Irish mates were not strictly 'conchies', that was how they were regarded by the public and so must have suffered some of the distasteful comments that were being voiced. The press was used to great effect by the RSA and others who supported conscription, to demonise those who refused to fight. The appeal board cases were widely reported in the media, no doubt as part of a name and shame campaign designed to deter people from appealing, and for those who had, to have second thoughts. Jingoism reigned.

In September 1941 at a special meeting of the RSA in Dunedin, one member linked the conscientious objectors to Labour Party politicians:

> If the conscientious objectors get away with it we know what will happen. It will be the same as last time and the objectors of that time are running the country today.[20]

In its quest to denounce the Irish and others who were in their eyes disloyal, the RSA failed to recognise that 150,000 citizens of Éire joined the British forces and a further 250,000 worked in Britain's war factories.[21]

Farmers' groups were at one with the RSA when it came to leading the charge against conscientious objectors. A meeting of the Southland provincial executive of the New Zealand Farmers Union condemned the conscientious objectors and supported a move by the Gore RSA to give evidence against them at appeals. At what appears to have been a rowdy meeting, the executive finally resolved that:

> Conscientious objectors who refuse alternative service be drafted into essential production at soldiers' rates of pay without soldiers' benefits and that they be deprived of their civil rights for a period of ten years.[22]

Later in North Otago another group of farmers quizzed Minister of Agriculture Bruce Barclay on whether men in the camps for conscientious objectors were 'having an easy time', and one asked, 'How many miserable damned crawlers have you got tucked away in the camps and why can't they be made use of?' Barclay said he didn't know how many men there were in the camps but said those in the local area were growing flax and vegetables.[23]

Interestingly, while farmers joined the chorus against defaulters, many successfully won appeals to stay on their land, as did specialist workers such as those in dairy factories, freezing works and meat slaughter facilities. While a number were prepared to fight, their skills as food producers were regarded as more valuable to the Allied war effort. Some of the Sons of Éire were in these roles and others had come to New Zealand under specific schemes to work on the land.

One of the ironies of the whole conscription issue in WWII is what happened in Northern Ireland. While New Zealand introduced conscription, Northern Ireland, Britain's little outpost in the Emerald Isle, did not. When the idea was mooted there was strong opposition from Catholics within Northern Ireland and from across the border in Éire. On 28 May 1941 the *Press* in Christchurch, New Zealand, quoted Irish Prime Minister Éamon de Valera, as saying:

> There could not be a more grievous attack on any fundamental human right than to compel an individual to fight by force for a country to which he objected to belong … the six northern counties have always been part of Ireland and the inhabitants are Irishmen. There is not an Irishman in the world who does not regard a continuance of partition as a deadly wound inflicted on the body of this nation. Nothing can alter that. More than a third of the population [of Northern Ireland] has vehemently protested at being cut off from the body of the nation.[24]

Other political parties in Ireland joined in support of de Valera. In essence, he was reinforcing his view that he did not recognise partition and that he regarded every person living on the island called 'Ireland' as Irish.

Before WWII broke on 1 September 1939, de Valera was on record during a debate in the Dáil saying that he didn't want territory in Northern Ireland 'but we want people's hearts'. De Valera's point that a third of Northern Ireland was opposed to partition raised other issues. Many Northern Ireland Protestants were in jobs deemed 'essential industries'. If conscription was introduced in the six counties, a disproportionate number of Catholics would have been called up leading to huge dissent and trouble – something that the German propaganda machine, via Lord Haw-Haw (aka William Joyce), could have seized upon. As a result conscription was never introduced in Northern Ireland. Religion, resentment and politics prevailed.

What makes the whole saga of the Sons of Éire so ironic is that if these men had been living and working in Northern Ireland under British rule, just a matter of hours travel from where they were born, they would not have been conscripted. Living on the other side of the world in New Zealand saw them treated completely differently. One has to ask why the Irish question was not thought about and resolved long before WWII broke out. War books to prepare and plan for WWII were created in both Britain and New Zealand, which makes it hard to understand why the Irish situation had not been raised and sorted at that time.

While the Sons of Éire awaited the decision from the appeal board, they would have probably been aware of what others, and potentially themselves, were facing for refusing to take up arms for New Zealand or Britain.

The setting up of the camps for defaulters was the subject of a debate in Parliament with Minister of National Service Bob Semple saying that those sent to the camps would be 'engaged in breaking in land for settlement, road making, tree planting, drainage, farming and other work in connection with maintenance of their camps'. But in response to a question by right-wing National Party MP for Waitomo Walter Broadfoot about whether people interned in such camps would lose their civil rights for at least 15 years, Semple gave an emphatic no. He went on to say that those in camps were in detention and it would not be policy to let them work on farms.[25]

In many respects the camps were akin to prisoner-of-war camps as there were guards, strict rules, and every attempt made to keep the internees isolated from family, friends and the outside world. The camps were controlled by patrolmen, roll calls, and checks heralded by the sound of a whistle. Newspapers were banned and leave was allowed only for family emergencies.

Camp for conscientious objectors, Hautū near Tūrangi, 1943.
A.C. Barrington collection, Alexander Turnbull Library, F-37730-1/2

Visits to internees were limited to family members, which were supervised and infrequent due to the remoteness of the camps. The men in charge of the camps could impose punishment such as solitary confinement and a diet of bread and water for disobeying an order to work. More serious offences were heard by magistrates and prison sentences were imposed.

Margaret Tate provides a vivid insight into two camps in the Manawatū/Horowhenua region – Whitaunui and Paiaka – in the *Manawatu Historical Journal*. She notes that the camps were located in the vicinity of Shannon and Foxton, around the flood-prone Moutoa area where flax was common.[26] (Today the area is mainly dairy farms.)

These camps were probably two of the better ones in the country because they were near the township of Shannon and the city of Palmerston North, which were on the main trunk railway line. Other camps, such as the ones at Reporoa between Taupō and Rotorua, and Hautū on the Desert Road, were more isolated.

The camps in the Manawatū were typical of others in terms of design. A barbed wire fence, which was well lit at night, secured the perimeter. The men lived in a mix of one- and two-man huts containing a stool, a small table, and a bed with a straw mattress, but no heating. In the early days the men sent to such camps lived in tents and were required to help build some of the camp infrastructure, such as drains. Vegetables for the camp were grown by inmates within the perimeter wire.

Some attempt was made to provide recreational facilities, such as a theatre where plays could be performed, and there were also some limited sporting facilities. But the detention camps were not holiday camps – the men in them suffered from being away from their families and the basic comforts of life. They were designed to replicate the privations that servicemen and women overseas were experiencing.

Some notable New Zealanders were imprisoned at Whitaunui and Paiaka, including Dan Long, who was later to serve as the President and General Secretary of the Public Service Association. Terence – the elder son of Archibald Baxter, one of New Zealand's most celebrated conscientious objectors in WWI and the subject of a book by David Grant [27] – spent time at the Whitaunui camp. At the same time Rex Hillary, the brother of the renowned mountaineer, Sir Edmund Hillary, was at Paiaka. [28]

When the men were released from the camps after the war ended, sanctions on conchies continued. They were not allowed to vote in the 1946 election, and so did not get to vote until 1951. Teachers were debarred from service until 1948 and in some institutions their contracts were not renewed. Families of conchies suffered as well, with sons and daughters being teased.

Despite their fears the Sons of Éire were not sent to the camps in the end, but they were invariably regarded as shirkers, unpatriotic and of low standing. I can recall my father and grandfather being denied admission to play bowls at the Tawa Flat RSA Bowling Club after the war because of Dad's refusal to fight. Perhaps the feeling of the time is best summed up in a letter to the editor of the *Press* in Christchurch on 7 June 1941 when 'Common Sense' wrote:

> Referring to the 'natives of Éire' who appeal against military service: I suggest that the government just collects them in one mob and send them back to Éire where they belong and leave the country [New Zealand] and the jobs they have been holding for our boys when they return. [29]

The public outcry against conscientious objectors, regardless of their reasons for refusing to take up arms, would have made it a stressful time of uncertainty for the Irishmen.

9

The unknown mates

The Sons of Éire case was set to define how all Irishmen in New Zealand were to be dealt with in terms of their appeals against conscription. It seemed that this was agreed to by officials and government early in 1941. But even before their case was heard, Irishmen in other parts of the country were appearing before their local appeal boards.

It is likely, at least initially, that not all Irishmen facing conscription were members of the ENA, or even aware of its existence. The ENA did not have a high profile and this was partly because the executive was trying to negotiate a special deal behind the scenes and considered that any publicity might prejudice this. Some Irishmen may have been aware of the ENA but, for whatever reason, decided not to join. It is impossible to say exactly how many men from Ireland living in New Zealand in WWII actually took their cases to court because the government records are incomplete.

It is known that before the hearing in Wellington, cases were heard by the No.1 Appeal Board in Auckland, and some of the appellants were represented by Fred Ongley, the Wellington lawyer who later represented Dad and his five colleagues.

One of the Auckland cases was Thomas Scannell, a fibrolite or asbestos worker at Hardies in Penrose, Auckland. On 11 November 1940 he lodged an appeal against serving in the New Zealand Territorial Service on the grounds of 'conscientiously objecting to serving with the armed forces'.[1] This appeal was recorded on an official form designed to deal with all manner of requests to avoid military call-up, including domestic circumstances and undue hardship as well as conscientious objection. His formal request was received by the Manpower Committee in Area 1 (Auckland), on 15 November 1940.

Scannell followed this up with a detailed letter received by the Area 1 Committee on 30 December 1940, in which he stated that he was a citizen of Éire which was a neutral state and claimed to honour the policy of that country while living in New Zealand.[2] In this three-page letter he stated, as Matt Burke would do later, that he was prepared to do any work other than combatant work 'as I realise that residing in New Zealand even as a "neutral", work must be done and the country's resources kept going and developed'.

Scannell went on to say that while being a citizen of neutral Éire was one reason, there were other more compelling reasons relating to the Troubles in 1919–21:

> I was a resident of Éire during the Black and Tans reprisals 1919–21. I saw then and experienced the brutalities committed in the name of British law and in conscience could not take part in the war [WWII]. My own house was broken into by the Black and Tan soldiers in the name of British law and order.

He went on to say:

> I desire to assure you that it is no cowardice that is the cause of this unwillingness to fight, but the fact that my people and myself went through oppression and outrage at the hands of the Black and Tan soldiers and how in conscience could I take part in this war … I feel strongly that Éire is cut in two and partitioned … I have no attachment to Germany or any country on the continent of Europe. My devotion is first to the country of my birth, Éire, and then to the country of my adoption, New Zealand … I am prepared to do any kind of work in New Zealand apart from combatant service. I say that I am a conscientious objector in the fullest sense of the word and I wish to be allowed to work in any class of work, other than combatant work.

Scannell further stated:

> I do not base my claim of conscience on anything that has arisen since war broke out in September 1939, but from what I saw, felt and experienced in 1919–21 in Éire and it is only those who have lived through that experience can realise how the memories of those frightful days have left something on one's mind that can never be blotted out. To ask me to wear the uniform of a British soldier would not only be cruelty but one against which my conscience rebels. I therefore ask that I be exempted from military service on the grounds that:
>
> As a citizen of Éire, a neutral state:
>
> That I be allowed to do any other useful work in New Zealand during the war.
>
> OR
>
> That I be permitted to leave New Zealand.

This letter by Thomas Scannell was virtually replicated word for word in the Sons of Éire's statements of evidence to the appeal board in Wellington seven months later. The link between Scannell's case in Auckland and the Sons of Éire case in Wellington was that Ongley was lawyer for both parties, which is the likely reason for the similarity in statements.[3]

What this letter does show is from an early stage there was considerable consistency in the messaging from Irishmen living in New Zealand about their objection to being conscripted into the armed forces. It is possible that Scannell was in contact with members of the ENA even though he was living in Auckland, as Michael Lafferty from Auckland was on the ENA Executive.

Thomas Scannell's brush with the authorities surfaced again in a report in the Christchurch *Press* on 10 June 1941, when he and 13 other Irishmen appeared before the No.1 Armed Forces Appeal Board in Auckland with Fred Ongley from Wellington, the ENA's lawyer, and a Mr Robinson.[4] The others were William Coleman, carpenter; Patrick Joseph Whooley, labourer; Michael Whooley, chamberhand; Michael Lafferty, bricklayer; James Thomas McDonnell, carpenter; Joseph McNamara, labourer; Michael John Luby, farm labourer; Patrick Egan, labourer; Patrick Joseph Lynch, porter barman; George O'Connor, labourer; and William Reidy, barman.

Speaking on behalf of his clients, Ongley told the appeal board that, with the authority of the government, he had written to Éamon de Valera, Prime Minister of Éire, asking for direction regarding men in the position of the appellants, but that no reply had been received. He said that he had hoped there would be a conference among the authorities to get a principle laid down. This was because some men had asked to be allowed to return to Éire while others had offered to do noncombatant work in New Zealand.

Fred Ongley made the comment that 'cases of this kind were never contemplated when the regulations were drawn up'. He went on to say:

> If the appeals are dismissed, the onus of saying what is to become of these men will be thrown upon the government and that may lead to a very undesirable position. We are then going to be faced with the fact that we are conscripting unwilling Irishmen.

The Chairman's response was that the matter was in the hands of the government and the military authorities, and not the concern of the appeal board.

Michael Lafferty made an interesting submission to the appeal board saying that he came to New Zealand in 1939 under a government contract guaranteeing him two years employment, but claimed they did not live up to their obligations. Lafferty stated that although he was only a child at the time of the fighting in Ireland, he vividly remembered certain incidents. He said his uncle, who had fought in WWI, was taken out and shot in the presence of his children by Crown forces during the Troubles.

Shipping records show that Lafferty, who came from Roscommon, arrived in Wellington on 29 June 1939 on board the *Rangitikei*, the sister ship to

The first party of 59 skilled tradesmen from England (including a number of Irishmen), brought out under a special arrangement by the government, are greeted by Minister for Housing H.T. Armstrong upon their arrival in Wellington on 29 June 1939.
Evening Post collection, Alexander Turnbull Library, N-P-2036-7/4

Rangitane which my father travelled on. Lafferty, a bricklayer, was one of a group of Irishmen on board that included William Coleman, Frank Kelly, Michael Molloy, John Joseph Moriarty and Thomas Walsh, all of whom were later to appeal their conscription. These men were part of a contingent of skilled workers recruited by the New Zealand Government to help build new state houses.[5] They were met by Minister of Housing H.T. Armstrong, who made a special trip down to the docks in Wellington to welcome the party.[6]

Yet within a year these men were battling the government on the conscription issue. Michael Lafferty, who lived in Auckland, was a member of the ENA executive and became the secretary while Aylward was overseas. He had asked to return to Éire but was told that because there was a war on and as he was a 'British subject' he must remain in New Zealand.[7] This highlights the trap the Irishmen found themselves in. The benefits of being British were few, if any. However the Chair of the appeal board adjourned his appeal *sine die* and said it was up to the Director of National Service to make a decision. A similar call was made in respect of James Thomas McDonnell.

The hearing continued with Thomas Scannell taking the stand and stating he was now 45 years old and had experiences with the Black and Tans:

Some of the Citizens of Éire. From left: Peter Melvin, Paddy Carr, Con Collins and Mick Sheridan, pictured here with Kate Carr.
Courtesy of Pat Sheridan

I was imprisoned without trial and got my release through hunger striking, was captured, escaped and recaptured and escaped again. I saw the burning of homes and the destruction of property.

He went on to say he would not bear arms even for the defence of Ireland. Scannell even went so far as to claim he would not assist the Red Cross or defend himself if attacked. McDonnell, McNamara, Luby and Egan also said they would not fight for Ireland, while the Whooley brothers and O'Connor said they would only fight for Ireland if she was attacked.

Official records show that Patrick Egan was working at the Westfield Freezing Works in Auckland and was living at 39 Avenue Rd, Ōtāhūhū. He had lodged his appeal against his conscription into the Territorial Service on 16 November 1940.[8]

According to the newspaper report, the appeals of Scannell, Lafferty, McDonnell, Luby, Egan and McNamara were allowed on conscientious grounds, while those of the Whooleys, O'Connor and Reidy were dismissed. Those of Coleman and Lynch were adjourned to allow them to give evidence.

Before this hearing on 10 June 1941, Egan had made an appearance before the Board on 4 June, at which his counsel noted: 'It was funny to hear of an Irishman who did not want to fight, but there were certain other circumstances.'[9]

The case was held over until 10 June, which was the day the No.1 Appeal Board officially sent Egan a standard form letter saying that his appeal had been granted on 'conscientious grounds'.

The appeals in Auckland did not go unnoticed by the ever vigilant public. In a letter to the editor of the *New Zealand Herald*, Lawrence Gee wrote about the appeals of the citizens of Éire:

> It would be interesting to know whether these same individuals are, or have been, receiving all the privileges of citizenship in New Zealand during the period of their residence here. For instance, did they exercise

their votes at the recent municipal elections? If so, then surely their claim to be citizens of another country does not stand. They cannot have it both ways![10]

Such letters to the papers were the order of the day, but the Irish did not respond, probably fearing further attacks. They were more interested in changing government policy towards them, than winning – or probably losing – trial by public opinion.

Other letters to the editor of the *Evening Post* supported the anti-Irish sentiment. A 'True Britisher' from Southern Ireland noted that:

Irish people in England were coming together to buy a Spitfire aircraft for the RAF. And I would be delighted to head the list in New Zealand to purchase an aircraft to help Britain.[11]

On the same day Mary O'Malley wrote a letter which included the following:

Let it be known that a vast number of Irish living in this land [New Zealand] are grateful to the British flag and are willing and happy to make the supreme sacrifice to keep it flying forever over our land.[12]

Another case of an Irishman opposing conscription in 1941 was that of Michael O'Connor, whose appeal was heard in the coal mining town of Westport on the South Island's West Coast. The area had a reputation for being a place of refuge for Irishmen, and many worked in the coal mines in WWI and WWII to avoid conscription.

O'Connor told the Board, consisting of Chair E.F. Reid, A.H. Kane and G.M. Hall, that he was born in Tralee, County Kerry on 13 April 1916, and came to New Zealand on 17 December 1938. His claim for exemption was again on the basis of status, as he was a citizen of neutral Éire. The report makes no mention of any events in Ireland, which is understandable as he would have only been a child when the Troubles occurred. The appeal board made no recommendation in his case and stated that it was up to the government, not the board, to decide his fate.[13] Apart from that one reference in the *Press*, O'Connor's name does not appear again until January 1942 when it is on the list of Irishmen – along with my father's – scheduled for deportation back to Ireland.

A law unto itself

The West Coast in New Zealand has always been a place where British law was seen as more of an 'advisory than an absolute.' Rough local justice was often meted to police trying to prevent after-hours drinking. The use of gelignite to blow up the chimney pots on the houses of the police was not uncommon. Coal miners knew all about explosives and probably could have taught the old IRA a few tricks during the Troubles.

Another Irishman who appealed against serving in the New Zealand Army on conscientious and status grounds was James Featherston, a milking hand on a dairy farm near Edgecumbe in the Bay of Plenty.[14] He was supported in his case by his employer, Maurice J. O'Flaherty, who was a sharemilker. O'Flaherty stated that Featherston was an excellent dairy hand and essential to the industry, and that if he was called up it would make it impossible to carry on milking the large herd.

In his statement Featherston declared that he would not take part in any military service but would help New Zealand in a civil capacity. At the age of 19 he had vowed to take no part in war, politics or class conflict. He went on to say he was a citizen of Éire who had come to New Zealand twelve years previously, and was an electrical fitter having only taken up farm work a year before. He also stated he was a member of the Roman Catholic Church.

The Crown representative asked Featherston how he in conscience could earn money and do work that assisted in sending other soldiers to fight, to which he said he had no control over this. The final word from the Crown representative was typical of what the Irishmen endured. He said:

> If his conscience is genuine, then he could cease earning and not take any part in the war and if necessary starve and die for his ideal.

Featherston politely replied that he disagreed with that notion.

Interestingly, Featherston's appeal was accepted and it seemed he remained in New Zealand – he was not on the list of 155 deportees in 1942.

As for Thomas Scannell, he was mentioned in memos in November 1941 for not turning up for medical examination, and then again on 16 January 1942, when in a memo from the National Service Director to the Under-Secretary for the Department of Internal Affairs, his name appeared on a list of 155 Irishmen who had been granted exit permits to leave New Zealand because they refused to join the armed forces. Scannell was living at 72 Grafton Road in Auckland in February 1943. I can find no record of what happened to him beyond that date, other than that he died in Auckland on 16 January 1966. His death notice, with 'NZR' (probably for New Zealand Railways), announced that a Requiem Mass was to be celebrated at St Benedict's Catholic Church in Newton, and Scannell was to be buried at the Māngere Lawn Cemetery. There is no mention of relatives in the death notice, so I assume he never married and had lost contact with Ireland.

The life story of Thomas Scannell and many other Citizens of Éire will probably never be told. For those who didn't marry their stories most likely went to the grave with them – far away from the homeland which they might have visited once or twice, or maybe never. Perhaps a photograph exists in a family home in Ireland, or these men may be lost and forgotten souls whose deeds for their country rest only in the libraries of heaven.

However, at a St Patrick's College Old Boys dinner a few years ago, I asked if any of my colleagues knew if their fathers were involved in these events. John Knox, who attended the school the same years as me, came forward with the story of his father. Later Mike Carr and his sister Elizabeth, who had heard about my research, also provided me with the story of their father, Mick Carr, who came from Galway.

John Knox, who I went to both primary and secondary school with in Wellington, had a fascinating story to tell about his father, Robert, who was not part of the original group of Irishmen involved in the appeals, but his story probably reflects what happened to the others.

Robert Knox was born in 1916 in Irvinestown, County Fermanagh, in Northern Ireland, and was one of a family of eleven who came to New Zealand in 1928. John takes up his father's story:

> It was a pretty rough boat trip and a lot of people got sick, so much so that the family were taken to Somes Island, a quarantine station in the middle of Wellington Harbour, before they were finally allowed to land. The day they finally set foot on New Zealand soil they caught the train to Hamilton city and then settled in Massey Road in Ngaruawahia where the family bought a farm. Dad never went to school in New Zealand. He immediately became a builder and he built a house for his parents on the farm. He loved his rugby and played the odd game for Waikato during the war.
>
> However I understood he was a conscientious objector. It seems he joined the army but deserted and refused to go to the war. After this he was chased by the police to be put away and imprisoned, and kept eluding them. He told me of a train trip down to Wellington where the police attempted to apprehend him, and he jumped off the train while it was still moving. In the end he went down to the West Coast of the South Island and was a coal miner for many years. I think he also had other brushes with the police but he didn't say much about this.
>
> He came back to Wellington where he met my mother. She came out from Ireland in 1939 to be bridesmaid at a cousin's wedding, Kate McGrath, and intended to go home but the war set in and, in the words of my mother, she was imprisoned in New Zealand for the rest of her life. Her name was Bridie Carr and she came from Oranmore near Galway City, and as a child experienced the brutality of the Black and Tans. Her family home was raided by them and as a two-year-old she was thrown into the burning fire. She had a burn mark scar on her face for the rest of her life.

Robert Knox.
Courtesy of John Knox

My parents got married at St Joseph's Church which was close to the old St Pat's College, and I was born in 1945. My father was eventually caught by the authorities and was sentenced to two years in prison for being a deserter. He was in Mount Crawford Prison in Wellington while I was just a baby.

Our family life was based around the friendship with other Irish families in Wellington such as the McCabes, Sheridans, Carrs, and the Wilsons who owned the Railway Hotel in Thorndon. We traipsed across town to socialise and of course I went to St Pat's with the sons of these families. A favourite meeting place for the Irish was the Basilica in Thorndon and I remember that after Mass on Sunday they would stand on the steps of the church and talk.

I do remember as a young lad when we went to the movies they used to play 'God Save the King' and everyone was expected to stand. My parents did not and I was not allowed to either. I wanted to join scouts but again there was strong opposition from my parents who saw the khaki uniform as a symbol of the British army.[15]

The case of Robert Knox came to the attention of the ENA later and was the subject of a letter dated 30 October 1945 from Maurice Aylward to Prime Minister Peter Fraser, where Aylward sought consideration of Knox's case. This presented some dilemmas for the ENA.

The story Mike Carr tells about his father, Mick Carr, and family is similar to that told by most of the sons and daughters of the Citizens of Éire. He knew, or knew of, some of the names on the list of 155 Irishmen who were to be deported, such as Mick Lafferty, Charlie McPeake, John Nally, John Clancy, Dan Culloty and Tom Grealish. He remembers Dan Crowley as a man who fought in 1916 and in later life was quite a good fiddle player, who played for Irish dances. He knew the Sheridans, Hickeys and Flahertys, who came from the Aran Islands.

My father, Mick, who was from Carnmore in Claregalway Parish, County Galway, came out to New Zealand in 1938. We knew he was conscripted and involved in some sort of court case and that later he was manpowered to work in the freezing works. On his first day there he was with 15 other Irishmen and a Māori man called Mulligan. The foreman came in and there were all these Irishmen standing there and he said, 'Which one is Mulligan? I want to talk to Mulligan.' He repeated it, but there was silence until finally the Māori lad stepped out from the back and said 'I'm Mulligan,' much to the amusement of everyone.

Dad never talked about the Black and Tans, but when I was in Ireland I was taken to visit his cousin's house and they said my dad's older sister was married to this fellow Kelly who lived with his two brothers and during the Troubles there were always guns in the house. The Kelly boys were quite active IRA men and they apparently burned down the houses of a number of landlords. When I visited my mother's folks who lived in Derry, I discovered that they were great friends with a relative of Francis Hughes, a well-known Provisional IRA man who died on a hunger strike in the infamous Maze Prison in May 1981. Hughes came from a prominent republican family – his father had been a member of the IRA in the 1920s and he is claimed to have killed four RUC men and one soldier. He was on a hunger strike at the same time as Bobby Sands.

My mother, Mary Keenan, was from Northern Ireland and my father was quite shy, but his fellow Irishmen somehow managed to get them together and they married in 1950. He was working on the waterfront in Napier and was obviously affected by the big 1951 waterfront strike. After the strike he left the waterfront and worked for Watties, the fruit and vegetable processors, then Fletchers, the building company, and finally he worked at the Tōmoana Freezing Works until he was in his 70s. He had his one and only trip back to Ireland in 1982.

Dad used to talk about going to South Canterbury with Mick Sheridan to do harvesting work with traction engines and threshing machines. They worked around Fairlie, Geraldine, and a place called Kerrytown which had a tradition of Irish music. I always thought it was a working holiday but now realise that he would have been manpowered and sent there.[16]

Mick Carr was on the list of the men to be deported back to Ireland in 1942. His son still has a copy of his permit to leave New Zealand, which was never needed. The story of Mick Carr is similar to that of my own father and I suspect most of the men who came to New Zealand in the 1920s and '30s. Like Mick, Dad went back to Ireland only once. Contact with families across the world was limited to letters and generally it was sporadic, sometimes only a Christmas card. As late as the 1980s not everyone in Ireland had a telephone and so communication could be difficult. To borrow the words of Bridie Knox, they had become imprisoned in New Zealand for better or for worse.

The option of going back offered few financial opportunities, and as immigrants they had to make the best of what they had in New Zealand, even though their families were, in many cases, only distant memories. Some became 'prisoners' in New Zealand, although some, like Maurice Aylward, loved their adopted country and were never tempted to return permanently to Ireland.

IO

Fight or feck off

Throughout 1941 there was much debate in New Zealand about conscientious objectors, and the rights and wrongs of that position. At the same time, behind the scenes, the special case of the Sons of Éire was still being put to the government. Contact was likely to have been with Acting Prime Minister Walter Nash, because Peter Fraser was overseas from May to September. It was on this trip that Fraser again met de Valera, after meeting with Winston Churchill.

The initial hearing of the Sons of Éire had taken place on 31 July 1941, but Fraser was home in time for the announcement of the decisions of the No.4 Armed Forces Appeal Board on 9 October 1941.

While Fraser and Nash did not seek to intervene in the case of the Sons of Éire or the decision of the appeal board, the matter was of enough concern for Fraser to send a cable to the British Secretary of State for Dominion Affairs in London, Viscount Cranborne, on 30 September 1941, just ten days before the announcement of the decision:

> Citizens of Éire who are resident in New Zealand in terms of National Service Emergency Regulations are deemed to be natural-born British subjects and liable for compulsory military service both in New Zealand and overseas. Large numbers of them are refusing to serve on grounds that they are citizens of the neutral state of Éire and ask that they be exempted from service or granted permits to return to Éire. Please advise policy followed in Great Britain in respect of citizens of Éire who are resident in Great Britain in terms of National Service Armed Forces Act 1939.[1]

The Fraser Government was obviously looking for an answer which could help resolve the issue, or provide a political answer which could potentially override any appeal board decisions. It should be remembered that while the boards were required to adhere to strict guidelines, and presumably take note of Semple's hard-line attitude, there was still inconsistency in decisions nationwide with some boards harder than others on conscientious objectors.

On 4 October 1941 Cranborne replied to Fraser:

> Liability of Éire Citizens to Military Service: Under section 1 of the United Kingdom National Service (Armed Forces) Act 1939, Éire

citizens who are British subjects are not liable for military service if they are not normally resident in Great Britain. They are not regarded as being ordinary residents if they have been a resident for less than two years, if they reside here only for the purpose of attending a course of education or if circumstances of their residence here are otherwise such as to show residence for a temporary purpose only. As regards Éire citizens who are British subjects and who become liable for service under these provisions an informal arrangement was made with the Éire Government in March 1940, whereby those whom the Irish High Commission in London certifies as having a home in Éire and belonging there are allowed to return there and so avoid being called up for service. An Éire citizen who returns to Éire under this arrangement is not allowed to return to this country unless he is willing to serve in the armed forces here. Should he return to this country he is not allowed to leave again unless he has served. This arrangement is widely known amongst Éire citizens in this country, many of whom have taken advantage of it, but in view of its informal nature care is taken not to give it general publicity.[2]

This response was interesting as it was to change New Zealand Government policy and set in train a series of actions over the next twelve months. It also begs the question why the government had not asked this much earlier when the Irish issue was first raised, or why the government didn't know about this policy given the representations made to it in 1940 by the ENA. Also noteworthy is that Britain wanted to keep the issue quiet – possibly because it would have compromised Churchill's hard line against Éire and his demands for Ireland to join the war, as well as his annoyance at the handing back of the Treaty ports to Ireland.

Had the government sought this advice sooner it may have also stopped ructions that occurred when some Irishmen were earlier refused permits to leave the country. It was not addressed in the War Book although Fraser and others in government were well aware of the issue. Instead they relied on the imperfect regulation regarding conscientious objectors to take its course.

Just before Cranborne's response arrived on 2 October 1941, a letter was sent by Ongley's office on behalf of Maurice Aylward to what appears to be the National Service Department. It stated that he had agreed to leave New Zealand if permitted to do so, or do noncombatant work.[3] It said Aylward was willing to be medically examined to see if he was fit for noncombatant service. The letter carried the caveat that Aylward reserved all his rights as an Éire national and asked that the letter be put on his file so his attitude was on record.

Despite all the last-minute cables and letters, the decision of the appeal board was released on 9 October 1941, both privately to the men via Ongley,[4] and publicly at the top of page 10 of that day's *Evening Post*.

'Sons of Éire – Appeals Dismissed' read the headline. It listed the names of the six: 'Maurice Leo Aylward, freezing hand; John James Moriarty, brewery labourer; Patrick Sullivan, freezing-chamber hand; Brian Kennedy, freezing hand; Jeremiah Allen, cellarman; and Matthias Burke, lorry driver.' It reported they were represented by Mr F.W. Ongley.[5]

The report stated that the appeals by the Sons of Éire were dismissed in a reserved decision and that the board held that the appellants, when called up, had not lawfully ceased to be British subjects, and being residents of New Zealand within the meaning of the National Service Emergency Regulations 1940, they were properly members of the General Reserve. It dismissed the men's claim on conscience grounds, but recorded that some of the six (it doesn't say who) failed to include the ground of status (the claim to being citizens of neutral Éire), but said that they considered this anyway. The report by the appeal board listed the names, where they were born in Ireland, their dates of birth and arrival in New Zealand.

In justifying its decision, the appeal board noted that when the Irish Free State Constitution Act of 1922 was passed, Ireland, broadly speaking, achieved the status of a free dominion within the British Commonwealth, and subjects born within his Majesty's dominions and allegiance retained the status of a natural-born British subject. At the same time it claimed they acquired an Irish Free State 'sub-nationality'.

In its judgement the appeal board went on to say that when the Constitution of Éire Act was passed in Ireland in 1937, the appellants claimed that Éire ceased to be part of the British Empire and that they lost their British nationality. But it said it could not find any legislative enactment that allowed for this change of status and the Board concluded that the men remained British subjects. It used this example to substantiate their findings.

> It is a matter of interest to note that as late as June 1940 when the form of registration under the [New Zealand] Social Security Act was complied with, Messrs Allen, Aylward, Burke declared they were British subjects by birth while Moriarty failed to declare and Sullivan declared for birth in the Irish Free State.

The decision, as reported, goes on to quote Clause 1 of the British Nationality and Status of Aliens (in New Zealand) Act of 1928 and the National Service Emergency Regulations. It finally concluded:

The Board feels bound to hold that the appellants, when called up, had not lawfully ceased to be British subjects and, being residents in New Zealand within the meaning of Regulation 5 of the National Service Emergency Regulations, were properly members of the reserve. Their appeals on the ground of status must therefore be dismissed.

It appears that the *Evening Post* was sent a copy of the appeal board's decision because the reported text matches exactly that sent to Ongley.

Reaction to the decision of the appeal board was swift, with Fred Ongley sending a letter to Fraser on 17 October stating that the ENA could not accept the judgement and the arguments used to justify the dismissal of the appeals by the men.[6] He stated that the Sons of Éire and those behind their appeal were not conscientious objectors as defined in the New Zealand regulations as they regarded it as 'their right and duty to fight for Éire'. The Ongley letter went on to point out that:

The regulations provide only for the case of those who 'hold a genuine belief that it is wrong to engage in warfare in any circumstances' and do not provide for those who do not believe it is wrong to defend their own country, but do believe it is wrong to engage in warfare in the defence or attack of another or some other country. The result is that because they do not believe it wrong to defend Éire they are called upon by the Regulations to disobey either the Regulations or their conscience.

Ongley said that the men he was representing were exercising their duty and regretted any embarrassment that may have arisen from their position. There was also reference to the comment in the appeal board decision which effectively dismissed the men's claim to Irish citizenship under the Constitution of Éire Act of 1937. Ongley said that was not a decision that should have been taken by the board – rather, as it was an international matter, it should be dealt with at least by the countries concerned. His final paragraph was telling:

They [the six Sons of Éire] wish to record that their case was given a fair and impartial hearing and they were courteously treated by the Tribunal before which they appeared. They express their appreciation of that. They feel that they have now exhausted all their immediate legal remedies and that there is nothing more they can do other than to bring the matter under your notice and to appeal to you to see that no wrong is done to them.

This concluding paragraph doesn't entirely reflect the exchanges that my father and his colleagues had at the hearing as set out in the transcripts. However, it would seem that this was a call to Fraser for help and to get him to use what influence possible to get the best deal for the men. Unfortunately I have been

**RULING ACCEPTED
"SONS OF EIRE"**
MORE APPEALS DISMISSED

At the request of counsel appeals made by nearly sixty "Sons of Eire" on the ground of status were dismissed by the No. 4 Armed Forces Appeal Board yesterday afternoon. This action followed acceptance of the ruling given by the board some weeks ago, when

Evening Post, 4 November 1941, p.9

unable to trace a response from Fraser to Ongley. Presumably there was one, as well as some personal discussion between the ENA and Fraser.

Even before Ongley had sent his letter to Fraser, a memo was sent by Lt Col R.H. Quilliam, the Director of Mobilisation, to the staff officer of the No.5 Army Area in Wellington.[7] It listed the names of 69 of the Citizens of Éire and stated that until further instructions were issued no action was to be taken to require them to comply with their military obligations. For some reason Patrick Sullivan was missing from that list, though the other five Sons of Éire were named. If a prosecution was underway against any of the men a stay in proceedings for one month was to be requested, and within that period he hoped to be able to issue instructions about the future of the Irishmen.

With no evidence of a response from Fraser to the letter requesting his intervention, or any apparent awareness of the government's dialogue with Cranborne, on 3 November the ENA asked for the appeals by the remaining 56 men behind the test case of the Sons of Éire to be dismissed. All had been scheduled to appear before the appeal board that day, but they did not, and left it to their counsel to speak for them. Among the 56 cases dismissed was that of Michael (Mick) Carr. Like all the appellants he received formal notification of the date and time of when the hearing would take place, and also a standard form response from the appeal board stating their decision, and the grounds on which it was based. Remarkably Mick Carr's family still hold these records.[8] The decision of the appeal board dismissing his appeal and the appeals by the other 55 was published in the *Evening Post* on 4 November 1941. They were represented by M. Dennehy, appearing for Fred Ongley, and C.J. O'Regan was the counsel in the remaining case, that of Michael Connolly.[9]

Ongley stated in a letter to the appeal board that the original appeals had been brought as test cases, and that the present appellants appreciated that it was no good going over the same ground again and that their appeals were governed by the ruling. Ongley asked that the appeals be dismissed rather than withdrawn, to which the board agreed, effectively demonstrating that the other 56 had put up a fight and lost – not just given up. O'Regan agreed with Ongley's position.

W.F. Stilwell, Chairman of the appeal board, remarked that the attitude by the 56 was very helpful, and went on to say that in the original cases there was an appeal based on conscientious objection but the statements of the six individuals put them outside the regulations. He said that the board would dismiss all the appeals on the grounds of status, as they had done with those involved in the test case. Only Michael Connolly appeared at the hearing, stating much the same as the others, but noting that he was only prepared to bear arms in Ireland. His appeal was dismissed on the spot.

With the appeals dismissed, the New Zealand Government set about dealing with the Irishmen. On 23 October 1941 the war cabinet largely adopted the UK Government's policy on Irish nationals as set out in Cranborne's cable of 4 October. The actions required involvement of a range of government departments including the departments of National Service, Mobilisation and Internal Affairs, with much communication occurring between them.

The direction was set out in a memo sent on 5 November from National Service Director J.S. Hunter to Director of Mobilisation Lt Col R.H. Quilliam.[10] This listed the conditions for dealing with any Irishman who refused to enlist in the military. Essentially it was a case of 'fight or feck off'.

The men born in Éire who did not wish to serve in the armed forces were to be given permits to leave New Zealand by 31 December 1941, or as soon as shipping was available. Those who were called up after 1941 and objected had three months to leave, in which time they had to produce tickets for travel to Éire by the most direct route. The direction also contained a clause that was not included in the Cranborne cable, which stated that once the men left New Zealand they could never return. The British did not impose such a restriction on the Irish, probably because they were aware that they would need labour for new building work and repairing infrastructure damaged during the war. The memo also stated that any citizen of Éire who refused to serve in the armed forces and who did not leave the country would be treated as a defaulter, which meant they would be sent to a defaulter camp in some godforsaken place in rural New Zealand.

Hunter reminded Quilliam to withdraw any cases against Irishmen who said they wished to return to Éire, and told him that he would shortly receive a letter outlining the names of the men requiring permits to leave. He sent a similar letter to the Under-Secretary of Internal Affairs the next day, 6 November 1941, regarding the role of the Internal Affairs Department in issuing permits to leave. But the memo also added that those leaving must give a written undertaking that they would not return to New Zealand:

> Such persons availing themselves of the permit to leave New Zealand, they be not allowed to return either during or after the war.[11]

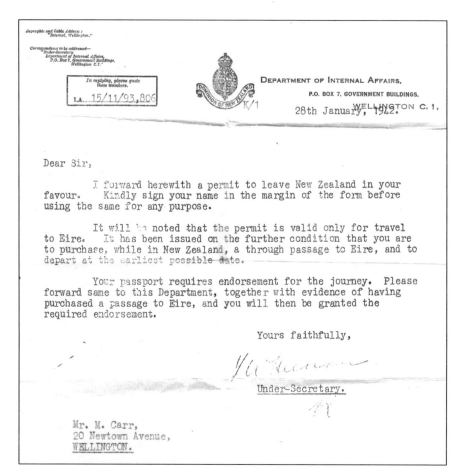

Geographic and Cable Address :
"Internal, Wellington."

Correspondence to be addressed—
Under-Secretary
Department of Internal Affairs,
P.O. Box 7, Government Buildings,
Wellington C.1."

In replying, please quote
these numbers.

I.A. 15/11/93,806

K/1

DEPARTMENT OF INTERNAL AFFAIRS,

P.O. BOX 7, GOVERNMENT BUILDINGS,

WELLINGTON C. 1,

28th January, 1942.

Dear Sir,

     I forward herewith a permit to leave New Zealand in your favour. Kindly sign your name in the margin of the form before using the same for any purpose.

     It will be noted that the permit is valid only for travel to Eire. It has been issued on the further condition that you are to purchase, while in New Zealand, a through passage to Eire, and to depart at the earliest possible date.

     Your passport requires endorsement for the journey. Please forward same to this Department, together with evidence of having purchased a passage to Eire, and you will then be granted the required endorsement.

     Yours faithfully,

Under-Secretary.

Mr. M. Carr,
20 Newtown Avenue,
WELLINGTON.

Official letter to Mick Carr granting permission to leave the country.
Courtesy of Michael Carr

Other memos fluttered around Wellington from office to office, reminding that any prosecutions against the Irishmen who had stated they wanted to leave the country should not be pursued. The process was moving at a pace probably not expected by the Sons of Éire. I wish I knew whether my mother and father were courting at the time and, if they were, what my mother was planning to do with all this uncertainty. Sadly she never spoke about this with me.

In Hunter's letter of 5 November there was a requirement that the Irishmen take the most direct route back to Éire. It would appear that this did not include a stopover in the United States, if a letter to the

Department of Internal Affairs by Michael Lafferty is anything to go by.[12] On 29 November Lafferty wrote that he was only prepared to travel via the United States and that the time by which he was expected to depart, 31 December 1941, was too soon, so asked that this be postponed to early in the New Year.

A week later Joseph Heenan, the Under-Secretary of Internal Affairs, told the Director of National Service about Lafferty's position and suggested that a ruling on the cabinet decision regarding the Irish would allow them to travel via the USA.[13] He also pointed out that there were difficulties getting passages across the Atlantic, no doubt due to the dangers from German U-boats. On Christmas Eve Lafferty got his wish – Hunter advised Heenan that travel to Éire via the United States was approved.[14]

One may surmise that Lafferty and others were possibly planning to jump ship and stay in the USA where most had friends and relations. My father had a brother and sister living in Boston, and a whole bunch of Bohan cousins from his mother's side of the family.

While Hunter had advised the Director of Mobilisation to withdraw cases against Irishmen who wished to return to Éire, there appeared to be some confusion. An example is the case of Scannell, whose appeal had been heard in Auckland in June 1941.

On 25 November Thomas Scannell is mentioned in a memo from L.N. Harris, the Secretary of the Manpower Committee to the Director of National Service in Wellington stating that:

> This man [Scannell] has failed to call in response to notifications and failed to submit to medical examination. I have it from his employer that he does not propose to take any notice of the correspondence emanating from this office as he intends returning to Éire.

Harris went on to say:

> I know that Scannell as a native of Éire is going to take the attitude that he is not subject to this country's laws and that he will want to go back to Éire in accordance with the arrangements approved by Cabinet ... It seems to me that Scannell wants to please himself what he does and there is no guarantee that he will return to Éire in the near future. I consider therefore that he ought to be called to appear before the Special Tribunal unless all cases of natives of Éire are going to be withheld until it is known whether the men will leave the Dominion.[15]

On the same day Harris penned a memo to the Director of Manpower and again referenced Scannell.

> I do not know whether the Director will consider it worthwhile taking further action in these cases until after the end of the year although, in the meantime, the men concerned may gain some advantage from continuing their present occupations at normal rates of pay.[16]

The reference to 'normal rates of pay' is significant as it had already been determined that so-called defaulters who were not sent to labour camps were to be paid soldiers' rates – £4 per week. Rates of pay were a contentious issue with understandable unhappiness that men who refused to serve in the armed forces were being paid more than soldiers. Hence the soldiers' rates arrangement was designed to placate and defuse some of the anti-conchie attitudes.

While a solution had seemingly been found to address the 'Irish issue', implementing it presented some challenges. However, this was set to become more difficult as the nature of the war changed in December 1941.

11

The 155 to go

The prospect of a safe passage across the Pacific and plans for the deportation of the Irishmen changed dramatically on the morning of 7 December 1941 when the Japanese attacked Pearl Harbor, in what was described by US President Roosevelt as 'a date which will live in infamy'.[1] There was now no such thing as 'safe passage' across the Pacific. New Zealand had another war front close to home as the Japanese army poured into South East Asia.

Pearl Harbor was the act that created the total world war and for the first time New Zealanders were faced with the prospect of conflict on their doorstep. Air raid shelters were built, aircraft patrolled coastal waters, and ports were heavily guarded as the country moved into defence mode. Interestingly Prime Minister Peter Fraser was in Washington for talks with US officials when the news broke about the Japanese attack.[2]

If my mother was concerned about what might happen to her future husband being deported, she would have also been worried about her younger brother, Jim Warren, who was in Malaysia and Singapore with the RNZAF's No.1 Aerodrome Construction Squadron. He and his colleagues were tasked with building airfields because of the lack of local labour and expertise. It was the first unit of its kind in the world when it was formed in July 1941. They arrived in Singapore three months later and then headed to Tebrau where they were to build their first aerodrome. The British commanders in charge of defending Malaysia and Singapore recognised the value of aircraft protecting the region. But while they built aerodromes they failed to supply modern fighter aircraft, so it was all a bit of a waste of time as the Japanese army quickly subdued the Allied forces. My uncle told me in reality his unit built airstrips for the Japanese.

Jim Warren, as a young man before the war.

A history of this squadron talks about how having just built the airstrips, they were forced to destroy them a matter of weeks later. In the light of their rapid retreat they nicknamed themselves the 'Singapore Harriers'.[3] They, like others, retreated to Singapore where they awaited evacuation as most realised that it was only a matter of time before the city fell to the Japanese. My uncle was one of the lucky men who managed to get out of Singapore, apparently on the *City of Canterbury*, on the night of 7 February 1942. Some of his colleagues were not so fortunate and suffered terrible treatment as prisoners of the Japanese.

On 15 February 1942, a week after Jim escaped, the commander of the Allied forces in Singapore, General Arthur Percival, surrendered to a much smaller Japanese force and consigned 130,000 men to captivity. It was one of the largest military disasters in British history and it had an Irish connection.

During the Troubles in Ireland, Percival was major of the Essex Regiment, which was well known for its lack of restraint. The legendary Tom Barry of the IRA's West Cork Brigade described Percival as 'easily the most viciously anti-Irish of all the serving British officers'.[4] Barry's Flying Column attacked Percival's regiment at every opportunity, but an attempt to assassinate the much hated British officer at Bandon in October 1920 failed.

Had Barry and his men been successful the outcome in Singapore may have been different. Although in fairness to Percival, the whole strategic defence of Singapore was a total shambles, not helped by the incompetence of the British military which had Churchill's finger in the pie.

Barry is said to have sent Percival an ironic telegram on his surrender of Singapore and one could assume that many of the Irishmen in New Zealand were delighted to see this individual get his comeuppance, although no doubt they would have shared the grief of New Zealanders whose men were killed and captured in this brief and bloody battle. General Percival's bravery, it seems, was confined to dealing with unarmed civilians and under-armed, part-time soldiers, but when confronted with a real army he threw in the towel.

More bad news followed on 19 February 1942 when Darwin, the northern-most city in Australia, was attacked by Japanese aircraft in what was a rerun of the attack on Pearl Harbor. This time it was the turn of the Australian military and civilian administration to demonstrate their incompetence in defending the town. What is worse, the Australian Government tried to cover up the extent of the raid, the resulting chaos, and the death toll. Peter Grose in *An Awkward Truth* estimates the death toll in the raid to be 297, and possibly up to 320.[5]

With the United States now in the war with Britain, Irish-American relationships had their moments. De Valera sent Defence Minister Frank Aiken to the States to supposedly garner support for Éire. But Aiken didn't follow the script and made inflammatory statements that annoyed President Roosevelt, who later asked whether Irishmen would ever get over hating England. 'Remember if England goes down, Ireland goes down too,' he said.[6]

The entry of the United States into the war also posed some problems for Ireland, as many Irishmen and Irish Americans joined the US armed forces. Two of my father's cousins, John and Arthur Bohan, served with distinction in the US military in Europe. De Valera was somewhat piqued when American troops started arriving in Northern Ireland, and in January 1942 issued a proforma complaint that he had not been consulted about their pending arrival. But this could have been as much for German consumption as anything else and to show that, publicly at least, Éire was neutral. The reality was quite the opposite because de Valera allowed Allied aircraft to use a narrow corridor across Éire, known as the Donegal Corridor, for their aircraft to patrol the North Atlantic. It raised the question: Who in WWII were the 'neutral' Irish against? The simple answer was Germany.

Back in New Zealand, the move by the authorities to deport Dad and his fellow Irishmen for refusing to fight started to gather momentum, even though leaving New Zealand by ship for Ireland had become a seriously dangerous proposition. This must have been a particularly worrying time for them.

A letter to Ongley from David Wilson, the Associate Minister of National Service, on 9 January 1942, stated that the government's preference was that the men travel on a British ship to the UK and then to Éire.[7] It said that in light of the recent developments in the Pacific, it could see no advantage in the men going via the US, but stated that this was up to them, and that they must book and pay for a passage as soon as possible and forward their paperwork to the Department of Internal Affairs to obtain a permit to leave.

The letter went on to politely reject an offer by the Irishmen to work in noncombatant roles in New Zealand, noting that 'while the action of the Éire Nationals is appreciated, it [the Government] regrets

J.S. Hunter, Director of National Service.
S.P. Andrew collection, Alexander Turnbull Library,
F-150642-1/2

that it is not possible to vary the decision which has already been made'. It also set out details of the procedures the Éire Nationals had to go through to get their permits.

On 16 January 1942 National Service Director J.S. Hunter sent a memo to the Under-Secretary of the Department of Internal Affairs (DIA) with a list of the names of the 155 so-called 'Éire Nationals' who were to be deported, and asked the DIA to issue them permits to leave.[8] On that list were the six Sons of Éire and the other members of the executive of the ENA: Thomas Cahill, Paddy Feeney, Patrick Hickey, Con Horan, Tim McCarthy, Joe Nally, Denis Roche and Edward Walsh. There are also names of people I knew, or knew their children, or heard my father talk about, including John Clancy, Michael Carr, Thomas Grealish, Thomas Lally, Michael Mannion and Michael Sheridan. The memo is quite a revealing document in that it shows the intent of the authorities to deal quickly with the issue.

A week later the DIA reported that the permits had been issued but that the process was not going exactly to plan. It said that on 4 February Mr Harbottle of the New Zealand Shipping Company advised that they were considering whether they would carry the men and wanted an assurance from the New Zealand Government that the British Government would allow the men to arrive at a British port and then be trans-shipped to Éire.[9] The Department noted that Mr Harbottle informed them that they could not book a passage to Éire.

Internal Affairs Under-Secretary Joseph Heenan recommended that the New Zealand High Commissioner in London, Bill Jordan, be asked to sort out the problem and come back with an answer.[10] In the end the issue was elevated up the political ladder with Prime Minister Peter Fraser asking the British Secretary of State for Dominion Affairs in London, Viscount Cranborne, for the answer. On 25 February 1942 Cranborne responded to Fraser saying that the men could tran-ship through Britain to Éire, but that in no circumstances could they stay in Britain, and that his officials must be furnished with a list of the men's names, their arrival dates and the port they would arrive at.[11]

What had started as a 'fight or feck off' arrangement had changed completely. The British Government's policy of allowing Irish people in that country to return home had only a hint of risk about it as there was minimum danger crossing the Irish Sea. But it was another thing running the gauntlet of German surface raiders and Japanese submarines in the Pacific and South Atlantic, not to mention German U-boats in the North Atlantic. Death by deportation was now a reality for the 155 Irishmen being sent home.

To that end, on 26 February 1942, Fred Ongley wrote to Prime Minister Fraser on behalf of the executive of the ENA on a range of matters relating to the pending deportation of the 155. In particular he pointed to the entry of Japan into the war and noted that the only route a ship could take to the UK was 'via Panama to some port in the United Kingdom'. This would have dangerous and serious implications for the men.[12]

Ongley went on to ask what action and response had come from a letter written by the ENA to David Wilson, Associate Minister of National Service, requesting that he formally tell the Éire Government of the plans to deport the 155 men, whether this had been done and what the response was. He also asked what steps had been taken to ensure the safe passage of citizens of a neutral country, and if the Irish Government hadn't been informed, Ongley requested that they be informed as soon as possible.

The lengthy letter also asked Fraser for permission for the ENA to write to Éire's Minister Plenipotentiary in Washington, Robert Brennan, about the planned deportation, and to seek his advice on how this might be best managed and what help he may be able to offer.

The issue of safe passage was again raised, with Ongley saying that under the existing process the permit to leave New Zealand would expire after just one month. In that time the men had to get the necessary endorsement for the voyage and provide evidence that they had paid for the passage at a cost of about £90. He said they had to pay this money upfront without knowing what arrangements had been made for the safe conduct and passage of their journey. He asked Fraser to amend the provisions so that the men did not have to pay any money until they got the guarantees they were asking for.

These comments were in effect a warning to the government that they risked bad publicity, not to mention diplomatic problems, if New Zealand sent the men to their deaths in a mass deportation. The challenge was finding an alternative that was politically acceptable, given the extent of anti-Irish sentiment in the country.

Ongley raised yet again the issue of the Irishmen swearing allegiance to the King. He pointed out they could not and would not do this, but were happy to do 'useful' work such as they were doing in the meat and allied industries, as long as this did not require them to take the oath of allegiance. The letter concluded that the ENA regretted that it was not possible for Fraser to meet with emissary Maurice Aylward to 'discuss these matters, and trust that whatever can be done will be done to protect and secure their rights as Éire Nationals or Citizens'.

As with all letters from Ongley, the wording is moderate and the ENA was going out of its way to try to find a workable solution and not offend the Fraser Government. They were probably aware that secretly Fraser was sympathetic to their cause and wanted to keep him on their side.

This letter was one of the most significant pieces of correspondence from the ENA to the government. It raised all the issues of 'concern' and was quietly warning the government that if any men were killed or injured during the voyage to Ireland, it would be held accountable.

On 3 March a form response to the Ongley letter was sent by Fraser saying the representation made by the ENA would receive 'due consideration'.[13] The copy of the document that I have is a file copy on which there are comments that make interesting reading, including that the Ongley letter had been referred to the United States Department of Internal Affairs and to the New Zealand Minister of National Service. A notation on the file, seemingly by Hunter of the Department of National Service, stated: 'The matter is again before the war cabinet and an early decision is likely and that no further action be taken until the war cabinet makes a decision'. This position is further supported by a memo from the Under-Secretary of DIA, Heenan, saying the same thing to Hunter.[14]

In essence, by taking the issues directly to Fraser, the ENA, through Ongley, was starting to get traction with a government that was clearly concerned at the implications of deporting the 155 Irishmen. They would have also been mindful of two other factors which in the end would work in favour of the 155. First, merchant shipping was in short supply as the American industry had not fully mobilised itself to mass produce ships as it did later in the war. Second, there was a manpower shortage, with New Zealand having a very high number per capita in its armed forces.

Time drifted along with little evidence that I can find of anything substantial being done by the government. Dissident Irishmen were obviously not a priority cargo, and unlike other men who refused to fight and were termed defaulters, the 155 could not now be sent to defaulters' camps. It was something of a Mexican standoff. Presumably the ENA, especially Aylward, were still quietly lobbying for their cause behind the scenes.

Meanwhile, the effect of Pearl Harbor was being felt in New Zealand. US forces had arrived in the UK and even in Northern Ireland after America entered the war. There was a similar American invasion of sorts in New Zealand from June 1942, when it began to be used as a staging post for the US forces, who were to become involved in some of the most brutal battles in the Pacific as they 'island hopped' their way to Japan.

The marine invasion

The Americans' presence was welcomed by the locals, with events and social outings organised for the men. The American soldiers were smartly dressed and attractive to the local female population. Romantic liaisons did occur and about 1500 New Zealand women married US servicemen. Not so happy were New Zealand males who considered that the visiting soldiers were 'overpaid, oversexed and over here'. Other problems were caused, it would seem, by the failure of the US military to brief their men that New Zealand did not discriminate against Māori in the way that white Americans did with African Americans. In Wellington in April 1943, tensions between local servicemen and US troops boiled over and a free-for-all fight took place in the city. Known as the 'Battle of Manners Street', it is believed that at one point at least a thousand men were involved in the fracas.

US military enjoying some rest and recreation at Oriental Bay.
Alexander Turnbull Library, F45134 1/2

The Marines who arrived on 14 June were based at two big camps near the small beachside township of Paekākāriki, about 40 kilometres north of Wellington. Most of these soldiers were in New Zealand to train for forthcoming battles in the Pacific Islands, and they practised landings and jungle marches. Others were returning from the battlefields of the Pacific for rest and recreation, or recuperation.

Despite a few ugly incidents, the short stay of the US soldiers and sailors was generally peaceful. The water supply system for Paekākāriki was built by the American troops and continues to serve the town. At nearby Queen Elizabeth Park there is a memorial to the United States Marine Corps, which continues to be visited by ex-marines and their relations.

Although New Zealand was a long way from the war in Europe and the Pacific, there were occasions when it came close to home. For example: two ships – the *Rangitane*, which brought my father to New Zealand on its maiden voyage, and the *Holmwood* – were sunk off the New Zealand coast. In early 1942 aircraft launched from a Japanese submarine flew over both Auckland and Wellington which reinforced the impossibility of 'safe passage' from New Zealand for the 155 Irishmen as a result of the military activity in the Pacific.[15]

The next time the issue of the Citizens of Éire surfaced was 30 June 1942. The Associate Minister for National Service, David Wilson, reported to Fraser a conversation he had with Ongley and Aylward in respect of the ENA attitudes to their call-up for National Service. In answer to his question: 'Would the members of ENA fight for New Zealand?' – Wilson said the answer was no, and they would not wear a New Zealand uniform.[16] His next question was: 'Would a minority of ENA members who disagreed with this decision fight to defend New Zealand?', and the answer was 'none', regardless of their personal opinions. Wilson then asked if the ENA accepted the government had no alternative but to either prosecute the men or deport them, to which Aylward and Ongley said yes, noting that the majority of their members would be of that opinion. Finally Wilson asked if the association still adhered to the pledge previously given that under no circumstances would it be a party to any obstruction or agitation if the government decided to deport them. 'Yes,' said Aylward, 'and the Association would do nothing and would endeavour to prevent individual action by members.'

Wilson, in his memo to Fraser, said he wrote down the answers and showed a copy of them to Ongley and Aylward, who agreed they were a true record of the conversation. He said they went further by expressing appreciation for the careful consideration that had always been given to their representations.

Wilson concluded by stating the law as it stood in respect to the men, and said that ENA members had even refused to serve in the territorials: 'There seems to be no course open but to deport them as previously agreed upon and I so recommend.'

This letter put the onus back on Fraser and the war cabinet to make a decision. The time for any further appeals or delays seemed to be at an end, given the sentiments in the memo.

With time running out and the ENA members anxious and concerned about their future, Aylward entered the fray with a letter to all members. There is no date on this letter but its contents indicate that it was written following the meeting with Wilson, with the knowledge that things were coming to a head, so members needed to receive clear directions from the executive of the ENA.[17]

The document is headed: 'Confidential – Éire Nationals – statement issued by the executive for the information and guidance of members' and in just one page Aylward eloquently summarised the ENA case and what members should now do.

> To obtain recognition of the independence and neutrality of Éire and our rights as citizens of Éire, the Executive has kept in constant touch with the authorities and with each development since the outbreak of war and particularly since the introduction of conscription. Éire is a free independent sovereign state and is neutral. We claim that Éire nationals cannot be conscripted into war by any other state.

He noted that while this claim had been rejected under British law the ENA had achieved a moral victory and had been active throughout New Zealand to protect the rights of its members.

> Its efforts have met with sympathy and consideration by those in authority. The present position is that all members have undertaken to do whatever essential noncombatant work the authorities require them to do pending a decision on whether or not they will be rehabilitated to Éire. Our members are loyally carrying out this undertaking and will continue to carry it out. The executive have also undertaken that its members will do nothing in any way to cause difficulty or embarrassment. That undertaking has been strictly observed and we ask for a continuance of that.

Maurice Aylward then went on to note that the executive of the ENA had some difficult situations to deal with caused by some people who had taken things into their own hands, and only last-minute intervention had got everything back on track, but at some embarrassment to all concerned. He asked all Éire nationals to stand together and not let matters drift, and to get in touch with members of the executive sooner rather than later to prevent trouble:

> We urge members to assist us in this direction and while we hope nothing untoward will happen, we feel that in times like this the safe course is to be prepared and we urge members to be ready to meet any contingency and to act philosophically in all circumstances. We feel that sacrifices will have to be made, but there must be no sacrifice in principle.
>
> When the story of this war comes to be written and national and international rights are adjusted, the actions and attitude of each one of you and of all Éire citizens in calling for recognition of our national rights and status will have a very important bearing. We ask for the wholehearted support of all Irishmen and lovers of freedom in this effort to maintain the principle that every nation shall be free to decide its own form of government – the great principle of the Atlantic Charter. Magna Carta enunciates the principle of men, the Atlantic Charter enunciates the principle of nations. The maintenance of both is vital to us all.

Aylward then referred to the ongoing troubles in Ireland and the injustice of partition. He said the ENA had lodged a protest with the New Zealand Government about this and that Ireland was fortunate in having Éamon de Valera as a leader to guide Éire to its destiny:

> We pray with God's help he may bring Ireland safely through.

His final message was extremely powerful, and a call to action by the ENA executive of its members:

> Irishmen, be true to Ireland and each other.

Aylward's letter was statesman-like, inspiring, patriotic and prophetic, following in the footsteps of Ireland's revolutionaries, including de Valera and Pearse. There was a call to action and sacrifice, and to not let past sacrifices be in vain. It was also a call for unity and comradeship, that in sticking together greater strength would rise. In my view, in 1942 New Zealand the humble man from Knockmoylan, Kilkenny, showed the leadership and political nous learnt from the great leaders of Ireland.

A copy of Aylward's statement must have somehow got to the New Zealand authorities because the copy I have has several annotations. One refers to Aylward asking his people to be 'true to Ireland'. The scribbled annotation reads: 'Why not true to NZ?' Another refers to the men refusing to be conscripted and says: 'Then they have no right to accept protection here from our soldiers'. Another commented on Aylward's words that the men should be rehabilitated out: 'It was decided to repatriate'. And one comment questioned

Aylward's right to raise the issue of Irish troubles, saying such a reference was 'fermenting Ireland's troubles in New Zealand'. Another described the contents of the letter as a 'sheer abuse of our hospitality'.

These comments show that some of the New Zealand bureaucrats were anti-Irish and did not necessarily share Prime Minister Peter Fraser's views. Aylward's words were well chosen and one suspects that he realised that sooner or later such a document would find its way into New Zealand Government circles. Maybe he even leaked it as part of a tactic to state his case to all concerned. Whatever is the case, this letter by Maurice Aylward was a final compelling plea for reason to prevail on all sides. It is significant because it links the sacrifices of the members of the ENA in New Zealand to past sacrifices made in the cause of Irish freedom.

Within just two weeks of receiving Wilson's 30 June memo, it appears that the war cabinet held yet another discussion on the situation of the 155 Citizens of Éire. The outcome of this was a cable sent at 8.30 am on 18 July 1942 by Peter Fraser to Clement Attlee, the Secretary of State for Dominion Affairs in London.[18] In the cable Fraser referred to the earlier advice sought from Attlee's predecessor, Viscount Cranborne, about the Éire Nationals, and Britain's policy of allowing Irishmen to be repatriated to Éire. But then he completely changed his approach and asked:

> … In view of the probability on the one hand that the shipping space that would be occupied by these people could be better utilised and on the other hand that the shortage of manpower in New Zealand affords a strong reason why the services of these people might well be utilised here in civil employment either at ordinary award rates or on soldiers' rates, the New Zealand Government are inclined to feel that there is on the whole little to be gained by repatriation. Before coming to any final decision on the matter, however, they [the New Zealand Government] would be glad to be advised whether the exemption of these men from military training and their utilisation as proposed above would in any way embarrass His Majesty's Government in the United Kingdom.

The cable was also copied to the ministers of Defence, Internal Affairs and National Service and noted by Head of the Prime Minister's Department Carl Berendsen.

There is no documentation to show whether Ongley and Aylward knew about the initiative, but it is likely that Fraser played this card close to his chest in case there was a problem with the UK, and the risk of any leak embarrassing Britain. It is unclear if New Zealand's High Commissioner in the UK, Bill Jordan, was told either, and I suspect that he may not have been, as he had a track record of not always being discreet.

The only hint of a possible change came in a memo dated 7 August 1942 marked 'confidential and not for publication' from J.S. Hunter to the men chairing the armed forces appeal boards, stating that he had been told that Prime Minister Peter Fraser and the war administration were giving further consideration to the Citizens of Éire. Hunter asked them to defer hearing any appeals until advised to the contrary.[19]

On 11 August 1942 Clement Attlee responded to Fraser by telegram:

> His Majesty's Government in the United Kingdom are most grateful to His Majesty's Government in New Zealand for the opportunity of considering possible repercussions of proposals set out in your telegram of the 18th of July as to policy as regards treatment of Éire citizens here. In view of differing circumstances here and in New Zealand as explained in latter telegram, [the] United Kingdom have come to [the] conclusion that the course of action proposed in New Zealand would not embarrass them.
>
> Signed: Secretary of State for Dominion Affairs.[20]

For Aylward and Fraser a compromise had finally been found. It was now a matter of getting the war cabinet to agree, and having a strategy to placate the opponents of the Irish, both in government and the country at large. A hint of what that compromise might be was contained in Fraser's original cable, which referred to the option of paying the Irishmen soldiers' rates, which were set at £4 a week and did not include the benefits that soldiers serving overseas received. This seemed a fair deal because to pay award rates would have been a bridge too far, and possibly what Aylward was alluding to when he said 'sacrifices may have to be made'. If this deal was signed off by the war cabinet, the Irishmen could stay, avoiding the risk of being killed on the journey to Ireland or being treated as defaulters and sent to a camp. They were in fact being treated as they had always wanted – as a 'special case'.

12

A secure future at last

Just imagine the celebrations and relief when Dad and his mates heard the news about the cable from Clement Attlee. It was the answer to their prayers. They may or may not have been aware of the cable immediately, although with their close links to Fraser and some of his colleagues they were likely to have been kept up with developments.

While it might have answered the prayers of the Sons of Éire, it was also probably music to the ears of Fraser himself, who was in somewhat of a dilemma dealing with the Irish 'problem'. Behind the scenes, the strong indication was that Fraser was quietly and positively disposed to the Irishmen and not part of the chorus of those who wanted them out regardless of their rights. However he was also mindful of the rule of law and the perception that Labour was being 'soft' on conscientious objectors.

Manpower was a major problem for New Zealand because there were not enough people to adequately farm the land and produce food for the troops. Fraser's decision to retain the Irishmen – who were willing and, by and large, not troublesome workers – was positive and pragmatic, thanks in no small part to the response from Attlee.

While Fraser now had 'permission' from Britain to keep the Citizens of Éire in New Zealand, he still had to gain support from the war cabinet to implement the decision. He would have been facing pressure from National Party members, as well as his officials and other civil servants, who were known for their opposition to the Irish. This is obvious when reading notations on some of the New Zealand Government documents, and in particular the comments on Aylward's 'True to Ireland' letter.

On 19 August 1942, just a week after Attlee's cable arrived, J.S. Hunter sent a two-page report to his minister, Walter Broadfoot, setting out the historical background relating to the Citizens of Éire.[1] Hunter noted the war cabinet decision on 23 October 1941, which effectively stated that the Irishmen had the choice of fighting, leaving New Zealand or being imprisoned as defaulters. The report emphasised the Irishmen's refusal to wear a New Zealand military uniform or to serve in the armed forces. He went on to tell Broadfoot (if he didn't already know) that Prime Minister Fraser had sent a cable to Attlee

Members of the New Zealand War Administration, 15 July 1942, clockwise from left: Angus McLagan, Arnold Nordmeyer, William Polson, William Bodkin, Paraire Paikea, Gordon Coates, Sid Holland, Carl Berendsen, Peter Fraser, Dan Sullivan, Frederick Jones, Walter Broadfoot, Adam Hamilton.

Alexander Turnbull Library, 1/2-045547-F

asking if keeping the Irishmen in New Zealand and working for soldiers' pay would 'embarrass the British Government'. He then quoted the response from Attlee and told the minister that the war cabinet was going to consider the following recommendations:

> That no special regulations be issued conferring any absolute right of appeal, status or exemption to citizens of Éire.

> That the war cabinet should issue a policy direction that those who have been called up for military service, or who may hereafter be called for service shall, if they refuse to undertake military service, be allowed to remain in industry upon satisfying the Director of National Service that they are a citizen of Éire. Whilst remaining in industry they are subject in all respects to the National Service Emergency Regulations 1940 and its amendments in relation to industrial mobilisation.

This paper and policy is what the ENA had been asking for all along and it seemed that after more than two years of lobbying and legal action, their wish was about to be granted.

When Hunter wrote this paper he would have had a fair idea how the conservative, pro-RSA and anti-conchie Broadfoot would react, which he did on 1 September by writing to Acting Prime Minister Dan Sullivan:

> With reference to the report dated 19th August submitted to the Director [of National Service] at the request of the Prime Minister without

reference to me, I desire to make it clear that as Minister for National Service I disagree with the recommendation.[2]

Broadfoot then went on to say that while other men were being conscripted from their businesses and jobs, their jobs were being taken over by others not prepared to fight for New Zealand. He further stated that he proposed to submit an alternative report in the next few days and asked that the war cabinet defer its decision:

> We have hundreds of New Zealand-born men in detention camps for their failure to observe their obligations. Why preference to the men from Éire who elected to come here and who incidentally stated in their petition that 'New Zealand was the land of their adoption'. Lately I have had letters from wives of men in camp asking why their husbands are taken into camp while Irishmen are filling well-paid jobs and refusing to assume their military obligations apparently with the concurrence of the government.

Broadfoot, a lawyer and an ardent Tory, was the MP for Waitomo, an area in the central North Island based around the farming service town of Te Kūiti. He was frequently quoted in the newspapers during the war, advocating for defaulters to be imprisoned. He even went so far as to suggest that defaulters and conscientious objectors should lose their civil or voting rights for at least 15 years.[3] Although Broadfoot was in the wider coalition cabinet, rather than the war cabinet, he was a fierce critic of the governing Labour Party. At one stage he claimed that there was a similarity between the Labour Party and the Government of Russia.[4] He was no friend of the Irish, or Fraser for that matter. Ironically, on 12 May 1942 two constituents in Broadfoot's Waitomo electorate – farmer John Bargh Swindell and milk vendor Norman Syme – were given the relatively light sentence of one month in jail for refusing to report to the local army office. Both claimed to be conscientious objectors.

However, it seems that Broadfoot's venting was to no avail, as on 28 August 1942 the war cabinet approved the policy as outlined in Hunter's letter, and note that it was referred to Broadfoot.[5]

Walter Broadfoot, MP from 1928 until 1954.
S.P. Andrew collection, Alexander Turnbull Library, F-43307-1/2

On 9 September Foss Shanahan from the Prime Minister's Department sent a memo to Hunter stating that he was aware of Broadfoot's objection to the war cabinet decision,[6] and that the cabinet had taken note of this. Shanahan had been asked to review the position, so he attached his understanding of the events in question and asked Hunter to make sure it was correct. He stressed the urgency of the matter and suggested that Hunter ring him if necessary to clarify the matter.

It appears that there was a conversation, because two days later a document emerged signed by Foss Shanahan to Dan Sullivan, which looks like a preamble to the final recommendations to the war cabinet.[7] The paper summarises the saga of the Citizens of Éire leading up to the request by Fraser to the British Government to let the men stay in New Zealand. Shanahan's note at the top of the document says that he had discussed the matter with Hunter and they were in agreement with the terms of the war cabinet decision. In essence this paper reinforced the decision made by the war cabinet and ignored Broadfoot's objection. So the situation was that the Minister for National Service was opposed to the policy of allowing the Irishmen to stay, while the head of his Department agreed with it.

To clarify things Hunter issued an eleven-page circular on 23 September 1942 to the chairmen and members of the armed forces appeal boards, Crown representatives and secretaries, in which he asked them to bring their work up to date.[8] He said that with Ballot No.17 just announced, all past appeals should be dealt with so that they could move onto the expected influx of new appeals. Hunter made reference to appeals of undue hardship, adding that a problem arose when the father of a family was called up, which was made worse when sons were later called up.

Hunter referred to problems in the production of certain foods, noting there was a shortage of the bacon products in demand by the Allied forces in the Pacific, and asked the appeal boards to 'give favourable consideration' to allowing the appeals of men with skills in this industry. He said the same about the fruit industry because the demand for fresh fruit, jam, canned fruit and juices was rapidly increasing, and skilled staff were required. The list was seemingly endless with recognised staff shortages in the tanning, sawmilling and engineering fields, as well as for plumbers, drain layers, electricians and opticians. The report gave advice on how appeal boards should deal with appeals by teachers and also with directing people into essential industries. It also briefly outlined the war cabinet decision and agreement regarding Irishmen living in New Zealand who did not want to be conscripted. He said a policy paper on this would be issued shortly.

Hunter's paper was timely, given the war in the Pacific and the need for New Zealand to be a food basket for the large US forces operating in the region. It has been said that the Americans were less interested in military assistance from New Zealand and more interested in the food that the country could provide. The Americans regarded the Pacific as their war and didn't trust Britain and the Allies in the wake of the surrender of Singapore.

However, the war cabinet's agreement was not the end of the saga as the ENA's attention moved to assisting the government to implement the decision, and also dealing with several other appeals that seemed to have slipped through the net and ended up in court proceedings. The list of 155 Irishmen who were to be deported probably represented about half the number who actually stayed in New Zealand and worked under the agreement between the ENA and the government.

Evidence of the role of the ENA was set out in a memo from Hunter to the Director of Mobilisation at army headquarters in Wellington on 29 April 1943, to which he attached a copy of the policy based on the war cabinet decision in relation to citizens of Éire.[9] Hunter stated that the ENA had supplied him with a list of their members, but warned that they regarded their list as incomplete, as not all Irishmen were members of their organisation. Hunter acknowledged that he did not have a complete record himself and suggested that the army obtain names from their area officers.

Hunter advised that all the names would be forwarded to the ENA to verify whether the claims of individuals were genuine and the ENA would contact the Irishmen concerned directly. This was significant and showed that the ENA had won the trust of the Director of National Service, and that both organisations were working together to help sort out what was probably one big muddle.

Essentially by default, the ENA Executive had become the unofficial but recognised representative of the Éire Government. That the New Zealand Government and the bureaucrats saw the value of working with the organisation says a great deal. This must be put down to the leadership of Paddy Feeney, the silver tongue and smart negotiating skills of Maurice Aylward, and the brilliance of Fred Ongley, in the way they had dealt with the government. Ongley, with his contacts in the Labour Party and his own Irish background, was pivotal to the outcome. At the same time there is no doubt that the friendship between Fraser and de Valera, which I will discuss in detail in Chapter 15, was also an influential factor.

A series of letters were exchanged between the ENA and the New Zealand Government on how the scheme to manpower the Citizens of Éire in New

Zealand would work.[10] One letter on 21 January 1943 from Ongley to Angus McLagan, the Minister of Manpower, asked about a potential problem raised by Aylward – what would happen to men employed in the freezing works when the season was over? He had been told that these men may be employed in flax works that were away from the main centres where the freezing works were located. He was happy for single men and maybe married ones without children to be moved to such places, but wanted to meet McLagan to talk further about this issue.

On 3 February 1943 McLagan wrote a detailed letter to Ongley again setting out the conditions for Citizens of Éire to remain in New Zealand.[11] Essentially this was a letter of record stating that the Irishmen either fight, work, or be deported, that the cost of the men returning to Ireland was theirs and that New Zealand would not help fund their journey. McLagan went on to say that as it was unlikely that shipping space would be available to return the men to Ireland, they would be manpowered – that is, directed to whatever industry the government saw as having the greatest need for labour, and he specifically mentioned flax cutting.

One of the major flax-growing areas was between the Horowhenua townships of Foxton and Shannon. This was also near one of the camps for conscientious objectors, so flax and conchies became somewhat linked in a New Zealand context. The letter also said that J.S. Hunter would communicate directly with those men who had established their claim to be Irish citizens and implied that he would ask the ENA to help the government verify this. Finally, McLagan told Ongley that the New Zealand Government would assist the ENA in making contact with the Irish Government to see if they could provide some financial assistance to those Irishmen wishing to return to Éire.

In February 1943 a letter from Ongley to McLagan confirmed that he and Aylward had met McLagan briefly and felt they had a sympathetic hearing and would be available to talk at any time in the future.

In April McLagan again wrote to Ongley about the request for the government to assist the ENA to obtain financial support from the Irish Government for men wishing to return to Éire.[12] McLagan made it clear that while the government had no objection to the ENA asking the Irish Government for assistance, the New Zealand Government was not prepared to act directly on their behalf. But what he did offer was that if the ENA drafted a letter to the Irish Government, he would send it to the New Zealand High Commissioner in London with the instruction to pass this on to the Éire envoy in London, John Dulanty, for forwarding to de Valera. There is no record of any further action on this matter and no evidence, one way or the other, as to whether the Irish Government did help, or was prepared to help, fund the return of any Irishman back to Ireland.

While a deal had been brokered, it seems the various departments were not adequately briefed about the situation as names from the list of 155 kept appearing in correspondence requesting status updates. For example, it was asked why Joseph Christopher Robinson had failed to be medically examined, but he was part of the group of 155 and did not have to undertake such an action.[13]

As promised in his letter of 3 February 1943, the National Service Director wrote to all those men who claimed to be citizens of Éire.[14] On 6 May 1943 Maurice Aylward received his copy of the letter that essentially asked him to confirm what he wanted to do in relation to previous correspondence, presumably about his decision to fight, provide manpower as directed by the government or leave the country. There was a form that the recipient was required to fill in and return to the office of National Service at P.O. Box 165, Te Aro, Wellington.

While the focus was on the 155 Citizens of Éire, there were other cases that surfaced that were not so clear cut. There was John Joseph Devoy, who got himself into a bind because he was prepared to join the New Zealand Territorials, but as he never appealed the initial call-up he was automatically called up for overseas service. In a letter from Hunter to the Director of Mobilisation at Army HQ on 12 October 1942, Hunter stated that Devoy was now represented by Fred Ongley and his associates.[15] He said Devoy, through his lawyer, had made it clear he did not wish to serve overseas and that he had been verified by the ENA as a genuine Irish national. Hunter suggested that Devoy not be sent overseas.

Another case which surfaced in 1942, long after the decision relating to my father and the Sons of Éire, was that of Frank Mitchell.[16] He was born in Tuam, County Galway on 14 September 1915 and came to New Zealand on a five-year tourist visa in 1938. Mitchell, who was a driver living in the Auckland suburb of Onehunga, was not aware of the existence of the ENA and its opposition to Irishmen being conscripted into the New Zealand Army. He duly registered for military service, was called up and drafted into the army, where he became a driver. Mitchell was under the distinct impression that the Irish Government supported people such as himself being drafted into the Crown forces and he had no objection to this. His commanding officer described him as a good soldier and neither a 'pacifist nor conscientious objector'.

However just before he was due to be sent overseas in June 1942, Mitchell discovered that his brother, who was also in New Zealand, had obtained an exemption from service as a citizen of Éire, as verified by the ENA. Mitchell it seems, had only just become aware of the ENA, the test case and its outcome. He wrote to the Secretary of the Manpower Committee in Auckland seeking release from the army. He stated he was prepared to pay his own fare back to Ireland or work in New Zealand for soldiers' rates.

Correspondence flowed between the National Service Department in Wellington and the No.1 Appeal Board in Auckland regarding Mitchell's status. Mitchell wrote to the Manpower Committee again on 29 July 1942 asking what was happening. He was told a decision was still pending. Finally, apparently frustrated by the lack of response from the authorities, Mitchell hired lawyers Herman and Thomson, who wrote to the appeal board on 8 October asking for answers as Mitchell was due to be sent overseas. It asked that the letter be treated as his appeal against conscription. The next day the board responded saying the army had deferred his posting. It was not until February 1943 that Mitchell learnt, through his lawyer, that he was to be discharged from the army and treated like other Citizens of Éire and manpowered on soldiers' rates.

Mitchell's situation was unusual and shows that while the cases of many Irishmen refusing to fight for Britain were addressed as part of the ENA process, others slipped through the cracks and were dealt with on a one-off basis.

There was one high-profile case that came to the notice of the ENA. It was John James Moriarty, one of the original six Sons of Éire who was part of the test case in 1941. On 19 November 1943 Fred Ongley wrote to the officer in charge of Manpower in Auckland saying that the ENA had been told that Moriarty, without permission, had left the place of employment he had been directed to by the New Zealand authorities, and that the association was concerned about this.[17] Ongley said that the ENA agreed that Irish nationals who refused to be conscripted gave an undertaking that they would either leave the country or work as directed, and this was the first case of someone breaking that agreement. He requested that he be sent the details of what happened so that the association would know how to deal with similar incidents.

It is apparent from the letter that the ENA had been in contact with Moriarty because Ongley said that they'd advised him of the association's position on such matters, which was that Irishmen stick to the agreement with the government to leave the country or work as directed – no exceptions.

Smoko time for manpowered Irish workers on a farm near Timarū.
Mick Sheridan is on the far right.
Courtesy of Pat Sheridan.

Ongley also said that the ENA sought to place the matter before Angus McLagan as soon as he returned to Wellington.

The ENA was obviously not happy with Moriarty for breaking the arrangement and was quick to distance itself from his actions and support the government on whatever measures they chose to take in relation to him. Despite extensive searching, I can find no record on what happened to John James Moriarty. In 1941/42 a J.J. Moriarty was one of two vice presidents of the Wellington Irish Society, and in 1943/44 is listed as being a member of the committee. It is not clear if this was John James Moriarty or John Joseph Moriarty, but this name does not appear again. It may be that he went back to Ireland.

The ENA had made it clear to Irishmen in New Zealand that they would not tolerate people who took matters into their own hands with the authorities, and the case of Moriarty demonstrates the extent that they worked with the government to retain the integrity of the agreement.

Another example of the ENA advocating for Irish citizens is the story of Robert Knox, who joined and then deserted the army. This case came to the attention of the ENA in 1945 and demonstrates the dilemma that the association sometimes found itself in.

Throughout its existence the ENA had been careful not to offend either the Irish or New Zealand governments and to comply with the laws of their adopted land. On 30 October 1945 Maurice Aylward wrote to Peter Fraser emphasising this point and saying that his organisation had always taken the stance that it would not try to dissuade any Irishman who wished to join the New Zealand Army, and only those who approached the ENA were accepted as members.[18] He noted that Knox did not know about the ENA and that when he was drawn in the ballot he went into the army. Aylward went on to say that while Knox was in the army he found out about the association and applied to join, which in theory he was entitled to as an Éire National.

Aylward explained to Fraser that the ENA's legal advisor had investigated Knox's case, but his advice was that the ENA should do nothing to get Knox out of the army because all his appeal provisions were exhausted, and that if the ENA attempted to get him out there was the possibility that the association could be accused of breaching their agreement with the government. The upshot was that Knox was refused membership of the ENA.

The letter retells what we know from John Knox that his father was tried for desertion, and that when Aylward wrote his letter Knox was serving time in Mount Crawford Prison in Wellington. Aylward concluded his letter to Fraser by saying:

> Knox is the sufferer. We would like to help him and consequently bring the matter before you for consideration and whatever help you can give in the circumstances.

Two weeks later Fraser responded briefly saying he had asked the Minister of Justice to look at the issues to see what, if anything, could be done.[19] I can find no documentary evidence about whether anything further happened in respect of Robert Knox, but as John says, his father was in prison while he was a baby.

It is evident that Aylward was embarrassed by this dilemma and the actions the ENA considered necessary to keep onside with the government. But to be fair to them, the risk of breaking such a deal could have resulted in repercussions for other Irishmen, so abandoning Knox was the price for this. The cries of the RSA and anti-Irish sentiment continued, and the ENA was probably seeking to ensure that situations did not arise that would inflame them.

While the main battle for the ENA was over, its role evolved. The association maintained its semi-official position with the government, ensured the integrity of the agreement so the Irishmen could remain in New Zealand, and represented those Irishmen who did not want to fight for the King and his Empire.

PART THREE

HISTORY MADE

13

Aylward's Irish odyssey

In 1943 war was still raging, although the tide was turning in favour of the Allies in Europe. In New Zealand the unthinkable happened – food rationing was introduced.

On 23 June 1943 a general election was held in Ireland in which Éamon de Valera only just held on to power with 67 of the 70 seats needed for a majority. In the end he formed a minority government, but he'd lost ten seats and the future of Fianna Fáil was on the line. The election was reported in the *Evening Post*, which said that owing to the ban on the use of motorcars due to the petrol shortage, voters in Ireland 'journeyed to the polls in wagonettes, jaunting cars, traps, coal, and milk carts'.[1] Necessity was certainly the mother of invention. Of course a lot would have walked and bicycles would have also been used. The election news is unlikely to have been well received by the Sons of Éire, most of whom, it would seem, were de Valera supporters.

Meanwhile in New Zealand, Fraser and his Labour Government were in the midst of their own hard-fought election campaign. On election day, 25 September 1943, the first results to be counted indicated that Labour would win, but as the evening progressed it seemed likely that there would be a victory for the conservative National Party. Ultimately it was the votes from

the troops in the Middle East that delivered Fraser his victory. During his trips away Fraser had made a point of visiting them, as well as the aircrew in Britain. The servicemen and women appreciated that Fraser took the time to meet them. Fraser is said to have quipped, 'It was not only North Africa that was saved by the Second Division.'[2]

With Fraser re-elected, the ENA would have heaved a sigh of relief, none more so than the power behind the organisation, Maurice Aylward.

Maurice Aylward (from the ENA executive 1945 photo).

Maurice Aylward's nephews, from left: Liam, Fr Eamon and Bobby.

A leader in both the ENA and the Irish Society, Aylward had an infectious, outgoing personality, as well as the gift of the gab. But above all, being a highly intelligent man who was politically well connected to Fianna Fáil and de Valera, he stood out from the rest. His brother Bob was elected to the Irish Senate in 1973. After Bob died in 1974 his sons Liam and Bobby became Fianna Fáil TDs (members of parliament) and have served their constituency of Carlow–Kilkenny consecutively since 1977.

On 10 September 1943 Feeney, Walsh, Lafferty and Cahill, members of the executive of the ENA, sent a confidential letter to the members.[3] It contained some interesting facts about what had happened, the people involved and their plans for the future.

First it confirmed that about 200 Irish citizens living in New Zealand elected not to serve in the armed forces, and of those, about 20 still had to decide whether to stay in New Zealand or go back to Ireland.[4] It also stated that they knew of 20 Irishmen who had agreed to join the New Zealand armed forces. It said that the Director of National Service had written to all Irish citizens living in New Zealand, not just those who belonged to the ENA, asking what they wanted to do – stay or return. The list of names was forwarded to the association and numbered between 350 and 400, including those who wished to leave. The ENA executive said it was still unclear what would happen to these people, but reiterated to all members that it was 'their duty' to honour the agreement they had with the government about undertaking whatever work they were directed to. This document indicates that around 500 Irishmen were involved in the conscription issue.

The main news of interest in the letter was that the executive had decided to send Maurice Aylward to Éire as the official representative, or emissary, of the Éire National Association, with the purpose of briefing the Irish authorities on what had happened in New Zealand on the conscription issue. The brief went beyond merely informing de Valera and the Irish authorities about the deal which the ENA had struck with the government and how it was working. He was also to inform the Irish Government that their laws and those of the British Government were in direct conflict on the issue of 'status'. That is, the claim by Britain that everyone born in Ireland was a British subject and therefore liable for call-up into the armed forces of Britain or a Commonwealth country, notwithstanding that Éire was neutral. He was asked to urge the Irish Government to raise this issue at the next peace conference.

The final point Aylward was asked to raise was the need for an accredited representative for Éire in New Zealand. The executive noted that this would enable any citizen of Éire living in New Zealand to have someone who could officially represent them to the government. In 1943 the ENA was the nearest Éire had to official representation in New Zealand, as the government recognised the ENA and had delegated some roles to it. There was also mention in the letter of fears the ENA had about what might happen after the war when servicemen and women returned:

> Difficult economic conditions may arise after the war and there may be unemployment and other difficulties to be met. If these difficulties and conditions arise, it is inevitable that distinctions will be made between those who accepted service and those who did not and between those who are British subjects and those who are not. We may find our members having to give up employment and that sort of thing. We must be prepared to meet that contingency.

The executive identified that there could be a problem for Irish people wanting to buy land in New Zealand, and Maurice Aylward was tasked with discussing this and the other issues while in Ireland.

While the briefing to the de Valera Government about the conscription problem was no doubt important, it was the other big picture issues that were more worrying. In 1943, two years before the war ended, the ENA was tuning into the political matters that were on the horizon by raising concerns of Irish living abroad, and seeking clarity and support from the Irish Government. They felt isolated in New Zealand, and every day they could read the vitriol in the newspapers being directed at conscientious objectors by the RSA and other like-minded individuals, and also at the neutrality of Ireland. They had a genuine reason to be fearful of what the future might hold for them in New Zealand post-war. They were particularly fearful of the National Party being elected to power, as there were well-known Irish-haters in the party, including Walter Broadfoot, who were backed by the RSA – whose members wanted outlandish punitive measures imposed on those who refused to fight.

Feeney, Walsh, Lafferty and Cahill all signed this letter, but it is highly likely that the author was Aylward because his address, 2 Murphy Street Wellington, was at the bottom of the letter. His visit to Ireland was seen as being akin to an ambassador of any country being recalled home to brief the government on current and future issues.

Evidence of Aylward's status was contained in a letter from the Minister of National Service Angus McLagan, to Fred Ongley on 4 September 1943.[5] In this letter McLagan referred to earlier correspondence in which he'd noted a request by the ENA for one of its representatives to be allowed to travel to Éire to consult with the government. McLagan had agreed but stipulated that such a person had to be beyond conscription age.[6] But he now recognised that Maurice Aylward was the 'most suitable and capable representative that the association could send' and so he had no objection to Mr Aylward being appointed as the representative. He went on to advise that he would ask his department to facilitate issuing a permit for Aylward to travel overseas.

Mr Aylward was now 'Mr Ambassador' – well, sort of.

Before Aylward left for Ireland, the ENA wrote two letters dated 12 October 1943 that set out the official status of Aylward as their delegate to represent them in Ireland and to the Irish Government. The first letter, addressed to 'The Government and People of Éire', established Aylward's credentials and that he was delegated to speak on all matters concerning the Citizens of Éire in New Zealand, their welfare and rights, and to make representations on their behalf to 'all persons and authorities interested and concerned with their well-being'. This letter was signed by all the members of the executive of the ENA, including my father and his long-time friend from Moycullen, John Clancy.[7]

The second letter was addressed to Éamon de Valera and alerted him to Aylward's impending visit.[8] It is a beautifully crafted letter that exudes Irish whim and sentiment and love of Éire. After setting out Aylward's role and status it went on to praise the Irish leader in glowing terms, Ireland's position on the world stage, and the Irish Government for the efforts they had made to further:

> Our country's claim to complete independence and to preserve and protect the neutrality of Éire in the present crisis ... and trust that your work and efforts will continue to bring success and that Éire and our people will be saved from the tragedy of war. We convey to you and your parliament and people our best wishes and assure you of our wholehearted support in whatever you may do to preserve the neutrality, integrity and independence of Éire. We further hope and trust that we

will soon see the stain of partition removed and our country once more free and independent and united.

Although we are a long way away we have lost none of our love for you and our native land and we pray that the day of destiny is close at hand when Éire will assume her proper place in the world and prove as of yore the shining light of Europe, and Ireland will be Éire, and Éire will be free.

With all the respect, admiration and love that Irish men can have and give, we send you this message through our delegate Mr M.L. Aylward. He should reach you about Christmas time and we take this opportunity of including Christmas greetings and felicitations to you and your government and to all our kinsfolk at home.

The shipping records show that Maurice Aylward left Wellington mid-November 1943 on the MV *Port Dunedin* and arrived in Avonmouth Docks, Bristol, on 30 December.[9] He is listed in the ship's manifest as a labourer. The voyage was across the Pacific Ocean and through the Panama Canal with a stop at New York. His nephew Fr Eamon Aylward recalls a story about this stopover:

> They weren't allowed off the boat but he jumped ship anyway and went looking for his brother's family because at that stage his brother Patrick, nicknamed Dexter, was dead and he knew that his sister-in-law and kids were living in The Bronx in the Carmelite Parish. So he went there and somehow found the family and that's how he met his sister-in-law and kids. He stayed talking to them until 4am, then went back to the boat and continued on to Ireland.

This demonstrates the enterprise and determination of Aylward. It must have been both a happy and sad moment for him seeing his sister-in-law and nieces for a matter of hours, knowing he would probably never see them again. Besides meeting relatives in America during the course of his trip, Maurice was also able to visit his aunt and youngest sister, both of whom were nuns in the UK. There is also a suggestion that Maurice was 'detained' overnight when he arrived in the UK before being released, though there are no further details. It is not known how he got to Ireland from Bristol.

Maurice Aylward's arrival in Ireland was the cause of much joy at the family home at Knockmoylan, close to Mullinavat, County Kilkenny. I can only imagine the moment when he walked through the door of his home to be greeted by his mother Hannah (née Raftis) and the rest of his family and friends. The prodigal son had returned. It was a big deal to travel across the world, especially in wartime with considerable risks involved.

It is evident that all of Knockmoylan and the nearby villages wanted to welcome Maurice home, so his younger brother Robert and sister-in-law

Maurice Aylward with some of his family prior to coming to New Zealand. From left: Ivan White (family friend), Mary Ann, Kathleen (who later became Sister Frances Clare), Ned, Hannah and Maurice.

Kitty took it upon themselves to host a big party at their place for Maurice in January 1944. It must have been some event because the local paper, the *Munster Express*, sent a reporter along to cover it:

A most enjoyable reunion was held at the home of the Aylward family Knockmoylan on the Wednesday 21st when Mr Maurice Leo Aylward was host at a large gathering of relatives and friends. It was a veritable gathering of the clans and many old friendships were renewed and new ones formed. An Irish atmosphere permeated the whole proceedings – every guest was made to feel at home and the genial Bob [Maurice's brother] and his winsome wife were untiring in their efforts to cater for the material comforts of their guests.

Hospitality was dispensed with a lavish hand and everything went as merrily as the proverbial marriage bell. While the older folk swapped reminiscences in the comfortable farm house, the younger element and some not so young tripped the light fantastic to the music of Jack O'Carroll's Band in a spacious outbuilding which provided ample room for the accommodation of upwards of fifty couples at a time. As is their wont the members of the band were most generous in the matter of encores. Songs and recitations were contributed by several guests but the titbit of the evening was undoubtedly the rendering by the 'bean a tighe' [woman of the house] of an old Irish haunting melody which recalled the bad old days when the emigrant ships took toll of the flower

Mullinavat on a quiet day.

of our Irish manhood and womenhood. Mr J. Ryan on behalf of the assembled guests returned thanks to Mr Aylward and members of the family for the splendid evening's entertainment they had so generously provided. Mr Ryan referred briefly to the object of Mr Aylward's mission to the homeland: its importance from an international viewpoint and the significant part their host had played in bringing the matter to a successful issue. 'We are very proud of the stand taken by Maurice Aylward and his Irish compatriots' said Mr Ryan – a sentiment which was received with prolonged applause. In conclusion, Mr Ryan asked Mr Aylward to convey to his brother William the best wishes of the assembled guests, especially of those of the Old IRA who campaigned with Bill during the Black and Tan terror.[10]

In reply, Mr Aylward expressed his pleasure at the way in which the guests had responded to the invitation. He said he was pleased beyond measure to see his old friends. He thanked Mr Ryan, his old school teacher, for his kind references to himself and to the cause for which he would carry back with him to the land of his adoption with many happy memories. This proved all too short and the midsummer's dawn wrote 'finis' to one of the most enjoyable functions it has ever been our good fortune to attend amongst the kindly generous-hearted people of the Walsh Mountains.

The *Munster Express* also published another article on Maurice's homecoming. Unfortunately the extract I have doesn't have a date, but given the content it is likely that it was published before the article about the big party.

Home from New Zealand

Mr Maurice Leo Aylward, Knockmoylan, Ballyhale who is home on business from New Zealand after an absence of fifteen years is secretary of the Éire National Association in Wellington which was organised at the outbreak of the war for the purpose of safeguarding the rights and interests of Irish Nationals in New Zealand in keeping with the status of Éire as a neutral state. Mr Aylward arrived home in December having travelled via the United States.[11] A son of Mrs and the late Edward Aylward, Knockmoylan he is the brother of Mr Bob Aylward, well-known Carrickshock hurler, Garda Ed Aylward (Dublin), Mr Wm Aylward (Melbourne), Mrs P. Hartley (Slieverue), Mrs Frisby (Waterford), Mrs Kenneally (Cotterstown), and Sister Frances Clare from St Mary's Convent, Lincolnshire.

He won the Kilkenny County Junior Hurling championships with Carrickshock in 1928 and subsequently played in Australia where the GAA had a firm foothold. Mr Aylward, who is a regular reader of *The Munster Express* in New Zealand, intends to return again to the latter when he has concluded his business visit to Éire in July.

This newspaper article gives some valuable insight into Aylward's mission, most notably that he planned to leave Éire for New Zealand in July, but this did not happen because he needed more time to be able to complete his brief.

One thing is clear: as soon as Maurice arrived in Ireland in January 1944 he headed to Dublin seeking to meet with officials of the Irish Government. This was even before his 'official' family welcome in Knockmoylan on 21 January. A detailed account of Aylward's contacts with the Irish Government is contained in documents from the Irish Department of External Affairs (Roinn Gnothai Eachtracha) and the Department of the Taoiseach (the equivalent of the New Zealand Department of the Prime Minister).[12]

On 13 January 1944 Dr Michael Rynne, Chief Legal Advisor for the Department of External Affairs, sent a detailed briefing paper to Department Head Joseph Walshe, about Maurice Aylward's visit. It gave the history of the Éire National Association and also covered what Rynne saw as other relevant issues pertaining to the situation of the Citizens of Éire in New Zealand. His paper was a wide-ranging, five-page document designed to brief de Valera on the issues that potentially would be canvassed when Aylward finally met with him. The day after the paper was written it was forwarded by Walshe to Miss Kathleen O'Connell at the Department of the Taoiseach.

The power of two

Miss O'Connell was de Valera's personal secretary from 1919 until she became ill and died in 1956. She was a much trusted aide of de Valera and witnessed many of the events in his illustrious career. According to Liam Aylward (former TD and European parliamentarian) Kathleen O'Connell was de Valera's greatest confidant and the matriarch of Fianna Fáil. Aylward says 'her word was law'. De Valera even wrote to her personally on his trip to New Zealand in 1948 telling her about the hectic time they had, and the enthusiastic reception he and Frank Aiken's received from both the people and government.

Dr Michael Rynne was a top Irish government official with a doctorate in international law from the University of Munich. He was a member of the IRA and it is said he was with de Valera at his home when the Treaty was signed in December 1921. He was a trusted aide of de Valera's – more so it would seem than his boss, Joe Walshe. It was Dr Rynne who was given the task by de Valera of defending Ireland's policy of neutrality in WWII. In essence he concluded that Irish neutrality actually suited Germany and Britain, and that for Ireland to take sides would have had more serious consequences than the policy of neutrality. Dr Rynne was assigned to meet with Aylward, which seemed appropriate given that the arguments advanced by the ENA essentially questioned the legality of Britain to 'brand' them as British subjects, whereas Ireland saw the men as citizens of Éire, who should be treated no differently to Swiss nationals.

There is no doubt that Maurice Aylward met some of Ireland's top officials and people who were close and trusted aides to Éamon de Valera, and was accorded the trappings of a visiting diplomat.

It is clear from Rynne's paper that he had met with Aylward and was told about the activities of the ENA. Rynne also revealed that Aylward had already delivered two formal messages of goodwill from the ENA to the Taoiseach's Department, including one personally to de Valera. (It appears that these were the letters written by the ENA dated 12 October 1943 before Aylward left New Zealand). Dr Rynne thought that Aylward was likely to ask de Valera for financial assistance to repatriate those Irishmen in New Zealand who did not wish to be manpowered, work for soldiers' rates or spend the rest of the war in defaulters' camps. This was consistent with previous discussions between the ENA and New Zealand Government about seeking assistance from the Irish Government for those who wished to return, even though repatriation would pose physical risks to people travelling by ship to the UK and Ireland.

There was a claim in a memo dated 29 March from Joe Walshe to Kathleen O'Connell that the idea of repatriation was put to the New Zealand Government by the ENA 'more or less as a bluff and it was not thought that the New Zealand Government would accept it'. There is no evidence of this interpretation by the ENA in New Zealand. Dr Rynne does confirm that the ENA had contacted the Irish Government in 1940 appealing for help to prevent Irishmen in New Zealand being conscripted. He noted that in 1941 Fred Ongley wrote to the Irish Department of External Affairs, again appealing for them to take the issue up with New Zealand, and that this resulted in a meeting between department officials and High Commissioner Bill Jordan, in London. Jordan replied that Fraser and his cabinet were considering the matter but were 'reluctant to take any hasty action'.

In his briefing paper Rynne noted that in a meeting with Bill Jordan in September 1943 (presumably in Dublin), the Taoiseach raised the subject of the way the New Zealand military laws were being applied to the Irish and asked why Irish citizens were being labelled British subjects. It would seem that Jordan stuck to the line that the Irish were still British subjects in law – a point that de Valera disputed.

Rynne's paper referred to the April 1942 judgement by Lord Chief Justice of England and Wales Viscount Caldecote, endorsing the status quo as regards the status of the Irish. De Valera responded in a press statement describing the British law as 'quite inconsistent with the present international position with Ireland' … and 'running directly counter to all recognised international principles governing such matters'. Rynne thought it likely that de Valera would convey his strong views on the status issue to Aylward when they met.

One of the issues that Rynne anticipated Aylward would raise with de Valera was the need for Ireland and New Zealand to have reciprocal diplomatic representation. Rynne suggested that the Taoiseach should inform him that this was not possible at the present time but indicate the possibility of an exchange of high commissioners with New Zealand soon after the war. Interesting here is the use of the words 'high commissioners' rather than 'ambassadors'. This would support the view of de Valera's grandson, Éamon Ó Cuív, that in his heart de Valera wanted to remain in the Commonwealth but allegiance to the King was a stumbling block. Also surprising is that it took more than 70 years for embassies to be established in the two nations. Until 2018, ambassadors in London and Canberra carried out this task.

Two months elapsed before there was any further recorded contact between Aylward and the Irish officials. In a memo dated 29 March 1944, Joseph Walshe, the Head of the Department of External Affairs, confirmed to Kathleen O'Connell that he had had 'a long talk' with Maurice Aylward the previous day, as a precursor to the ENA representative's formal meeting with Éamon de Valera on 30 March. He said he had briefed the Taoiseach on this discussion and that Aylward left 'a pile of papers' but they did not raise any new points. But Walshe said they did show that the 'New Zealand Association acted very diplomatically vis-à-vis the New Zealand Government, and the latter have behaved extraordinarily well towards the Irish citizens under its jurisdiction'.

Walshe noted that Aylward would be asking de Valera to try to devise a plan to allow the Irishmen to remain in New Zealand and relieve them of their obligation to fight.

The next day, 30 March 1944, Éamon de Valera and Maurice Aylward finally met. I have been unable to find any records of what was actually said at that meeting other than what was contained in the briefing notes, and later in Aylward's report when he returned to New Zealand. For Aylward, the meeting with de Valera was mission accomplished, but the war in Europe entered a new phase with the invasion of Europe by the Allies, so he ended up remaining in Ireland for about a year.

Aylward was still there when de Valera decided to call a snap election in May 1944 born out of the frustration of having to manage a minority government. The gamble paid off, with de Valera and Fianna Fáil winning 76 seats, comprehensively beating the main opposition, Fine Gael, who won 30, and the agrarian party Clann na Talmhan, who claimed 10 seats. Dev, as he was affectionately known, was back in charge again with a big mandate.

Following this election result Maurice Aylward received a cablegram from the ENA in Wellington, and again news of it made the *Munster Express*:

> Mr Maurice Leo Aylward who is home on a business holiday from Wellington New Zealand has received the following cablegram from the Éire National Association.

> 'Convey to Mr de Valera heartiest and sincere congratulations splendid election victory on behalf of the Éire National Association, New Zealand. Signed: M. Lafferty Acting Secretary.'

> Mr Aylward who is Secretary of the Association which has a membership of over 500 is at present in Éire and has interviews with the government on the question of safeguarding the rights and interests of Irish nationals in New Zealand.

Dev in second heaven

When Éamon de Valera and Maurice Aylward met in March 1944, one can assume it was a very friendly and positive meeting, especially given Aylward's Fianna Fáil connections. Maybe Dev even told some of his stories about the Rising – one of which his grandson Éamon Ó Cuív relates:

> He was in charge of Boland's Mill and Pearse Station and one of the things he was trying to guard against was reinforcements coming in from along the railway line. One night he was patrolling the railway line and he got very tired as he'd been up for a few nights. He saw a carriage on a siding and he broke into it and fell asleep. When he opened his eyes he thought he was in heaven because he saw seraphims and cherubs over his head. He then realised he had broken into the royal carriage of the King, which was built especially for him when he came to Ireland. Interestingly the carriage is preserved and my grandfather actually used the carriage when he was President of Ireland in the 1960s.[13]

Aylward finally sailed from Liverpool on the *Akaroa* on 10 February 1945, bound for his adopted home of New Zealand. It's assumed he arrived in Wellington in late March or early April. By then the war in Europe was all but over, and in the Pacific the Americans were closing in on the Japanese.

During his stay in Ireland Aylward spent time with family and friends, as well as fulfilling his obligations to the ENA by forging strong links with Fianna Fáil and de Valera as well as government officials. These links would have further strengthened the relationship between Ireland and New Zealand, especially as Aylward and the ENA had close links with Fraser and the New Zealand Labour Party.

Maurice Aylward's trip was fully funded by the ENA, and he was paid a fee for this and other work he undertook in his role as delegate. This was Maurice's one and only trip back to Ireland, like many of his compatriots.

On 15 May 1945, a week after VE day, Maurice Aylward sent out a report to all ENA members from Mrs Fitzgerald's boarding house at No.2 Murphy Street, Wellington. It detailed the outcome of his trip to Ireland and the meetings he had with Taoiseach Éamon de Valera and government officials regarding the position and status of Irish citizens in New Zealand.[14] He thanked members for their loyalty to Michael Lafferty and the executive of the association during his absence and assured them that their role was much appreciated. He said that his 'voyage to the "little green Isle" was dangerous and difficult, but thanks to kind providence I arrived there safely after a very adventurous nine weeks at sea'.

He then apologised for the delay in returning to New Zealand caused by 'political considerations pertaining to neutral Ireland'. The latter part of this letter succinctly sums up his meeting in Dublin with de Valera:

> I was very cordially received by Mr de Valera and the Éire Government and our problems here [in New Zealand] received a favourable and sympathetic hearing. Mr de Valera fully appreciates the difficult time through which members of our Association have come. The difficulties which have arisen he says were no doubt inevitable in the transition period of Irish history when Ireland was acquiring the full legal status of an independent sovereign state.

> Both himself and the Government appreciate the just and broadminded attitude of the New Zealand Government for its treatment of Association members during the war period. He looks forward to the day when the two governments will be in a position to arrange for an exchange of representatives, and when the government of Éire will be able to convince the New Zealand Government that Ireland is not only a 'mother country' in the full sense, but is an independent sovereign state with her own citizenship laws which make it clear that her citizens are not British subjects.

> He [de Valera] went on to say – Members of our Association are quite right when they say that Ireland is in no way subject to British legislation and that to describe Éire citizens as British subjects is wrong, legally and historically.

Aylward noted that de Valera asked that, while making their protests on the issue of status, members of the association should still give their loyalties and affection to the country of adoption and obey the laws and regulations of the Parliament and Government of New Zealand. He said all matters pertaining to citizenship had been discussed with de Valera and his departmental officials and everyone had a common view on the subject. The Éire Government planned to take the matter up with the New Zealand Government, but reiterated the need for members to honour their agreement with the authorities and do whatever jobs they were allocated.

His letter ended with a message from Éamon de Valera to members of the Éire National Association:

> Mr de Valera asked me to convey to each and every member his very best wishes for your future welfare, and was very pleased to hear from me of your interest at all times in the welfare of the Homeland. He believes that

those among you who wish to settle down in New Zealand will want to take your due share in winning for your adopted country still greater happiness and prosperity and that you and your children will always be ready to defend its interests.

Aylward concluded by thanking members for the support that they had given during 'the crisis'.

This letter is significant because it confirms the Irish Prime Minister and officials were fully briefed in person on the situation regarding Irish nationals in New Zealand. The trip was made possible as McLagan, Minister of National Service, approved Aylward's appointment and visit on behalf of the ENA and authorised permits to travel.[15] In doing so the New Zealand Government had essentially sanctioned the trip, knowing that Aylward intended to meet with members of the Irish Government. Maybe the government, and in particular Peter Fraser, were also using Aylward as an emissary to Ireland to ensure the two countries had a special relationship unimpeded by Britain.

The wording and tone of Aylward's report is carefully crafted. It is factual, unemotive, perhaps a tad lyrical, and written so that even the most ardent critic of the Citizens of Éire could not take offence at its contents. Aylward was probably aware that sooner or later the letter would get out in the public domain so he wanted to convey to the members of the association, despite their difference of opinion on the issue of status, that they were committed to obeying the laws of New Zealand.

De Valera's final comment about those who planned to remain in New Zealand was paternalistic in a nice sense. He recognised that once they took up citizenship in New Zealand it was acceptable for them to defend their adopted home country.

Aylward's trip was a successful mission and it would have been of much comfort for the ENA and their supporters to know that the Irish Prime Minister was on their side. The trip was a diplomatic mission in every sense of the word and set the stage for New Zealand establishing formal diplomatic ties with the Republic of Ireland.

Yes, Maurice, you were 'Mr Ambassador'!

14

The Columbans and the family

Having won their major battle, the Éire National Association continued in a holding pattern. However, its achievements were not realised in isolation as there was a wide group of supporters – family, friends and organisations – who gave strength to the ENA and its fight for justice.

Members of the ENA were also involved with Irish societies, and the men lived in two worlds – the social world of the Irish society, where they could enjoy a quiet ale and mingle with friends and relations, and the politically charged ENA. The only Irish society records I have relate to Wellington during the war years, with my father, Sullivan, Lafferty, Feeney, Traynor, Walsh, Cahill, Hickey, Horan, Roche, Nally and Aylward all appearing as office holders. From 1941 until 1943 Paddy Feeney was president of both the Irish Society and the ENA, so there were clearly close links between the two.

One of my father's best friends was Fr Jim McGlynn of the Missionary Society of St Columban, an order set up in 1916 by Fr Edward Galvin and Fr John Blowick, specifically to conduct missionary work in China, and later in the Far East, including Korea, the Philippines and Japan.

In August 1942 Fr McGlynn, who was based in Australia, was sent to New Zealand to look at the possibility of establishing a seminary for training priests for the order. The *Evening Post* published a lengthy article in which

The clergy and WWII

Many of the Catholic clergy in New Zealand were Irish and members of Irish societies. They were a source of comfort to the men who felt isolated in a country at war. There is no evidence to suggest, though, that the Catholic priests were 'pro' the ENA. After all, the majority of their parishioners had friends and family in the armed services. My own school, St Patrick's College, Wellington (fondly known as St Pat's Town), quite rightly honoured and recognised those who fought in WWI and WWII so that others may enjoy the rights we have today. 'When you go home tell the people that for their tomorrow we gave our today' is a fitting recognition of all those who fought for freedom.

Fr McGlynn talked about the work they'd been doing, in particular in China, Korea and the Philippines, which at that stage were occupied by the Japanese.[1] The article quoted him as saying Wellington had been selected as the headquarters for the society and that he had already taken up residence in the country. He bought a large piece of land with a sizable home in central Lower Hutt, about 20 minutes drive from Wellington. At that time it backed onto a golf course. He established a small seminary and the Columbans are still based there, though much of the land has been sold.

Soon after arriving in New Zealand, Fr McGlynn, who was renowned for being a very persuasive character, enlisted the help of young Irishmen, including my father, to create and maintain the beautiful gardens at the site. He had a soft Donegal accent, was tall and somewhat craggy, and a passionate Irishman.

Fr McGlynn was born at Glenfin, County Donegal. In 1922, after studying at Maynooth,[2] he went to Dalgan Park, the main house of the Columban Society, and was ordained in 1923. He served as rector and vice-rector at St Columban's Seminary in Melbourne, Australia, before opening the Columban house in Lower Hutt. He later went back to Australia and also served two terms as superior in New Zealand before finally retiring back to Dalgan Park in County Meath, where he died in January 1988.

In our household Fr McGlynn was much revered and loved, and this was true of all the Irishmen who got to know him in New Zealand. As a child I remember the frequent visits to see him at Lower Hutt. He was a strong supporter behind the scenes of the ENA as well as a paid-up member, with their final financial accounts listing him as having paid the sum of £6 to the association.

Fr McGlynn would have met the Most Rev Daniel Mannix in Melbourne, and coming from the Maynooth seminary, where Mannix had been president, McGlynn was likely to have been influenced by him. The controversial Archbishop of Melbourne vehemently opposed conscription in Australia in WWI and is regarded as the person who mobilised the anti-conscription forces, making him a much hated man by the Australian Government of the time and, of course, the British. From the correspondence I have read it would seem that Fr McGlynn was on good terms with Dr Mannix and probably shared his anti-conscription and republican sentiments.

From 1939 until 1949 Dr Mannix is listed as a life member of the Wellington Irish Society. Fr M.A. Brennan is listed as the patron and then, in 1945, Fr Jim McGlynn is listed as an honorary member. Archbishop Mannix visited the club in 1940 and one presumes that is how and why he was made a life member.

Éamon de Valera with Archbishop Daniel Mannix of Melbourne.

The *Evening Post* reported his official reception, noting that Monsignor Connolly represented Archbishop of Wellington Thomas O'Shea.[3] The welcome addresses outlined the ecclesiastic and Irish national achievements of Dr Mannix, and he was presented with an inscribed chalice and paten. Dr Mannix spoke for about three quarters of an hour and it was reported that the evening closed with singing the Irish national anthem.

Dr Mannix had many brushes with the British. When he was at Maynooth he was told to put up decorations for the King's visit. But the story goes that Dr Mannix would not put up any bunting with a Union Jack on it, and instead – rather smartly – put up bunting that conformed to the King's racing colours, thereby neatly sidestepping a diplomatic incident. Apparently the King nodded to Dr Mannix, said hello and moved on.[4]

The connection between Mannix and de Valera was strong and goes back to the days when Mannix employed the future Irish leader at Maynooth. Perhaps the most famous meeting between the pair, who were great friends and admired each other, took place at St Columban's Missionary College in 1920 in Omaha, Nebraska, when Archbishop Mannix was on his way through the United States on an abortive trip to Ireland. Within sight of his destination the ship he was on, the *Baltic*, was stopped by a British warship and Mannix was unceremoniously detained and stopped from landing in Ireland. The British feared he would stir up trouble, perhaps with good reason. During his US trip Dr Mannix gave a speech in which he said:

> England was never a friend of the United States. When your fathers fought, it was against England. Ireland has the same grievance against the enemy only ten times greater. I hope Ireland will make a fight equally successful.[5]

The Columbans, Mannix and de Valera were pretty much on the same page.

Apart from Fr McGlynn, only two other clergy, Fr Hanrahan and Fr Purcell, made small donations to the ENA. In general, the New Zealand clergy either supported the war or were neutral. At St Patrick's College in the late 1950s and early '60s when I was there, I cannot recall a single mention of Irish history and, in fact, we had a cadet corps which all boys had to be a part of. Although I cannot recall my father saying anything, I suspect the sight of his son in a 'British uniform' was anathema to him.

I am sure that both my parents and a large contingent of their Irish friends, including Maurice Aylward, were present at the opening of the St Columban's Seminary in Lower Hutt by Archbishop O'Shea in May 1943. Despite the war it would have been a gala occasion. It was opened on a Monday, the Feast of Our Lady Help of Christians, the patroness of Australia and New Zealand, with Fr McGlynn presiding.

My association with the Columbans started at my birth in January 1946, when Fr McGlynn obtained permission from Archbishop Mannix to be my godfather, and has continued right through to the present day when each month I get Masses said by the St Columbans for relations and friends. In my childhood we had a little cardboard box called the 'Jackie mite box', where spare pennies were placed to support the St Columban Missions. The Society's magazine, the *Far East*, was a popular family read and I still have copies of this.

When I was born Fr McGlynn wrote to my parents from Melbourne, where he was then based, congratulating them on my arrival and apologising for not being able to get over for my baptism. In the typed letter he said he was in the process of seeking permission from Archbishop Mannix to be my godfather and at the end there is a handwritten note saying he had got that permission. It is also clear he had some say in my being named Peter, saying in his letter that 28 January was the feast of St Peter. Then Fr McGlynn, the prolific writer that he was, had this to say to my father:

> Please ring up Maurice Aylward and ask him to bring you to the best tailor in town for a new suit and also to Hill Bros in Lambton Quay for a new hat – your other one will fit you no longer!!! Also, Matt, have a beer with Maurice and I'll pay the bill when I meet both of you.[6]

Fr Jim McGlynn with Éamon de Valera.

Fr Francis Douglas

There is another family and Wellington connection with the Columbans. My parents and grandparents lived for five years in the Wellington suburb of Khandallah and the church that I was christened in was St Peter and Paul's, in the adjacent suburb of Johnsonville. This township was the home of Fr Francis Douglas, a Wellington-born Columban missionary who was murdered by the Japanese in the Philippines on 27 July 1943. He had been a prisoner for more than a year before he was martyred. He was only 33 when he died.

Fr Douglas had served in parishes in Taranaki, including in Ōpunake where Maurice Aylward lived the latter part of his life. After a period at the St Columban's Seminary in Melbourne, he was sent to the Philippines in 1938. Fr Douglas is commemorated at Dalgan Park, and Francis Douglas Memorial College in New Plymouth is named after him. The Catholic boys college was founded in 1959 by the De La Salle brothers, and in recent years it has produced some notable All Blacks, namely Conrad Smith and the three Barrett brothers, Beauden, Scott and Jordie.

Fr McGlynn was a popular high-profile Irish priest who is still widely remembered by those who knew him, however vaguely, and spent his time between Australia and New Zealand over the years. In his time in New Zealand there is evidence to suggest that he became well connected politically, and I assume that he met Peter Fraser and other government ministers at some stage, especially as he was invited to a special government-hosted lunch for de Valera when the former Taoiseach visited Wellington in May 1948.

My father and godfather's involvement with the ENA was not the extent of my family's support for the organisation. My mother was also an ENA stalwart.

Mary Warren, like her mother, Sarah (née Milligan), was born at the coal mining town of Denniston on the West Coast of the South Island. It is a desolate place and a ghost town now, but in its heyday it was a large coal-producing centre, with coal taken 2000 feet down the mountain in tramway wagons, on what was called the Denniston Incline. It was a hard life on 'the hill' and, with the ground just rock, the dead could not be buried there. They had to be taken on the wagons down the incline to be buried in either Westport or the township of Waimangaroa. Mining was dangerous work then, as it is today. But 'coasters', as they call themselves, are a hardy breed.

Denniston, the birthplace of my mother, Mary Burke.

In some way I liken Denniston to the Twelve Bens in Connemara and the mountains around Maam Cross.

Denniston was a Labour Party stronghold and the miners were among the party's staunchest supporters. My grandfather John Warren, originally from Dilmanstown, near Hokitika, was a blacksmith in the Denniston mines and shod the horses that brought the coal from the pit face to the surface. Granddad was a Labour man through and through, and I can recall him listening avidly to Parliament on the radio, taking in every word of the Labour Party MPs.

Mum and her family left the West Coast in the 1920s and moved to Wellington where there were jobs of sorts. Mum managed to get work in Lindsay's Shoe Shop on Wellington's Lambton Quay, already a popular shopping area and not far from the Basilica which my father would have attended. Although Mum lived in Wellington for most of her life she always regarded herself as a 'Dennistonian'.

In February 1940 my mother was one of the organisers of the Eucharistic Congress held in Wellington that year. She was the president of the Children of Mary and throughout her life she spoke often and fondly about her involvement in this event. Mum was also a member of the Wellington Irish Society, where she met my father.

Mum told me that in late 1943 she feared being drafted into a job at an ammunition factory, and decided this was not for her because she wanted to support her husband-to-be's stand against war work. So she bought a small shop in Courtenay Place and set it up to sell baby clothes.[7] That was enough to prevent her from being manpowered. She had the whole family knitting baby clothes for the shop, though I am not sure that it was a great money earner.

On 19 February 1944 my parents, Matt and Mary, were married at the Basilica of the Sacred Heart in Wellington. My mother said it was a small wedding with just close family and friends, including some of her aunts who lived in a large two-storey house next to the church in Guildford Terrace. They were married by her uncle, Fr Dan Milligan, with Monsignor Connolly and Fr McGlynn also present. Mum's bridesmaid was her sister, Margaret Therese (Peg) Warren and the best man was John Clancy from Moycullen, who was boarding with my aunts. Mum's parents, Jack and Sarah Warren, were there as well as her brothers, Bill and Jim. My mother's family were musical; Mum was a fine singer and her sister, Peg, was a fabulous pianist and organist. Peg was my godmother and a lovely individual who died young. My great-aunt, Jo Milligan, was the organist at the Basilica and played at the wedding.

I've been told that the wedding reception was held in a restaurant nearby and that it was a low-key affair. Mum did not want an engagement ring, but instead asked Dad for a fox fur, which I still have.

My parents' wedding took place at about the same time as the Benedictine Monastery at Monte Cassino in Italy was bombed, an act which some Catholics saw as a deliberate act

The Bridal Party, 1944, from left: Bridesmaid Peg Warren (Mum's sister), Matt and Mary Burke, and John Clancy (best man).

of bigotry, although the generals, including Freyberg, claimed it was necessary. History proved them wrong, and in fact the bombing of Cassino is now seen as a mistake that cost the lives of many New Zealanders, especially men from the Māori Battalion.

After the wedding. This photo is likely to have been taken in the garden of the house in the Wellington suburb of Khandallah, where Mum and Dad lived with Mum's parents for the first five years of married life. At the back from left: Monsignor Connolly, Fr Dan Milligan (Mum's uncle), Fr Jim McGlynn. In front: John Clancy, Matt Burke, Mary Burke, Peg Warren.

Churchill had just returned from his meeting with Stalin and Roosevelt, and separately met Deputy Prime Minister Walter Nash. Around the time of my parents wedding the *Evening Post* carried extensive coverage of the British leader's view on the progress of the war. 'We will smite the Hun,' Churchill proclaimed.

Not long after the wedding, it was announced that meat rationing was to be introduced in New Zealand, so Mum and Dad at least managed to get in a decent wedding breakfast before this happened.

While the war was still far from over, there was a sense that the enemy was being pushed back and people like my parents were looking, hoping and praying for more peaceful times. Each day the newspapers reported on the latest developments from the battlefield, with news of big air raids on Germany, and published the casualty lists. But there was still gardening news and advertisements for such everyday things as gladioli bulbs, nylon toothbrushes, slippers and suitcases.[8]

As far as the ENA were concerned it was business as usual, sorting out arrangements for Irishmen who did not want to fight for Britain and wanted to stay in New Zealand. The ENA was in effect the first Irish embassy in New Zealand and its base was No.2 Murphy Street – the residence of Maurice Leo Aylward.

15

The Fraser and de Valera connection

The Éire National Association's success in winning the right for Irishmen to stay in New Zealand and work, albeit at soldiers' rates, was due to many factors. Their legal representative, Fred Ongley, played a huge part with the consistent line he took throughout the Irishmen's case. This was evident in every court case in which he was involved, and in particular, the test case. Maurice Aylward's contribution was massive and in him the association had a man of tremendous skill as a writer and negotiator, with a beguiling and charming personality.

However, even with all their combined skills, it is questionable whether the ENA would have had the same success but for the special relationship between Éamon de Valera and Peter Fraser, something the Irishmen would have realised.

Fraser's role in achieving a favourable outcome for the Éire National Association is highlighted in a letter he received from Maurice Aylward, dated 30 August 1945.[1] In it Aylward said that the executive and members of the ENA wished to place on record their appreciation for the fair and considerate treatment accorded to them by the government during the trying and difficult times imposed on everyone by WWII. He thanked Fraser, his ministers and officials for the kindness and consideration shown to them.

Aylward then referred to his visit to Ireland in 1944–45 and his meetings with de Valera and his cabinet ministers:

> I gave them full information of the fair and considerate treatment we received from your [Fraser's] government and the respect that has been shown for the views and neutrality of Éire. Mr de Valera and his Ministers were moved by gratitude to an extent that I am not able to express. In a recent communication from Mr de Valera to my Association, he expressed 'his Government's appreciation of the just and broadminded attitude of the New Zealand Government – in particular of the Prime Minister Mr Fraser and the very fair treatment Association members had received during the war'. He wishes to convey this to you.

Maurice Aylward then went on to praise Fraser for his efforts at the San Francisco Peace Conference and, in particular, his advocacy for small nations.

This was something that was also close to the heart of de Valera. Aylward said that Fraser's advocacy earned him the 'admiration and everlasting gratitude of the Irish people, not only in New Zealand, but throughout the world'.

Finally, Aylward made a clear statement of where the ENA stood politically:

> In conclusion, we once again thank the Prime Minister and his colleagues and pledge ourselves to continue to work in the interests of Labour [the Party] and assist the Government in any undertaking which aims at improving the lot of the community in general.

Aylward's endorsement of Fraser, and also the strong and sympathetic disposition of de Valera towards Fraser, indicates the close bond between the two leaders.

Until now little has been made by historians about the de Valera–Fraser relationship. In fact, in Ireland most have probably never heard of Fraser, while in New Zealand only fleeting references have been made to the friendship. Drawing together references from a multitude of books and papers paints a new picture about the relationship between the two men in what were very difficult times. To do this we need to investigate what each of them did in their early lives, as well as concentrating on the events from the time they first met in 1935, until the end of 1948. But we must also highlight certain historical facts and actions about each to provide context and gain an understanding about what they did, and how that impacted on the decisions taken in respect of the Irish in New Zealand during World War II. It is difficult in a few words to adequately critique two famous, complex, consummate politicians on whom numerous works have been published over many years. The objective of this narrative is to show how the pair contributed to the eventual outcome for the ENA members faced with conscription into the armed forces.

I found two books invaluable in exploring this relationship: *Peter Fraser* by James Thorn, a Labour politician who served as an Under-Secretary to Fraser, published in 1952, soon after Fraser's death; and *Éamon de Valera: A* 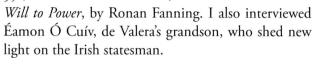 *Will to Power*, by Ronan Fanning. I also interviewed Éamon Ó Cuív, de Valera's grandson, who shed new light on the Irish statesman.

On a superficial level you may ask what does a deeply devout Catholic Irish prime minister have in common with a Scottish-born Presbyterian prime minister of

James Thorn, former President of the Labour Party and Under-Secretary to Peter Fraser during the war years.
Alexander Turnbull Library, F-20105 1/4

New Zealand? The likely answer is not a lot. But as you will see the pair were an example of the 'perfect mixed marriage'. Fraser and de Valera both had their critics then, as they do today. The Irish leader, in particular, was a polarising individual and did not enjoy the same affection as perhaps his opponent Michael Collins, who has almost achieved sainthood in Ireland.

The first meeting of de Valera and Fraser was in Dublin in 1935. It was here that a friendship began that was to transcend Ireland's political differences with Britain and WWII, and culminate in some special moments when de Valera visited New Zealand in 1948 and Fraser visited Ireland later that same year. De Valera was accorded a state welcome in New Zealand despite no longer being Taoiseach, having lost power in Ireland in the February elections to a coalition government. In December Fraser travelled to Ireland where de Valera, in his capacity as Chancellor of the National University of Ireland in Dublin, conferred a Doctor of Laws on Fraser. These two events, at the end of a tumultuous period and only months away from Ireland declaring itself a republic and cutting ties with Britain, show just how close the two men had become. It was more than just a political friendship of convenience. It was a genuine and enduring personal friendship born out of having much in common and also sharing a worldview, in particular that small nations should not be marginalised by larger ones.

At their first meeting Fraser was still an opposition MP. He had gone to London with his wife, Janet, as part of a parliamentary delegation to attend a conference of the Empire Parliamentary Association in July. Staying on for the British Trade Union Congress at Margate, he then travelled to Dublin where he met de Valera.[2]

It is interesting that Fraser went to Ireland in 1935 because the British spin doctors had painted de Valera as an evil, anti-empire, anti-British leader who had no right to challenge the authority of the British Tory ruling class. Churchill, in particular, appeared obsessed with de Valera and the Irish. Fraser, when he became prime minister in 1940, had to work with Churchill and he did this well, but at the same time it didn't appear to compromise his friendship with de Valera.

While we know they 'had a cordial discussion about social and economic issues' at their meeting we can also surmise that they would have touched on their similar backgrounds. Fraser may have recounted his life history of being born in Hill of Fearn, near Tain, north of Inverness in the Scottish Highlands, and how his grandfather on his mother's side had been evicted from his small holding, a victim of the Sutherland Clearances in the early part of the 19th century. And he may have spoken about how his parents emigrated to Canada and then returned to Fearn, and later how the family went their own ways – a sister to South Africa, a brother to Canada, and he to New Zealand, while his other brother was in London. Fraser would have talked about his political life in New Zealand and his role in founding the Labour Party in 1916 at about the same time as de Valera was a leader in the Easter Rising.

Fraser may have mentioned rising through the ranks of the Labour Party and his role as editor of the party newspaper, the *Maoriland Worker*, and his overriding personal ideals to see the poor treated fairly and workers' rights protected. He may have also mentioned his links in the early 1920s with the Irish Self-Determination League of New Zealand, which supported Irish self-government. This involvement at an early stage of his career indicates a clear affinity with Irish issues. One of Fraser's closest friends, poet Eileen Duggan, was also a member.

De Valera would have recounted his own background of being born in New York to a Spanish father, Juan Vivion, and an Irish mother, Catherine (Kate) Coll, being sent back to Ireland to live with his grandparents at the age of two, and never seeing his father again. He would have talked about his education, his love for mathematics, and then his conversion to Irishness, thanks to the woman who taught him the Irish language and whom he married in August 1909, Sinéad Ní Fhlannagáin. He may have recounted that it was Sinéad who politicised him, and told of his own rapid rise in the republican movement, his role in the 1916 Rising, the Troubles in 1919–21 and the Civil War of 1922; also his time as leader of Sinn Féin and the founding of Fianna Fáil, and finally his election as prime minister in 1932 – the transition from warrior to statesman. He may also have talked about founding the *Irish Press* in 1931 as a vehicle for promoting 'truth in the news', and to counter the other newspapers, which he saw as not supporting Fianna Fáil.

The power of language

Dev's love of the Irish language served him well when he made a 24-hour visit to Galway before the Troubles began. He was watched closely by the RIC Galway County Inspector, G.B. Ruttledge, who noted that Dev stayed at the Railway Hotel and addressed a crowd of 500 people, and later that de Valera addressed the Galway District Council and a gathering of Irish Volunteers. But the policeman designated to follow de Valera had a problem, which he later admitted to, because de Valera spoke Gaelic to his people and the sergeant didn't understand a word as he couldn't speak the language.

From this background it is clear that they had much in common. Both were foreigners by birth in the countries they led, and probably shared a dislike for the British aristocracy because their ancestors had suffered at the hands of English landlords. Due to their humble beginnings in life they would have held similar views on social and international issues. They also shared a passion for education and language, and both had been imprisoned for causes they passionately believed in. As time went by the two men were significant social reformers in their respective countries.

The pair were also quiet men, thinkers, yet men of action. Both suffered from poor eyesight. Fraser never drank alcohol and neither did de Valera. Fraser rarely went to dinner parties and had few leisure pursuits apart from walking, reading and visits to art galleries or the theatre. In their biography, Bassett and King say that 'chintzy hospitality' had little appeal.[3] One of Fraser's more unlikely activities once he was in government, and especially when he was prime minister, was to attend a lot of funerals.[4]

Who knows whether at that first meeting they talked sport, but just days after they met, the All Blacks began a tour of the British Isles that included a test match with Ireland on 7 December at Lansdowne Road in Dublin, which the All Blacks won 17–9. De Valera had been a keen rugby man in his youth and played mainly at fullback, but occasionally at centre. At Rockwell College in Tipperary, his rugby career blossomed and he was in the senior team. He played for his college in the Munster Cup competition and in 1905 was in the team that reached the semi-final.[5] Perhaps due to the influence of his wife, Sinéad, and his commitment to all things Irish, he developed a huge interest in the Gaelic Athletic Association (GAA), that runs all forms of Gaelic sports including hurling and Gaelic football – which has a much bigger following in Ireland than rugby.

From that first meeting in Dublin the two men went their separate ways, neither with the knowledge that in just over four years both would be leading their respective countries through the war years, or in the case of Éire, the Emergency.

On 6 December 1935 the New Zealand Labour Party, led by Michael Joseph Savage with Fraser as his deputy, swept into power to become the First Labour Government. Their election sparked a burst of revolutionary social reforms, with Fraser playing a major role as both the Minister of Education and of Health. For example, in March 1937 he set up a scheme for school children whereby they got a free half-pint of milk a day at school, and where milk was in short supply, children received milk powder for making cocoa.[6] He made secondary education more accessible, improved school buildings for

Māori children, and initiated education reforms for Māori relating to culture and language. He instituted the Country Library Service, which made books available to people living in remote areas. The reforms came at a breathtaking pace and were applauded by teachers and educational administrators.

Sharing de Valera's love of language, Fraser was a strong supporter of the Māori language and a friend of Māori, including those in opposition parties, such as Sir Āpirana Ngata. Fraser likened the tribal organisation of Māori to the Clans of Scotland and even drew a comparison between the kilt and Māori traditional dress. Māori seldom bestow special honorary titles on non-Māori, but in Fraser's case he was referred to variously as 'te kōtuku rerenga tahi', meaning he was as rare as the white heron of a single flight, and 'te matua o te iwi' – the father of the people.[7] Janet Fraser was also held in high regard by Māori.

Fraser would have seen a parallel between the Irish and Māori, who have intermarried almost from the first days that Europeans arrived in New Zealand. I call it 'Ngāti Irishness', but it could equally be 'Ngāti Scottish'!

The New Zealand Prime Minister's Catholic connections were also part of the mosaic that was his relationship with de Valera. This is identified in two references in the Bassett and King book. The authors say Fraser 'warmed to the Irish cause and liked his many Catholic friends, who in turn learned to trust him'.

> Over the years any bigotry or anti-Catholicism that he might have brought with him from the Scottish Highlands had long since evaporated. He enjoyed the company of Catholics and liked the Irish sense of humour; the Catholic Church in turn regarded him as an excellent Minister of Education. He was always welcome at St Patrick's College which was in his electorate.[8]

In April 1935 Fraser attended the Golden Jubilee celebration of that college. He attended the annual prize-giving in December 1938, and speaking to the gathering in the assembly hall stated that he read with interest the history of the college, which had a great tradition behind it, and noted that it had produced some distinguished champions of personal liberty and self-determination. He also paid tribute to the archbishop, saying if ever there was a great Christian, it was Thomas O'Shea.[9] Another such visit was to open the new gymnasium at the college in 1941, which is mentioned several times in the college archives. While Fraser's relationship with the Citizens of Éire is well documented, it is also important to note that many St Patrick's College old boys served in senior roles in the New Zealand armed forces, including Air Commodores Frank Gill and Stan Quill, and Fr Wil Ainsworth, who was the first chaplain of the RNZAF.

Eileen Duggan, in 1937 – writer, poet and friend of Janet and Peter Fraser.
Alexander Turnbull Library, 1/4-049917-G

The Frasers were also close friends with the New Zealand author and Catholic, Eileen Duggan, for whom Peter Fraser secured a small annuity of £240 per annum in 1942 to assist her writing.[10] Fraser wrote to Duggan in June 1943 congratulating her on being made a Fellow of the Royal Society of Literature. Eileen was a friend of my mother and a member of the Irish club in Wellington. Her poems were published in the Catholic weekly newspaper, the *New Zealand Tablet*, and she famously wrote a poem to commemorate the death of Prime Minister Michael Savage in 1940.

Fraser's links to Catholics were further enhanced when he met Pope Pius XII in Rome in June 1944 after the Eternal City fell to the Allies. He also met with several priests who had helped New Zealand prisoners of war.

Prime Minister Peter Fraser outside the gates of the Vatican, Italy, before his audience with Pope Pius XII in June 1944. From left: Fr Owen Snedden, Sir Darcy Osborne, Fraser, General Bernard Freyberg, Fr John Flanagan, unidentified Vatican official, Mr Montgomery (Secretary British Legation) and General Edward Puttick.
Alexander Turnbull Library, DA-06186-F

The other action of Fraser and his wife, Janet, that endeared them to the Catholic community was his offer in 1943 for New Zealand to take 733 Polish children and 105 adult caregivers who had been displaced by the war in Europe. The children had lost their parents following the German invasion of Poland and later occupation by the Soviet Union. In October 1944 the children arrived in Wellington and Peter Fraser was there to greet them. The children were housed in a special camp at the country town of Pahīatua, 160 kilometres north-east of Wellington. In theory they were only supposed to be in New Zealand's care for the duration of the war, but most stayed on and integrated into local society, attending Catholic schools in the area, while others went to boarding schools. The camp closed in 1952 but a plaque commemorating it stands in the main street of the town. New Zealand and Poland have a special relationship as a result of this great humanitarian act by the Frasers.

While Peter Fraser was busy introducing a flurry of social reforms in New Zealand, Éamon de Valera was busy in Ireland dismantling the Anglo-Irish

Countess Wodzicka, Peter Fraser and Mrs Kozera during the official welcome for Polish refugee children arriving in Wellington, 1 November 1944.
Alexander Turnbull Library, 1/2-003635-F

Treaty signed by Michael Collins in 1921, and setting Ireland on a course that would ultimately lead to it becoming a fully fledged republic in 1949. De Valera never tried to position Fianna Fáil to the left or right of the political spectrum, rather for him it was a case of being for or against the Treaty and the partition of Ireland. In his case, it was clearly against the Treaty and all its sidebars.[11] In 1932 he effectively abolished the position of governor-general in Ireland by forcing the incumbent to resign and replacing him with a nondescript 1916 veteran and shopkeeper Domhnall ua Buachalla, who reduced the office of governor-general to a joke by rejecting the vice-regal lodge for a simple house in Dublin.[12] Later the role of governor-general was replaced by an elected president.

De Valera abolished the controversial oath of allegiance to the King embodied in the Treaty, something he regarded as 'an intolerable burden to the people of this state'.[13] As well, de Valera refused to pay land annuities to the British Government. These were interest payments on loans that the British Government had advanced to Irish tenant farmers at the end of the 19th century so they could buy their lands.[14] At that time these were estimated at about £5 million, but by 1938 had grown to an estimated £75 million.[15] Britain retaliated and imposed a 20 per cent duty on all goods entering the UK. It was game on, with Britain taking exception to what they saw as belligerence by de Valera and Ireland. But what they failed to see was that while the Irish leader had issues with the historic and much hated constitutional powers Britain sought to impose and retain over Ireland, he recognised that Ireland's economy was then (and is today) heavily dependent on Britain. In fact, in 1953 de Valera revealed at his first meeting with Churchill that he had no objection to Ireland remaining in the British Commonwealth, but that the barrier to this was the oath of allegiance.[16]

The other major issue that de Valera had to deal with was the so-called Treaty ports, another hangover from the 1921 Treaty. The three deep-water ports were Lough Swilly in northern Donegal, Berehaven in Bantry Bay at the southern tip of Ireland in West Cork, and Spike Island in Cobh (then known as Queenstown). The ports were seen by the British as strategic bases for the Royal Navy to defend shipping in the Atlantic, but de Valera wanted no British military presence on Irish soil. On 25 April 1938 de Valera and British Prime Minister Neville Chamberlain signed an agreement to hand back the ports to Ireland. They also ended the trade war between the two countries. The first of the ports, Spike Island, was returned on 11 July 1938 and the others by October that year. This was a triumph for de Valera, and historians consider that it was instrumental in helping preserve Ireland's neutrality in WWII.

Churchill was furious at the agreement, describing it as an astonishing triumph for the Irish leader. It was to be a sore for Churchill that never healed and increased his dislike for Ireland and de Valera. Churchill apparently even objected to de Valera's constitution, which renamed Ireland 'Éire' – its Irish name. According to Churchill's world every name should be in English, 'Do we call Paris Paree?' he squawked. If he were alive today presumably he would object to New Zealand being called Aotearoa, its beautiful and appropriate Māori name.

While Churchill had his critics, there is no doubt that he served the British people well, at least in a public relations sense, in WWII. In the words of the American journalist Ed Murrow:

> Winston mobilised the English language and sent it into battle.[17]

Churchill certainly lifted the morale of the British people with his speeches, but many believe he was more of a hindrance than a help in matters military.

Much has been written about de Valera declaring Ireland neutral in WWII – a key issue for the Sons of Éire in their case against conscription in New Zealand. As far back as 1936 after the Italian invasion of Abyssinia and the likelihood of a greater war, de Valera told the Dáil: 'We want to be neutral.'[18] But he deliberately did not enshrine this in the Irish Constitution for fear it could constrain future government foreign policy.[19] While de Valera was the undoubted architect of Ireland's neutrality, Tim Pat Coogan states that during the 1921 Treaty negotiations Michael Collins had raised this very issue. Collins is reported to have said: 'England would be more safeguarded by a friendly and neutral Ireland than by an Ireland resentful and in spirit hostile as she had been in the last war.'[20]

In 1943 Churchill recounted to Clement Attlee: 'The Irish conduct will never be forgiven in this war by the British people … we must save them from themselves.'[21]

De Valera's son Terry is reported to have said that Britain, rather than Germany, was the most likely invader of Ireland and that Britain's intentions were less benign than those of the Nazis.[22] Churchill did have a penchant for meddling in matters military and, by and large, a history of failure, although he did preside over some glorious retreats with his involvement in the unsuccessful Gallipoli campaign in WWI, and the Norway, Greece and Crete campaigns in WWII.

Interestingly Churchill's dislike of Ireland was not shared by all his colleagues. For example Viscount Cranborne, the British Secretary of State for Dominion Affairs, published a list of 14 specific things that Éire did for Britain as part of its friendly neutral policy in 1945. These included providing meteorological information, internment of German personnel in Éire while Allied servicemen were returned to Britain, establishment of a radar station in Donegal, and de Valera's silence on people from the Irish Free State who fought for Britain. The Americans were even higher in their praise for de Valera's friendly neutral policy and were planning to give a number of Irish army officers the American Legion of Merit for their help during the war, but they backed off, fearing it might embarrass the Irish Government.[23]

Against all the odds and perils of the war, and busy agendas, Peter Fraser and Éamon de Valera continued their friendship and met again on at least one occasion during the war. This was during a four-month trip Fraser made in 1941 when he met with New Zealand servicemen in the Middle East and Britain.

Fraser was in Cairo when the Allies' campaign in Greece and Crete, in which New Zealand played a major role, fell apart, suffering heavy casualties and with many soldiers taken prisoner. Had it not been for Fraser's intervention, demanding an extra ship be sent to rescue more New Zealanders from Crete, the toll would have been higher.

Later Fraser went on to London for talks with Churchill where he spent the weekend at Chequers discussing a range of issues, including the Crete debacle. Fraser was not in the Churchill mould of being a big drinker and a finicky eater, but it seems he coped with the situation.[24]

Churchill's unusual eating habits are the subject of a complete book, which lists his favourite champagne as Pol Roger – nothing less – and notes he also had a liking for plover eggs, which he would go to great lengths to acquire.[25] But if Churchill disliked the Irish, it seemed he enjoyed their food. Ironically, Irish stew was one of his favourites – even reheated.[26] It's said that Winston Churchill 'was easily satisfied by the best'. What Fraser was served at Chequers is not recorded, but its possible Irish stew was on the menu.

The meeting with Churchill would have been interesting as a day or so after, Fraser was on his way to meet Éamon de Valera.

On 24 August 1941 Fraser flew to Baldonnel Aerodrome near Dublin on-board a BOAC De Havilland DH.91 Albatross Transport Frobisher aircraft which could carry up to 22 passengers. At the time this four-engine passenger aircraft, constructed mainly of wood, was considered one of the most modern medium-range aircraft, and in fact the Mosquito military aircraft was based on its design. According to Carl Berendsen, who was travelling with Fraser, the windows of the aircraft were frosted over, presumably to block out any possible light from showing, which might attract the attention of enemy aircraft. This trip to Ireland would have been carefully planned to avoid a

Peter Fraser with Winston Churchill outside No.10 Downing Street, London.
Alexander Turnbull Library, PA Coll-5547-049

diplomatic spat with the UK, not to mention the risk of the aircraft being deliberately or accidentally shot down. It's not known whether the flight took place at night or during the day, or whether it was a scheduled service or a charter from the British Government. Flights between Britain and Ireland during WWII were few, with Aer Lingus operating a limited service from Liverpool or Manchester to Dublin.

In Dublin Fraser and de Valera had a convivial few days together, briefing each other on what had happened in their countries since they'd last met in 1935. We can assume that Fraser also mentioned his Catholic and Irish friends back in Wellington, and presumably the topic of the Citizens of Éire was raised, as Fraser had been personally briefed by the ENA on this. The New Zealand Prime Minister would probably have spoken of his recent adventures in the Middle East and in Britain, where he spent a large part of his time meeting New Zealand servicemen and women. He may have also referred to his meeting with Churchill, which would have been of special interest to de Valera. This meeting of Fraser and de Valera would have helped pave the way for Maurice Aylward's meeting with the Irish Prime Minister in 1944.

In turn, de Valera would likely have briefed Fraser on the economic situation in Ireland and how his policy of friendly neutrality was working out. Dev, with his Irish charm that Fraser would have loved, probably told some stories of his past life and presumably there was much laughter. Bassett and King claim that 'Éamon de Valera regaled Fraser's party with stories about the revolution.'[27]

Carl Berendsen comments in his memoirs:

> We were entertained by the remarkable Irish leader, Éamon de Valera, and then at Adare in the West before leaving from Foynes via Gandar for Chesapeake Bay and Baltimore in our huge 160-foot wingspan Boeing Clipper [flying boat] with its eleven cabins.[28]

Berendsen, who was an intellectual and quick to criticise, must have been impressed with de Valera to describe him in the way that he did. After their meeting with de Valera, Fraser and Berendsen would have likely travelled by train from Dublin to Adare in County Limerick, and either stayed there or at Foynes, a village on the Shannon Estuary near Limerick, the departure point for the flying boats going to and from the United States during WWII.

For a few short years during the war when land-based aircraft were incapable of safely flying across the Atlantic, it was the huge flying boats that made this journey. Only the rich and famous were able to afford such a trip. Today there is a wonderful museum at Foynes set up by the famous Irish actress Maureen O'Hara and her flying-boat pilot husband, Charlie Blair. The museum book lists some of the celebrities who flew on these gigantic luxury aircraft, such as Douglas Fairbanks, John F. Kennedy, Bob Hope, Humphrey Bogart, Gracie Fields, Eleanor Roosevelt and, yes, Peter Fraser, Prime Minister of New Zealand. Incidentally, Irish coffee was invented by Joe Sheridan, the chef at Foynes Hotel in 1943, as a means of warming up passengers after their long journey on a flying boat.

Given this background of de Valera and Fraser, it is interesting to gain some insight into their personalities, characters and *modus operandi* through the eyes of people who knew and worked with them.

Éamon Ó Cuív, grandson of de Valera, rejects claims from writers who describe his grandfather as austere and withdrawn:

> I think whoever met him gave testament to the fact that he was warm-hearted, personable and very gracious. One thing that stuck out for us was the absolute attachment of all of his staff to him. He also treated them with respect and kindliness. I have heard stories from family members of people who worked for him that when he rang someone to have a chat with them about something important he'd first have a chat with the young person who came on the phone and ask how they were getting on. He had no airs and graces and was a very warm person. My mother used to get annoyed about him being portrayed as cold and not good at personal relationships. She said that he was a very soft person and we, as grandchildren, had a great relationship with him. He also had a great sense of humour. My mother had a particularly great father–daughter relationship with him.

A Boeing B314 'Clipper' long-range flying boat moored at Foynes on the Shannon Estuary, c.1940s. This is similar to the one Peter Fraser travelled on when he flew from Ireland to the United States in 1941. The aircraft carried 35 passengers in luxury conditions.
Foynes Flying Boat Museum

The big thing in his life was mathematics and here again there is another interesting side. My eldest sister, Nora, was special in that way and when she was very young Dev started doing mathematics with her and so she developed a huge interest in the subject. My memory at home on Sunday afternoons, until she went away on scholarships abroad, was of the two of them heading down to his study. He had a big blackboard because he couldn't read anything on paper because of his blindness. The two of them spent the afternoon doing higher mathematics and when she went abroad she'd write these long letters with all the newsy parts but also with some fancy mathematic equations she was doing for his benefit. She went on to be a Professor in Mathematics in Canada and some of that was due to his encouragement of her.[29]

On de Valera's relationship with Churchill, Ó Cuív says his grandfather described him as a great British leader, but that he was empire-driven, mercurial, and that saner heads in Britain were more realistic and understanding of Ireland's neutrality policy, recognising that if Éire had entered the war it would have split the country.

Renowned Irish historian Ronan Fanning notes: 'Éamon de Valera's vision was powerful but blinkered. Powerful, because his conception of an Irish republic satisfied the nationalist appetite for independence. Blinkered, because he saw independence as an end in itself, rather than as a means to an end.'[30]

Éamon Ó Cuív, TD for Galway West.

This is borne out by de Valera's persistence in pursuing the issue of the partition of Ireland, and one of the reasons for his visit to New Zealand was to gain support for his view. On the other hand, Fanning praises de Valera for not responding to Churchill's persistent attacks on Irish neutrality during WWII by saying, 'Éamon de Valera never received, nor would he have ever wanted or expected, gratitude for his comprehensive secret support for the Allies during the war.'[31]

Finally, Ronan Fanning makes a perceptive comment on why the British never warmed to de Valera: 'A reason why de Valera has always had such a persistently bad press in Britain is because he so signally fails to fit their stage-Irish stereotype: rumbustious, fun-loving, hard-drinking, colourful and larger than life ... but which never fitted the austere and pedantic de Valera.'[32]

Much has been said about Fraser's personality, and he was described by Carl Berendsen, Head of the Prime Minister's Department in the early war

Dev and Collins

Éamon Ó Cuív provided some insight into de Valera's relationship with Michael Collins. He said his grandmother talked about Collins as 'my boy – it's a pity he went the wrong way'. Ó Cuív said he and his siblings were brought up to have huge respect for Collins and that his own mother played with Collins's nieces and nephews and went swimming with them at Blackrock. When Ó Cuív was in charge of the Co-operative in Connemara he got a bank loan for the organisation from the chairman of the bank who was a nephew of Michael Collins, having disclosed that he was de Valera's grandson. This, he says, debunks the theory the two families bore grudges.

years and who worked closely with him, as 'one of the soundest thinkers on world problems.'[33]

He went on to say: 'Fraser's contribution to the war effort was greater than that of any other man. He was intelligent and quick but also honest and courageous. The problem lay in his methods, they were impossible.'[34]

Perhaps the last words should be left to Winston Churchill and Clement Attlee. Churchill said of Fraser, 'The Prime Minister of New Zealand is as honest and straightforward as you make them,'[35] and Attlee said, 'He never showed any weakness even when things were at their darkest.'[36]

Finding out what Churchill thought of de Valera uncovers an array of interesting comments. Historian Diarmaid Ferriter says:

> The two crossed swords on many occasions and there are a variety of colourful quotations one could cite to encapsulate the essence of the relationship between them, and in particular Churchill's view of de Valera. At various stages, he called him a liar, a fanatic, a murderer, a perjurer, a Bolshevist, and, perhaps most insultingly, a bore.[37]

One such colourful comment is in the Churchill minute (22/11/40) in which he suggested that Irish Taoiseach Éamon de Valera, should be allowed to 'stew in his own juice'.[38] David Freeman describes it thus:

'Churchill saw de Valera as both a malignant force and shameful opportunist who disgracefully used the sacrifices of his countrymen to advance his own career.'[39] Yet the relationship between de Valera and Fraser transcended the 'man in the middle' with whom they both had very different interactions.

Genealogist Geraldene O'Reilly at the Irish Parliament, 2016.

Peter Fraser being greeted by New Zealand Ambassador Walter Nash
at National Airport, Washington DC, April 1944.
War History collection, Alexander Turnbull Library, DA-02000-F

Finally, the pair had one thing in common – exceptional wives who supported their respective political careers with love and dedication. Janet Fraser even had an office in Parliament next to her husband, and Sinéad de Valera coped uncomplainingly with her husband's long absences, both in jail and overseas. Without Janet and Sinéad it is doubtful whether Peter and Éamon would have achieved what they did or the accolades that went with their political careers.

The literature of the WWII leaders tends to focus on the big three – Roosevelt, Churchill and Stalin. No room at the inn, it seems, for others.

But there is a place for recognition of the leaders of smaller nations, such as Ireland and New Zealand, who made a contribution well above most people's expectations. Both Éamon de Valera and Peter Fraser deserve recognition for their determination not to allow smaller nations to be marginalised.

16

The final meetings

Politics after WWII produced change. People who had endured the privations of the war were looking for a better future, but leaders who had served their countries well in wartime were not always seen as the agents for change. Winston Churchill was unceremoniously dumped in 1945 in a landslide loss and replaced by Labour's Clement Attlee. De Valera's days were also numbered. In New Zealand Fraser was re-elected in 1946, but with a reduced majority.

Bearing in mind the political sentiments expressed in the letter from the ENA to Fraser on 30 August 1945,[1] it's likely my father and most of his Irish friends would have voted Labour and supported its re-election.

By the time de Valera and Fraser next met, Dev had lost the election in February 1948 to a new coalition that saw John A. Costello of Fine Gael installed as Taoiseach. The former Irish Prime Minister, accompanied by his trusted friend and former Defence Minister Frank Aiken, then embarked on a tour of the United States, Australia, India and New Zealand to address what was a fundamental issue to him, verging on an obsession – the partition of Ireland. The purpose was to mobilise support from people in all four countries and get them to put pressure on Britain to make a united Ireland 'a nation once again'.

On 9 March 1948 Wellington's *Evening Post* reported that 3000 people turned out to farewell de Valera at Shannon Airport.[2] On 19 April the same paper hinted that he may visit New Zealand after spending time in Australia.[3] Such news, if they didn't already know it, would have been greeted with much joy and enthusiasm by the local Irish community, most of whom had not been back to their homeland for many years, if at all.

By this stage the ENA had seemingly disbanded[4] and the National Irish Society took up de Valera's cause by writing to Peter Fraser on 22 April 1948.[5] They wrote of the 'tragic story of the division of Ireland by a British Act of Parliament, the proscription and disenfranchisement of nationals in the six counties not being well known, even in Britain'. The letter went on to say that New Zealand was a leader in the way people from Ireland, England, Wales and Scotland got on well together, and questioned why this couldn't happen in the island of Ireland. It stated that partition of the north and south of Ireland was 'unnatural' and posed the question: how could the British Foreign Secretary accept democracy, yet allow partition to still exist? The letter then stated that the partition was regretted by all fair-minded people around the world, 'resented by Irishmen and women wherever they may be', and noted that the Atlantic Charter called for the rights of all nations to determine their own form of government 'without pressure or interference from any outside power – surely this cannot be denied to Ireland'.

Finally the letter reiterated that partition was wrong and a source of evil for both Britain and the Irish nation:

> We believe that it could be ended without injustice to the Unionist minority in Ireland, indeed its undoing may well prove to be the beginning of new, more fruitful and more influential life than that minority has ever known. We tender this protest and respectfully ask that it be forwarded to the imperial authorities.

The letter was signed by David O'Connell, M.M. Cooney, Michael O'Connor and Maurice L. Aylward.[6]

There was a perfunctory acknowledgement of the letter by the prime minister's office four days later,[7] followed by another letter on 5 May signed by Foss Shanahan of the Prime Minister's Department. In it he said the protest had been noted, but the request to pass the letter on to the British Government was declined:

> In questions of this kind, which are primarily the concern of another government of the British Commonwealth, it is not the practice of the New Zealand Government to act as a channel of communication for messages from New Zealand citizens.[8]

It suggested that the Irish club was free to make its own representations to the British Government.

There is no record of whether this was done and it is likely that nothing was. After all, the protest had been made to Prime Minister Fraser and he would now be aware of their views, if he hadn't been already.

The de Valera roadshow was already on the radar of the New Zealand Government in early May 1948, with reports of the Irish opposition leader's speeches in the United States being channelled back to them. One such report noted that in the US, de Valera's speeches were more or less confined to the history and injustice of partition, but as the tour went on he had 'ridiculed the idea that Britain had any claim to lead the forces of democracy and justice'.[9] Britain's representative in Ireland, Lord Rugby (formerly Sir John Maffey), reported that there was considerable objection in Ireland to de Valera, as the opposition leader, speaking out on the issue to gain popular support. 'The spell is broken and de Valera would have difficulty in getting back to his former pinnacle,' he asserted. He later described Ireland as 'a Scotland gone wrong'.[10]

It seems that while the New Zealand Irish societies were aware of de Valera's upcoming visit and had some plans in place, the government had not been involved. That was until Rev Dean William Murphy from the Auckland Parish of Balmoral sent a telegram to Peter Fraser on 5 May.[11] In it he said that de Valera and Frank Aiken were arriving at Whenuapai airport on Tuesday 25 May, and asked if the government had any official plans for the visit, or whether the Irish National Society should proceed to make arrangements. What followed was a flurry of correspondence between the Prime Minister's Department and the New Zealand High Commissioner in Australia, James Barclay. They asked him to contact de Valera and Aiken to offer them an official invitation to visit the country as 'guests of government'. On 13 May Barclay responded by saying that de Valera 'deeply appreciates and gratefully accepts your kind invitation'. He went on to say that de Valera would arrive in Auckland from Sydney on 25 May and would then fly to Wellington, with their only plans being a public reception organised by Archbishop McKeefry on Wednesday evening 26 May, and a similar function arranged by Bishop Liston in Auckland on Saturday 29 May, after which the pair would fly back to Australia. In the telegram Barclay told Fraser that de Valera would be pleased to 'fall in with any arrangements that he made and said that they would like to talk to him [Fraser] about housing and social services'.[12] This had a certain logic to it, given that New Zealand built its first state house in 1937 in Wellington and Fraser's government was regarded as a pioneer in the provision of social services.

The wheels of bureaucracy spun into action and within a week Foss Shanahan advised the Under-Secretary for Internal Affairs of the plans, which included a luncheon for de Valera and Aiken on 25 May at Wellington's Hotel Waterloo, to be attended by members of cabinet and under-secretaries.[13]

On that evening there was to be an official welcome for the pair at the Wellington Town Hall, and the government decided to hold an afternoon reception at Parliament on 26 May. Shanahan's memo said the Prime Minister wanted the following people on the invitation list: Professor McGechan, Professor Wood, Fr McGlynn and Dr Herlihy from St Columban's, two archbishops (Peter McKeefry and Thomas O'Shea) and a selection of Catholic clergy, Dr O'Regan, Mr and Mrs P. Callaghan, Eileen Duggan, Tim Cleary, Sir William Perry, Mr and Mrs Lenniston, Mr J. Cummings, Mr J. Madden and Mr and Mrs T. Sherrard. As well, Fraser said that he would like a wide representation of first, second and third generation Irishmen. If the invite list was anything to go by, even at an early stage, Peter Fraser was making sure that the Catholic community was well represented. The specific inclusion of Fr McGlynn, my godfather, gives me a special sense of pride.

What is unusual about de Valera and Aiken's visit to New Zealand was that they were accorded 'guest of government' status, making their visit to Aotearoa akin to a state visit. This was not so in the United States, Australia or India, where de Valera was treated like any tourist or business person. Again it was Fraser who turned what might have been an informal trip to New Zealand into a state occasion with all the trappings that came with it. Predictably the Grand Orange Lodge of New Zealand sent a letter to Fraser protesting that de Valera was being accorded a state visit and demanded it be cancelled, but plans carried on nevertheless.[14]

There was much media interest in the de Valera visit, which my parents would have followed avidly. His arrival in Sydney from San Francisco was reported in the *Dominion* on 28 April, with mention that he was then going to Melbourne as guest of Dr Daniel Mannix, the controversial archbishop. De Valera and Aiken were to spend a month in Australia making speeches and spreading their message on the partition issue.[15] On the day before he arrived in New Zealand, the *Evening Post* published a significant story on de Valera, headed 'Mathematician Who Led Sinn Féin'. The article recounted his childhood days, his marriage to Sinéad and his interest in the Irish language, but was mainly about his political career, including his part in the 1916 Easter Rising, through to the present day. The story carried no byline or date and I suspect it was put together using previously published material.[16] But Dev would have been pleased with the article as it included some of the key messages that he wanted to get across on this worldwide propaganda expedition. On the issue of partition the article quoted him as saying about the British Government: 'All they have to do is to abandon the insane ambition to dominate the Irish', and 'there could be no real reconciliation between Éire and Great Britain while the British occupied Northern Ireland'. There was a big build-up in the press for his visit, with reports in other newspapers previewing his arrival in Auckland and the plans for his stay in New Zealand as guest of government.

When de Valera finally arrived on the overnight DC4 flight from Sydney to Auckland on 25 May, he received a rousing welcome from members of the Auckland Irish Society who waved Irish flags and banners.[17] He and Aiken were met by J. Clarke, manager of the Government Tourist Department,

An Irish welcome for de Valera and Aiken at Auckland, 1948.
Vincent McHale collection, Alexander Turnbull Library, PAColl-7422-1

representing the government. Also there to welcome them was the President of the Auckland Irish Society, Mr Robinson, and Fr Lavelle and Fr O'Reilly. De Valera and Aiken went on a brief tour of Auckland before catching their flight to the aerodrome at Paraparaumu, about 50 kilometres north of Wellington that served the capital.

The welcome in Auckland was repeated a few hours later when they arrived at the beachside town of Paraparaumu, and this time it was the Wellington Irish who waved the flags, green ribbons and banners, and greeted Dev in Gaelic. The official welcoming party was the Patron of the Society Fr Brennan, President David O'Connell and Secretary Kitty O'Shea. The *Evening Post* reported that the welcome was demonstrative and that some people had come all the way from the South Island to greet this great Irish leader. He was quoted as saying that 'visiting New Zealand was a boyhood ambition fired by accounts of the country gained from a neighbour'. He went on to say that he was anxious to visit New Zealand as it had been held up as a 'model country with a model administration'. He said he brought greetings from Ireland to all Irish residents in New Zealand.[18] He then posed

Dev takes in Tawa Flat

The drive from Paraparaumu would have taken about an hour and they would have driven through my hometown of Tawa Flat, in those days without even its own Catholic church although it did have a cinema of sorts, and today is a typical middle-class suburb. They would have also driven down Ngāūranga Gorge past the freezing works where many Irishmen worked, including Maurice Aylward, and would have seen for the first time the beautiful harbour city of Wellington. But they were on a tight schedule so it's likely the pair had little time for sightseeing before their first official function in the city.

for photographs before he and his entourage headed to Wellington and a parliamentary lunch with Fraser and his cabinet.

Lunch would have been a formal, jovial, intimate occasion at the Waterloo Hotel just across the street from the Wellington wharves, where a lot of Irishmen worked, and where many had landed when they arrived in New Zealand. Opposite the hotel is the Wellington Railway Station, an imposing building just a few blocks from Parliament, and from the hotel you could see the Basilica of the Sacred Heart. In 1948, the Waterloo Hotel would have been the height of luxury (in fact it still was when I began work in 1963).

After lunch Fraser and de Valera had a formal two-hour meeting followed by a press conference. When asked about an 'all-Ireland policy', de Valera responded by saying: 'You have two islands here, would you like to have part of one cut off?' When asked if the threat of communism would bring Éire closer to the Commonwealth he replied, 'partition would still be a disturbing factor and that he had no hope that members of the United Nations would work together. They were without a will to co-operate'. In terms of his present visit, de Valera said he wasn't asking for material aid, just moral support. He defended Éire's right to refuse access to the Treaty ports in WWII, saying the time to ask that question was when Ireland got complete independence. A reporter at the conference noted that de Valera had a pleasant manner and his way of speaking had a distinct resemblance to Fraser.

As well as discussing the main political issues, such as whether Ireland would stay in the Commonwealth, it is hard to imagine the pair did not have time to chat informally about what had happened in their lives since they last met. Janet Fraser had died in 1945 and post-war political life was hard. Knowing de Valera's interest in all things cultural, it's possible that Fraser mentioned that just two years earlier his government had decided to fund the setting up of the National Symphony Orchestra under the umbrella of the National Broadcasting Service.[19] They would likely have had some light-hearted and convivial moments before getting back to business.

It had been a long day for the two Irishmen, but there was more to come. That night de Valera and Aiken were guests of honour at the official public welcome in the Wellington Town Hall. This function was open to all Wellingtonians, not just members of the Irish Society, and a large crowd attended. Newspaper reports stated that long before the reception, the hall was full and 'hundreds were unable to obtain admission'. Dr P.P. Lynch, a well-known Catholic doctor and a member of the Victoria University Council, presided over the proceedings which included speeches by Peter Fraser and Archbishop O'Shea.[20]

De Valera and Aiken were given a rousing reception as they walked onto the stage at this impressive venue. It had a main ground floor and mezzanine which together could seat up to 1600 people, and was decorated with green ribbons and Irish flags, adding to the spectacle of the evening. The clergy, priests, nuns and brothers would have all been there, along with members of the Irish Society and anyone with a 'green' connection. Cheers and prolonged

Peter Fraser hosts a reception for Éamon de Valera and Frank Aiken at Parliament.
Alexander Turnbull Library, F-16079 1/4

applause were the order of the night as the city turned out to get their first and, as it turned out, only glimpse of this Irish patriot and leader whom they had heard so much about.

Fraser said it was a great pleasure to welcome a great statesman and that New Zealand would be failing in elementary hospitality if a 'most cordial welcome were not extended to so distinguished a visitor'. Fraser went on to say that he hoped Ireland would remain a member of the British Commonwealth. (This was an interesting comment, knowing de Valera had declared that he wanted to stay, but that he could not do that while the oath of allegiance to the King was a precondition for membership.)

In holding the function to honour de Valera and Aiken, Fraser added that they were also honouring Ireland, a nation the two men had done so much for. Fraser then recalled that 30 years ago he had held office in the Irish Self-Determination League, which again drew sustained applause. Archbishop McKeefry welcomed de Valera and Aiken on behalf of the New Zealand Catholic Church –'especially those of Irish blood born in this country'. Brian O'Brien welcomed the pair on behalf of the Irish community.

When de Valera came to the podium he spoke first in Gaelic, and there is a suggestion that he also gave a greeting in Māori. He used the opportunity to raise the issue of partition, describing it as 'a grievous wound that was deeply resented by the people of Ireland' and as long as the wound remained open it would prevent the establishment of good relations with Britain. He went on to say that 'only on the basis of justice could one have good relations with neighbours'. The speech was vintage de Valera rhetoric and he had a large and influential audience to hear his message. One newspaper reported that the evening began with the playing of 'God Save the King', but ended with the Irish national anthem, 'A Soldier's Song', that many in the audience 'sang lustily'.

De Valera and Aiken had little time to rest. The next morning was devoted to an official round of meetings at Parliament. The *Dominion* reported they had meetings with Minister of Housing Bob Semple and Minister of Justice Rex Mason.[21] Dev would have enjoyed meeting Mason as he had an MA in mathematics from Victoria College, Wellington (now Victoria University), as well as a law degree.

There had been some suggestion that de Valera would give a lecture at Victoria College, but this did not eventuate. Instead, three members of Victoria's Political Science Society, who also worked for the Students' Association magazine *Salient*, turned up at the Waterloo Hotel to interview de Valera. The magazine reported that this took place in a passageway at the hotel and that de Valera was deeply interested in university affairs, telling the

The Irish community celebrating the visit of de Valera and Aiken at St Francis Hall, Wellington, 1948, with Maurice Aylward in the centre foreground.
Photo by Dan Kelly

journalists that economics and political science held considerable prominence in Irish universities.[22]

When questioned on student organisations, he stated there was plenty of vigorous student activity in the universities: 'It is well that it should be so'. The article concluded:

> Mr De Valera, himself a mathematician and Chancellor of the University of Ireland, has kept in touch with mathematical developments in New Zealand and remarked on the excellent work of the late Professor Somerville. He regretted that he did not have time to visit the mathematics and physics departments at Victoria College.

After the interview it was a short walk to Parliament with one or more of their New Zealand minders. Hopefully de Valera and Aiken had a chance to see something more of Wellington too, the surrounding hills all offering splendid views of the compact city and its natural harbour.

At 3.30pm they attended the large reception for special invited guests at Parliament. Being an official government occasion it would have been attended by members of parliament, diplomats and government officials, as well as invited clergy, business people, academics and the Irish community. The Māori community representatives included Lady Pōmare and Princess

Te Puea Hērangi, a leader in her own tribe of Tainui in the Waikato, an outspoken critic of the government conscripting Māori in WWI and a friend of Peter Fraser's. Attendance by Māori leaders was once again a manifestation of Fraser's high regard, love and respect for Māori. No doubt Maurice Aylward and other members of the executive of the ENA would have also been present, and the ever charming Aylward could well have sidled up to de Valera for a quiet chat. The *Evening Post* reported the hall was crowded. There was the usual social and networking time and then official speeches.[23]

In his introduction, Fraser referred to the democratic outlook, courage and foresight displayed by the former Prime Minister of Éire:

> Whether it has been in the matter of Italian aggression against Abyssinia, Japanese aggression in China or the actions of Germany, Mr de Valera has never hesitated to speak his mind at the Assembly of the League of Nations and has shown a great democratic outlook.

In reply de Valera said that it had been a great privilege to meet such a number of prominent New Zealanders, and he commented that to a large extent Ireland and New Zealand shared political and social ideals. He told the gathering that the world was fortunate in having a country that had developed so freely.

At the conclusion of this function, Aiken and de Valera would have only had time for a quick meal before they headed off to the final function of their stay in Wellington – the official welcome by the Wellington branch of the Irish Society at St Francis Hall in Hill Street, next to the Basilica. This was a large hall that was used for a range of Catholic activities in the capital. Regular dances were held there well into the early 1970s.

This was a night for the Irish to celebrate, although my parents were probably not there. My younger brother died at just two weeks old a few days before de Valera arrived, and looking at the photograph of the St Francis Hall function I cannot pick them out. On the other hand they may have just shied away from the camera. The night was probably great craic with music, dancing and all things Irish, and a chance for the locals to get up close with Éamon de Valera and Frank Aiken.

There were more speeches, this time from Irish Society President David O'Connell, Patron Fr Brennan and Archbishop McKeefry. De Valera also spoke, but his speech was not reported in the newspapers. It was the most informal gathering on the Wellington leg of the trip, and one he and Aiken would have enjoyed.

The next day the pair drove north and spent a night at the tourist city of Rotorua to see the thermal activity. Finally they spent a day in Auckland where

The reception for de Valera and Aiken held at Auckland Town Hall. Bishop Liston is fourth from left in the main party next to Éamon de Valera. Frank Aiken is seated next to the New Zealand Deputy Prime Minister, Walter Nash.
Vincent McHale collection, Alexander Turnbull Library, PAColl-7422-2

there was a large Civic reception hosted by Bishop James Liston. He was born in New Zealand of Irish parents and when he was the Coadjutor Bishop of Auckland he was reported as telling a St Patrick's Day gathering in 1922 about 'the men and women who in the glorious Easter of 1916 were proud to die for their country – murdered by foreign troops'.[24] This angered the Auckland mayor and civic leaders and led to him being charged with sedition, but he denied it in court and was eventually acquitted by an all-Protestant jury.

What set de Valera's New Zealand visit apart from the other places he visited was that he and Frank Aiken were officially welcomed by both the state and the Catholic Church. Whether the trip was a success in terms of gaining support for de Valera's anti-partition movement is a moot point. There was no outpouring of support in the media during his visit, but hundreds of Irish, or people of Irish descent, saw and met de Valera and loved the events they attended. Once again, the visit highlighted the close relationship, friendship, respect and genuine admiration Fraser and de Valera had for each other, and created a positive legacy between the two countries that remains today. As visionaries, the two men saw the similarities in each other's cultures and highlighted these to good effect.

Six months later, in December 1948, Peter Fraser was to be on the receiving end of some equally fine Irish hospitality in Dublin. This was at the end of a long three-month trip beginning on 30 September 1948, during which he visited Britain, France, Germany and Canada. He did not return until January 1949.[25]

The main purpose of Fraser's trip was to attend the British Commonwealth Prime Ministers' Conference in London, but he took the opportunity to visit Paris and then Germany, where he went to Berlin, Hanover, Cologne, Essen, Frankfurt and Dusseldorf, and met with refugees who had endured terrible suffering in the war. It was said that such sights 'pained and distressed him'.

Back in London on 12 December 1948, Fraser had tea with the King and Queen at Buckingham Palace. While they were doing this, Princess Elizabeth came to the door and asked Fraser if he'd like to see the baby. A few minutes later he and others gathered around the cot to admire Prince Charles, who was then just a month old. Fraser could well have been the first New Zealander to meet the prince.

The meeting was special for Fraser because in January 1946 he had been invested as a Companion of Honour by King George VI at Buckingham Palace.[26] This was one of many awards Fraser had received, but there was one more to come.

At 10.30am on Saturday 18 December 1948, Fraser left the plush Savoy Hotel in London, where he had been staying, and headed to the airfield at Northolt about 25 kilometres away.[27] He and his party, which included New Zealand High Commissioner Bill Jordan and two other staff, drove there to catch an Aer Lingus flight to Dublin. Northolt was normally an RAF base, but was used for civil flights while Heathrow airport was being built. They left at 11.45am and the approximately 450-kilometre flight on the DC-3 took a full two hours. The last time Fraser crossed the Irish Sea in 1941 he would not have seen much as the windows on the aircraft were effectively blacked out. This time, presuming the weather was reasonable, he would have had a superb view of the Irish coast and the green fields of Ireland, which later provided the inspiration for the famous song by Johnny Cash 'Forty Shades of Green'.

Peter Fraser's visit to Dublin had been signalled in the week preceding his arrival. All three leading newspapers – the *Irish Times*, *Irish Press* and *Irish Independent* – carried stories of his impending state visit and that he would be guest of President Seán T. O'Kelly and having discussions with Minister of External Affairs Seán MacBride, who acted as his official host during the three-day stay.

When he arrived at Dublin Airport Fraser told the *Irish Press* that he accepted the invitation to revisit Dublin to 'see how things were going'. He said he hoped to see Frank Aiken, and Éamon de Valera, 'an old friend whom I have known for 14 years'. He would also discuss the issue of trade between the two countries if it was raised, but declined to comment on the repeal of the External Relations Act which, with the passing of the Republic of Ireland Act 1948, finally and legally made Ireland a republic and cut all constitutional ties with Britain. Fraser was asked whether New Zealand was considering appointing a diplomatic representative to Ireland to which he replied, 'I cannot say at the moment, but I do not think so'.[28]

This was a state visit, and while his friend de Valera was no longer in power, the government of John A. Costello rolled out the red carpet for the New Zealand Prime Minister. Fraser was greeted at Dublin Airport by Seán MacBride and other officials and taken to the residence of the President of Ireland at Phoenix Park. O'Kelly was a long-time friend and associate of Éamon de Valera's, and had actively participated in the 1916 Rising for which he was jailed. He was a member of Fianna Fáil and something of a controversial character with little love for Britain. He had served in de Valera's cabinet until resigning in 1945 and was elected President of Ireland later that year.

A state dinner was held for Fraser that evening at Iveagh House, the headquarters of the Department of External Affairs. Iveagh House is at St Stephens Green and close to the historic Shelbourne Hotel. It is a beautiful building with an exquisite interior – especially the ballroom where the dinner was held. In his diary Fraser makes no mention about whether de Valera was present and there is no record of a guest list, but the dinner was hosted by Prime Minister Costello and included government ministers and perhaps members of the opposition, as well as other special guests. There would have been speeches and toasts, and a chance for Fraser to meet a wide cross section of Irish society, enjoying the company of the people of a country he loved.

Sunday 19 December was a more relaxed day for Fraser, and it appears that he and Bill Jordan took in some of the sights of the city between appointments. At 10am he met with Dr James Ryan, who had served in a variety of capacities in the de Valera governments – most notably as Minister for Agriculture – and then lunched with Seán MacBride. Finally he had afternoon tea with Senator James Douglas, who had chaired the committee that drafted the Irish Constitution after the War of Independence. The topics most associated with him during his work as senator were international refugees and the League of Nations – topics dear to Fraser's heart.

That evening O'Kelly hosted a dinner at Áras an Uachtaráin, the official presidential residence where both Fraser and Jordan were staying. It was once the vice-regal lodge where the British viceroys lived, but became the residence where Irish presidents have been based since the last governor-general was removed from office by de Valera. The residence is large, with 94 rooms, and somewhat resembles the White House in Washington DC. In his diary, Fraser made specific mention that his friend Éamon de Valera would be present at this function.

O'Kelly was one of 'Dev's men' so it's likely this function had more Fianna Fáil people present, and was in effect the unofficial state dinner for Fraser, with perhaps a little less formality than the official one.

On Monday 20 December there were official talks with MacBride, and undoubtedly top of the agenda would have been Ireland's pending departure from the British Commonwealth. MacBride would have been aware of the New Zealand Government's position as of November 1948 that said Irish citizens would not be treated as aliens and Ireland would not be treated as a foreign country – in other words, the status quo would prevail. The final departure of Ireland from the Commonwealth was a complex legal issue, much like Brexit is today. It was an issue that was to drift on over several years as Irish people living in New Zealand sought to clarify their rights and obligations, but in the end matters were resolved.

That day Fraser was the guest of honour at a luncheon at the Shelbourne, and he noted in his diary that the contact for the event was President of the Irish Labour Party, Mr Connor. The party was a major partner in coalition with Costello's Fine Gael and by its very name had an affinity with Fraser's own Labour party. William Norton, Tánaiste (or Deputy Prime Minister), presided over the luncheon, and the other guests there included the Lord Mayor of Dublin John Breen, the Labour ministers in the coalition, Labour TDs (members of parliament), Seán MacBride, and a member of Irish republican party Clann na Poblachta. All told there were about 14 people in attendance.

William Norton welcomed Peter Fraser, describing him as a 'brilliant ambassador who had blazed a trail which was bound to coerce governments everywhere to raise the standard of life of the plain people'. Norton was a former trade unionist in Dublin. In reply, Fraser said that he and his colleagues, many of whom traced their ancestors to Ireland, 'watched with interest and sympathy the developments that were taking place in Ireland'.

It would have been a fairly quick lunch because Fraser's next appointment was a ceremony conferring his honorary doctorate at 3pm at Iveagh House, about two kilometres away. Fraser carefully noted in his diary:

> 3pm: Ceremony of conferring Honorary Degree of Laws at National University of Ireland by Chancellor Mr de Valera at Iveagh House. Ceremony followed by afternoon tea.

According to reports in the local papers, the ceremony at Iveagh House was attended by a who's who of Irish politics: President Seán T. O'Kelly and his wife, Phyllis, along with Taoiseach John A. Costello, Tánaiste William Norton, External Affairs Minister Seán MacBride, Minister for Industry and Commerce Daniel Morrissey, Minister for Health Noel Browne, Lord Mayor of Dublin John Breen, Britain's Ambassador Lord Rugby, Canadian High Commissioner William Turgeon, President of Maynooth Rt Rev Monsignor Edward J. Kissane, and former Finance Minister Frank Aiken. There were also a number of other parliamentarians and officials present.[29]

Professor Michael Tierney, Senior Pro Vice-Chancellor and President of the University College of Dublin, presided over the ceremony and began the proceedings by saying that if they could not claim Mr Fraser as an Irishman, they could certainly honour him as a Gael. Professor Tierney outlined Fraser's political history and that he had been a member of parliament in New Zealand since 1918, was a founder of the New Zealand Labour Party and that he had 'won his way to his present eminence by sheer hard work starting at the bottom of the ladder'. He described Fraser as a man of 'high culture and real intellectual distinction with a serious interest in music and drama that was not acquired within the walls of a classroom or lecture hall, but in the harder school of the waterfront and the mill'.

Professor Tierney spoke of Fraser's presence on the international stage and his stance at the San Francisco Conference where he ensured that the 'rights of smaller nations were safeguarded'. Tierney noted that the 'glorious record of New Zealand in the war [WWII] will always be connected with Mr Fraser's name'. He also referred to Fraser's special relationship with the Māori people saying: 'There is no one else in public life in his country who has enjoyed the confidence and affection of the Māori people to such an extent as Mr Fraser and they have given proof of this by conferring on him the title – "Father of our people".'

Degree for New Zealand Premier

Mr. Fraser Honoured by U.C.D.

Mr. de Valera, Chancellor of the National University of Ireland, and the President of U.C.D., Mr. M. Tierney, look on as Mr. Peter Fraser, Prime Minister of New Zealand, signs the register after receiving the honorary degree of LL.D. at Iveagh House, Dublin, yesterday.

Peter Fraser receiving his Doctor of Laws at the National University of Ireland while Chancellor de Valera and Professor Michael Tierney look on.
Irish Independent, 21/12/48

Finally Tierney said:

> Mr Fraser is thus worthy by reason both of his personal qualities and action of the highest honour we can pay him. He deserves it further as the democratic leader of a great and gallant nation which we in Ireland have very special ties in kinship and common interest. Mr Fraser has already stressed himself that these ties are more real and intimate than any expression of them in changing constitutional forms. We Irish are proud to have had some share in the growth and development of a noble, generous and progressive people.

The newspapers reported that Éamon de Valera, as Chancellor of the National University of Ireland, conferred the doctorate on Fraser, and they published a photograph of the signing ceremony. No mention was made of other speeches, but I assume that Peter Fraser and other dignitaries spoke too. I have been unable to trace the actual citation for the degree, but what is clear from the newspaper reports is the high esteem in which Peter Fraser was held by politicians of all persuasions in Ireland. This hour-long ceremony was the last time Fraser and de Valera would meet. Both men had honoured each other with dignity and genuine affection. History had been made.

Shortly after the ceremony Fraser met briefly with former West Coaster 'Slim Byrne', his diary records, and then he was guest at a reception of the diplomatic corps in Dublin hosted by Seán MacBride. Bill Jordan would have been there, as would John Dulanty, Ireland's High Commissioner to Britain. Another cocktail party where Fraser would have been the centre of attention.

Later Fraser spoke on Ireland's national radio network, Raidió Teilifís Éireann (RTÉ), during which he talked about New Zealand's social services.[30] This was another first for Fraser and showed just how highly regarded he and New Zealand were in Ireland – he was invited to speak to the Irish nation at peak listening time, 6.45pm.

After his broadcast Fraser and Bill Jordan had a final dinner with President O'Kelly at Áras an Uachtaráin. Next day they drove to Belfast to meet with Premier of Northern Ireland Sir Basil Brooke, and Governor Earl Granville, before going to London, Scotland, and back to New Zealand via Canada.

When he arrived in London on Christmas Eve Fraser sent a telegram expressing his thanks to the Irish President and his wife: 'I greatly enjoyed my stay with you and it will be long remembered. I extend to you both and your household my sincere good wishes for a happy Christmas and a prosperous New Year.'[31] The visit to Ireland would have been one that Fraser enjoyed, especially having time with Éamon de Valera. Ireland was clearly impressed with him because immediately after he left, MacBride sent a cable to Walter Nash in Wellington saying:

> Peter Fraser has created a feeling of understanding and sympathy between the two countries even stronger and deeper than had ever existed before. In the course of his short stay, Peter Fraser met representatives of every section of our national life, on all of whom he created a deep and abiding impression.[32]

Peter Fraser was held in high esteem in Ireland and his death on 12 December 1950 was reported in the *Irish Press* the following day. It quoted messages of condolences sent by the Irish President, the Taoiseach and the Minister of External Affairs.

MacBride described Fraser 'as a man whose character and personality transcended the political arena and commanded the respect of all who knew him. Throughout his life he was a friend of the Irish people who valued his friendship. As one whom he counted as among his friends I feel a sense of loss at his death'.

Costello noted of Fraser that 'the passing of this great statesman who never ceased to show friendliness to Ireland fills with a sense of loss his many friends in this country.' Finally Seán T. O'Kelly said in a message to New Zealand's Governor-General Lord Freyberg:

> I wish to convey to you my profound personal sorrow and that of the people of Ireland on the death of Mr Peter Fraser. I deeply regret the passing of this great New Zealander whose statesmanlike achievements won him respect and friendship everywhere, and whose amiable qualities are warmly remembered in this country.[33]

Through friendship, mutual respect, understanding and tremendous political astuteness and nous, Peter Fraser and Éamon de Valera had forged an enduring relationship that continues to grow with the establishment of embassies in each other's countries in 2018. From their first meeting in Dublin in 1935, they created a powerful legacy between two small island nations.

17

Farewells

In May 1945 the war in Europe ended, and although the fighting still raged on in the Pacific, the Éire National Association realised that its time was coming to an end. It had been set up for a specific purpose – to oppose the conscription of Irishmen in New Zealand into the armed forces – and had succeeded in this goal. The Allies had beaten Germany, so the restrictions on the men in terms of manpower were soon to be lifted. The Irishmen had won their battle with Britain, and they had helped lay the foundations for positive long-term relations between Ireland and New Zealand.

In July 1945 the ENA published a final report on its activities and finances,[1] although there is no conclusive evidence to show it immediately went out of existence. The association continued to work in an informal manner to ensure that the agreement they had struck with government was upheld, and Maurice Aylward kept up a dialogue with Fraser and other government ministers.

The ENA report, signed by Maurice Aylward as secretary and Thomas Cahill as treasurer, was sent to all members and included some overall commentary on the activities of the ENA since it was formed in 1940. As the organisation would be disbanded, they believed that all members needed to know how their money had been spent. They also noted that some members 'failed in their duty to the association' by not paying their dues and that this put pressure on others to pay more. It is a 'name and shame' document as it shows exactly who paid what, although presumably any members who signed up later in the war would have been liable to pay less overall.

Just over £800 was paid out in professional fees, with most of this likely to have been to Fred Ongley and other lawyers. The biggest single expense was £1130 to Maurice Aylward 'for wages from 4.6.41 to 1.4.45', which shows that he was paid about £280 per year or just over £5 per week. This suggests that in the period leading up to the trial and until he returned from Ireland, he was working close to full-time for the association. He supposedly was manpowered during some of this time and it's apparent that the ENA paid him for the work he did at the weekends and after shifts. This would have been reasonable as there was a lot to do as secretary and the association needed someone to sign up members, write newsletters and brief lawyers, ministers and officials. Aylward was the brains behind the ENA and was rewarded for that. The other large ticket item was travel at £471. I assume much of this would have been done by Aylward, but possibly also by Ongley and others – such as Michael Lafferty who was based in Auckland but came to meetings in Wellington. Board and lodgings of £236 were accounted for in this way. In the final report, Aylward and Cahill also noted that some of their members had died and others had lost relatives back in Ireland, and money was spent on headstones and tributes.

The accounts also reveal that the subscriptions varied from year to year, presumably because of the need to expand ENA activities. Instalments were set at £3 in the first year and brought in £461. The following year the instalment was £5 and revenue was £715. The next instalment was also set at £5 but revenue rose to £857, and then it reached its peak in the fourth payment that was set at 'between £10 and £5', bringing in £1101. Quite why this is so is not set out in the documents. In the final year the subscription was reduced to £4. There were also donations from the Irish National Club and some special collections. Over the four years the ENA collected a total of £3755.10.03. There is evidence that the Irish National Club gave the ENA a loan of £50 to help set up the organisation. In the accounts there is money going out to repay the loan.

What this report demonstrates is that the ENA was a professionally run organisation, not only in what it achieved for its members in persuading the government to allow them to stay in New Zealand, but also in terms of their governance, finances and general accountability. That must have counted in their favour in discussions with the government.

The report also pointed to the difficult times that members had gone through, acknowledging the problems they had to solve, and that dealing with this 'called for the best that was in each and every one of us'. The sympathy of the New Zealand Government was mentioned as a key factor in achieving their success ... 'an achievement which is unparalleled in the history of Irishmen outside their native land'. Aylward and Cahill then went on to say:

> As a result of the Association's policy in relationship to citizenship we have brought our country a long way nearer to its final goal – recognition in the Southern Hemisphere and throughout the world as a free independent sovereign state.

The final paragraph is vintage Aylward. It is poetic, political, warrior-like – the words of a true and lifelong republican patriot:

> In conclusion, by our efforts here we have helped the cause, marching in step with that little green isle and our folk across the ocean. Let us each

try to hold fast to the fruits of our country's endeavours and our efforts here in New Zealand. For that reason we should resolve to carry out all our undertakings and do our duty in accordance with the wishes and in the interest of our native land. Be true to one another and continue to keep warm and living, love and fidelity to the great nation of Ireland.

Finally, he wrote again about his meeting with Taoiseach de Valera who he said 'was very impressed with the legislation that the New Zealand Government had enacted', and concluded on the positive note that 'Ireland is on the move and reborn with new life and vigour to face the future'.

These were the prophetic last words written by Aylward in his role for the ENA, a man who could be called 'Mr Éire National Association'.

Aylward's passion for promoting Ireland never ceased. He often wrote letters to newspapers extolling the progress and virtues of his native land. One of these, dated 7 August 1945 and titled 'Achievements in Éire', is extensive and lists in detail Éire's political and economic achievements, including removing the oath of allegiance, providing farmers with a guaranteed milk price and establishing 900 new factories. He also touched on social reconstruction – the building of 150,000 new houses, and new laws (including the Factories Act) – and went on to talk about the mark the war had left on Ireland with 'thousands of young men losing their lives on foreign battlefields'.[2]

Though active in the ENA, most of the men had maintained their links with Irish Societies. Paddy Feeney was president of the society from 1940 until 1943. Likewise Tom Cahill was treasurer in those years. Maurice Aylward served on the committee and executive during the war years and was elected president in 1946–47, and then disappears from the records, which sadly end in 1949. My father, Matt Burke, served one term on the committee in 1939–40 and does not appear again in Irish club records. I know that he and others were still involved for many years because as a young boy I was taken to the annual feis.

So what happened to the Sons of Éire and their associates? I have selected a few whom I knew, or knew of, to trace what they did later in life. Most just seemed to melt away into relative obscurity and rarely, it appears, talked much about their experiences.

Paddy Sullivan never married and ended up in the town of Ōtaki, about 70 kilometres north of Wellington. He owned a small block of land just out of town on which he grew vegetables and also worked in various local jobs. Friends say he used to go to the Irish club every Saturday and was a keen reader. He died on 28 July 1989. His Requiem Mass was held at Ōtaki's historic Pukekaraka St Mary's Church, and he was buried at

the Ōtaki Cemetery. With the help of a local funeral director I finally tracked down his grave, and much to my sorrow found it was unmarked. I had a small plaque made and installed on the grave site which acknowledges him as 'A True Son of Éire'. Paddy still has cousins in Moycullen.

John Clancy was also from Moycullen and a great family friend who boarded with my grand-aunts at 11 Guildford Terrace in Wellington. He had a sleep-out at the back of what is still an elegant house. His accommodation was far from flash and by today's standards would probably have been condemned. John never married, although I think he had eyes for Mum's sister, Peg, but any overtures from him were rejected. He devoted his life to the Catholic Church and, in particular, the Basilica of the Sacred Heart next door, where he took up Sunday collections and helped the clergy in a multitude of ways. He once featured in a local newspaper collecting for the Sisters of Compassion.[3] The article talked about his Irish background and how he went home to Ireland once, but was back in time for the Home of Compassion collection. He was a lovely, kind man who died on 27 August 1989, aged 81, and is buried at the Makara Cemetery. John still has relatives in Moycullen.

Top: Paddy Sullivan in Ōtaki.
Courtesy of Anne Richardson

Left: Kevin Richardson of Moycullen, at the grave of his grand-uncle, Paddy Sullivan, Ōtaki Cemetery New Zealand, 28 July 2018 – the anniversary of Paddy's death.

The challenge has been tracing all the members of the executive of the ENA, not to mention all the Citizens of Éire. Quite by chance at a conference on the meat industry I was chatting to Bernie Gardiner, who noticed the Irish flag badge I was wearing. It turned out his grandfather was Joseph (Joe) Nally, from Galway and a member of the executive. Bernie was able to give me details of his grandfather's life:

Joseph Nally (Popa Joe to his grandchildren) left his home in Ower, Headford, in County Galway, when he was 18 and arrived in Invercargill, New Zealand in 1939. His older brother, John, had arrived in New Zealand a year earlier, and sent money home to fund Joe's passage. Joe and John were the sons of Peter and Catherine Nally. They had two other brothers and three sisters.

Eventually Joe moved to Wellington and married Hanna (Joan) Myers, also the daughter of Irish parents.

Joan and Joe Nally.
Courtesy of the Nally family

The couple had six children with five surviving to adulthood – Kieran, Mary, Margaret, Rosaleen and Brian. During his early years in New Zealand Joe worked as a bricklayer and carpenter. After contracting polio he changed occupations to become a taxi driver.

The retention of the Irish culture was a strong feature of the family, with Joan and the children becoming involved in Irish dancing to a high level. Weddings and wakes were full of Irish song and dance.

Popa Joe never spoke of any historic grievances back home, nor did he speak of the deportation risk he and his brother had faced.

He was a quiet, gentle and kind man. So much so that his involvement with the Sons of Éire and the impact they had was a surprise to his family once it was discovered. I would imagine that while he remained silent on the issue, he was also proud of his involvement and that the stance he took helped to obtain a positive outcome for a large number of Irish New Zealanders. Popa Joe never returned home, and I now wonder whether the past threat of deportation played a factor in this.[4]

Fred Ongley, predictably, went on to greater things. He was appointed a judge of the Compensation Court in 1945, and was Chair of the Waterfront Industry Commission and a judge of the Land Sales Court dealing with land sales for returning soldiers. He died on 28 June 1969, aged 90. At a memorial service in Wellington, C.H. Arndt, one of the former partners in his law firm, described Fred as 'a man of outstanding intellect, forceful character, and an unusual kindness of heart'.[5]

Columban priest Fr McGlynn went back and forth between Australia and New Zealand over the years, but there was one memorable occasion when he was nearly a victim of one of this country's most deadly maritime disasters, the sinking of the interisland ferry *Wahine* on 10 April 1968, which claimed 51 lives. His story is told by journalists Max Lambert and Jim Hartley in their book *The Wahine Disaster*. Fr McGlynn, who was 69, was a friend of the captain on that fateful voyage. In the early part of the journey he spent time with Captain Robertson on the bridge and later had supper with him. Fr McGlynn had been in Christchurch the previous day visiting priests and nuns and was returning to Wellington. By the time the *Wahine* was about to enter the harbour one of the fiercest storms on record was pounding Wellington and, despite the efforts of the captain and crew, the ferry was pushed onto Barrett Reef. Fr McGlynn was saying his daily prayers when the ship hit the rocks and was pitched to the other side of his cabin.

The ship was holed and as the day wore on it began to fill with water. Fr McGlynn said many rosaries but to no avail, so when the order to abandon ship was given, he and others sought refuge in the lifeboats. Further misfortune followed when Fr McGlynn's lifeboat sank and he was left floating in the cold and windy harbour. With his mouth shut he kept praying, and these were answered when someone from a rescue tugboat threw him a line and the exhausted Columban priest managed to summon enough energy to hold on and be hauled aboard. 'I got a fit of shivers, but after a while my body seemed to generate a certain amount of heat and then all was well.'[6]

Fr McGlynn was taken back to land and on to the Wellington Railway Station, where he was given a cup of tea. He then ambled out to the public area to see if anyone was looking for him. No one was, so he took a taxi back to St Columban's at Lower Hutt. 'I could have said Mass, but the long gospel for that day made me a bit doubtful about myself,' he said.[7]

This amazing Irish priest had survived a terrible tragedy. As it turned out I was working for the New Zealand Broadcasting Company at the time, and shot some film of the storm, helping edit it for the news that night.

Fr McGlynn eventually returned to Ireland to live out his remaining years, and died at Dalgan Park, County Meath, Ireland, on 12 January 1988, where he is buried.

In 2017 I travelled to Dalgan Park and saw Fr McGlynn's simple grave. My family's long involvement with the Columbans, and in particular Fr McGlynn, meant this visit ranked for me along with arriving in Ireland for

Fr Neil Collins beside Fr McGlynn's grave at Dalgan Park Ireland.

the first time in 1978. It was an emotional morning being guided around the headquarters of the society by Fr Neil Collins, who knew Fr McGlynn when he was in the retirement home at Dalgan Park. He invited me for lunch and then to walk around the buildings where my godfather had lived, which was really special. I must admit to shedding a few tears that day. Fr Collins told me this story:

> The first day I met him was during a snow storm and we were actually snowed in here at Dalgan and our receptionist couldn't get to work. Some of us priests were trained to be telephonists and to run the front office. Fr Jim was down in the retirement home and each morning he would appear with four or five letters for people 'down under'. He'd look for incoming mail and I had to explain that as we were snowed in the postman couldn't come. But the next morning he appeared with five more letters and this went on for several days until the snow thawed.[8]

Fr Collins is a fine historian and his book on the Columbans, *The Splendid Cause*, makes excellent reading.

Peter Fraser and Éamon de Valera continued to correspond after their meeting in 1948, but for Fraser time was running out in all ways. His health was failing generally and his eyesight was so bad he could not read reports.

Fraser and the First Labour Government eventually fell victim to post-war desire for change, and in December 1949 Labour was defeated by National at the polls. Fraser continued on in opposition, but on 12 December 1950 he died at the age of just 66. Eighteen thousand kilometres away, his friend Éamon de Valera remained part of the political landscape for many years. He was re-elected Taoiseach in March 1951, which he held for three years, then lost the next election. He regained the position in 1957. In June 1959 he

Fraser's funeral procession though Willis Street, Wellington.
Alexander Turnbull Library, 114/239/05-G

resigned and became the third president of Ireland, a position he held until he retired in 1973. He died in Dublin on 29 August 1975, at the age of 92.

Peter Fraser and Éamon de Valera, two of the world's great leaders, visionaries and humanitarians, left indelible legacies and changed their small islands forever. The price may have been high by some people's standards, but the outcome was an outstanding achievement. As in the words of a memoriam reflection: 'Grieve not that they have gone, but celebrate that they were.'

Maurice Aylward never lost his zest for life but, like a lot of his ENA colleagues, he resumed a simple and peaceful life. After the war he never went back to Ireland, but in 1967 he went to Melbourne, Australia, to visit his older brother William with whom he had stayed before moving to New Zealand in 1939. Not long after the ENA was disbanded, Maurice moved north to Taranaki where there was a large Irish population. He settled into rural life, doing a variety of jobs around Ōpunake and never married. He worked as a fencer and was especially friendly with Tom Hogan, whose daughter-in-law

Josie has many fond memories of Maurice from when he came to live with their family in the early 1950s.

Josie's father was Paddy Foskin, who came to New Zealand from Kilkenny in 1927. She says her father said little about the Troubles in Ireland, but was very proud that de Valera slept at his family's house in Riverquarter one night, and that his older brother rowed Dev across the River Suir into County Waterford in the early hours of the morning. Josie recalls:

> After leaving Wellington, Maurice lived with my father and I for several years. He was MC at my wedding to John Hogan in 1956. John came from Nicholastown, Mooncoin in 1949. John's parents also came to New Zealand and when his father got sick and could not work, Maurice was able to get him a sickness benefit through his Labour Party connections, and in particular the MP Mabel Howard. When he came to Taranaki Maurice worked on the Bracken farm [John's sister and brother-in-law]. He also worked at a dairy factory at Kāpuni. When Maurice's farming days were over he lived in a small cottage at the back of our house and built fences for local farmers.
>
> The Wellington Irish crowd would come up and they used to have all-night parties. Maurice was the leader of the sing-along and a great man for using words I had never heard of. He was also a foundation member of the Taranaki Irish Society in 1967.
>
> I remember Maurice as a great ladies' man. He had a girlfriend called Ruth, who came down from Auckland. He liked to put on a big show and was the life and soul of any party even though he wasn't very well off.[9]

Kevin Bracken's family was another household where Maurice visited and worked as a fencer on the farm. He recalls that Maurice, along with eight other people in Ōpunake, formed a club where they would meet to solve the problems of the world, drink, and eat oysters, cheese and pickled onions. He says Maurice lived life to the full, but died almost penniless.

Maurice's life was cut short when he contracted cancer. His sister Kathleen, Sr Frances Clare, came to New Zealand on a Churchill Fellowship in July 1969 and spent time with Maurice. She was headmistress of St Joseph's Residential School at Severn Stoke, Worcestershire in England, and was in New Zealand to study techniques for teaching those with mental disabilities. Her fellowship also included visits to the United States and Australia, and she was accompanied on the trip by her deputy, Sister Ursula.[10]

Sister Clare's meeting with Maurice that July was the first time they had seen each other since 1944, when Maurice went to Ireland on his mission to meet Éamon de Valera. She told the local media that she tried to persuade Maurice to return home with her, but he loved New Zealand so much and

Maurice Aylward with his aunt Sr Clare Raftis, taken during his visit to Ireland and the UK.
Aylward collection

wanted to stay. 'He is still very much an Irishman, but he thinks there is no country in the world like New Zealand,' she said.[11]

Sr Clare stayed on for as long as she could to help nurse him, but in the end she had to return to England. Maurice obviously loved his sister and started to write her one last letter in December, probably knowing his days were numbered. Sadly he died before he managed to finish it, but that letter, along with Maurice's papers, found their way back to Fr Eamon Aylward, his nephew, who is the Aylward family historian and thankfully they are preserved today. These papers have been a rich source of information for this book.

Maurice Aylward died on 6 December 1969, at the age of 60, and is buried in the Ōpunake Cemetery.

My parents, Matt and Mary Burke, lived with my grandparents in a rented house in the Wellington suburb of Khandallah before they bought a gorse-covered section in Tawa Flat in 1949. With the help of his Irish mates and others, Dad cleared the section and then took six months off work to help a professional carpenter build a house. He was the typical hard-working Irishman, who built a solid home with lots of concrete walls to deal with the sloping section. But this hard physical work took a toll on his weak heart and soon after the house was built he had to take clerical work, which did not suit him and left him frustrated. Dad also suffered from epilepsy that added to his woes.

Dad made one trip back to Ireland in 1957. On the way he saw his brother Tom in Boston and then stayed with his twin brother, Malachy, in Galway. Departure records show that he left Auckland on 24 April on Canadian Pacific Flight 302. In those days the jet age was not quite here and there were frequent stops along the way. By all accounts the flight was via Fiji, Canton Island, Honolulu, Los Angeles, New York and Boston and then to Shannon. Dad was a great letter writer and it wasn't until the last few years that I have re-read the letters he sent to Mum and me while he was away. They were newsy, kind, caring and loving. His first letter to me was written at Auckland Airport just before his departure and asked me to 'look after Mum'. Then followed letters from Los Angeles and New York, the latter saying he flew in a jet from LA to the Big Apple. He talked about the marvellous reception he got when he arrived in Boston, where he met his brother Tom. This was followed by numerous letters from Ireland, with one describing a trip to Thurles in Tipperary for the opening of a school that Malachy's firm had built. He also talked about watching hurling being played and how much he enjoyed this. I must have sent him letters too because he says he enjoyed hearing from me. What is impressive about his letters is that they are beautifully

Matt Burke (third from left) and brother Malachy (far right) at the presentation of a golf trophy in Galway 1957. Malachy was a golf champion and died at his beloved Galway Bay Golf Course on 15 August 1980.

Malachy Burke, nephew Frankie Burke (son of Tom who emigrated to Boston) and Matt Burke – Ireland, 1957.

written, spelt perfectly and interesting. He wrote about every three weeks.

His visit was not confined to Galway – I have a copy of his diary that records the names and addresses of Maurice Aylward's brothers, including Ned in Dublin, who is Fr Eamon Aylward's father.

Most of my cousins in Ireland were young when Dad visited and only have fleeting memories of him. Geraldine O'Sullivan, Malachy's eldest daughter, was seven and she remembers him at Threadneedle Road in Salthill, Galway, where they lived and says there was huge excitement upon his arrival. She says he bought presents for her mother and father, but she also remembers him collapsing in an epileptic fit, which was disturbing. Her father was an extremely successful and wealthy businessman, and this must have been hard for Dad whose income was modest, to say the least. Malachy was a keen golfer and part of the elite set in the city.

Dad also visited his sister Maria and her husband, Lal O'Connor, who owned a small farm in the townland of Corcullen, about ten kilometres from Galway. Their cottage was small and, almost unbelievably, didn't have electricity connected until the early 1960s. Cousin Tommy recalls the visit and says that Matt bought a bicycle for him so he could cycle to secondary school in Galway. His memory of Dad was that he was a refined and gentle man. It was wonderful that he went home and saw his family. It was just a pity that his parents had died many years earlier.

While Dad was away my mother took it upon it herself to renovate the house, and I am not sure that was a totally popular decision. Dad arrived home at the end of September 1957, at which stage his health was in a state of decline. My memories are of a man who loved to work hard, but was frustrated by the afflictions of a bad heart and epilepsy. He was off work for months at a time and in hospital for long periods. He died in hospital on 21 October 1962 at the age of 53. My schoolmates from St Patrick's College formed a guard of honour at the Basilica where his Requiem Mass was held, while his Irish friends formed a guard of honour at his graveside at Wellington's Karori cemetery. A week later, my maternal grandfather, Jack Warren, died suddenly and so we had another funeral.

Mum never remarried and focused her attention on her shop, which she ran in partnership with her sister, Peg. The pair developed a love of horse racing, which my mother never lost. She died in February 2005 at the

Courtenay Place, c.1950, where my mother had her shop, two doors right from the corner.

tremendous age of 96. She was an amazing woman who worked in the shop until she was 80 years old. Her life in Courtenay Place could make another book!

My first pilgrimage to Ireland came quite by chance in 1978. I was working as the agricultural correspondent for New Zealand television and out of the blue I was offered a six-week trip to Europe courtesy of the New Zealand Meat Producers Board. It was at the time when the country was facing difficulty with the European Economic Community (EEC) over access for butter and lamb, so the Wool Board and the Meat Board decided to sponsor a journalist each and let them research the issues New Zealand was facing. I persuaded TV One to fund an additional side trip to Ireland so that I could produce a series of stories in that country, as well as Britain, France, Germany, Holland and Belgium.

I will never forget boarding the Aer Lingus aircraft at Heathrow – I was very excited. As I looked out the window when we crossed the Irish coast I felt a welling up inside me that is hard describe. The thought that in a few moments I would be meeting my Irish relatives for the first time almost reduced me to tears. But it got worse. When I walked out from Customs at Dublin Airport I instantly recognised my Uncle Malachy, Dad's identical twin brother, and cousins whom I had read so much about but never seen. Seeing Malachy was surreal. He looked like my old man (although he was more portly than Dad) and he talked just like him. We hugged each other, and I hugged the others. Also there to meet me was another fantastic man, Joe Murray of RTÉ, who had kindly agreed to loan me a camera crew for two days to film my stories. We all retired to a nearby pub and I had my first taste of Irish Guinness and Paddy's Whiskey, and then a meal before heading into Dublin, where somehow I managed to get myself booked into the Shelbourne Hotel.

After two days of filming, which ended at a sheep mart near Galway, I had about five days with my Irish clan, staying at Malachy's house at Salthill, where Dad had stayed. Malachy rushed me around to meet everyone. I was over the moon and in love with Ireland. I went out to Ballydotia, where Dad was born, and met his brother John aka 'Cheeser' – a real character – and his family.

It was a cultural and family immersion that I could never have dreamed of, and which laid the foundation for more than a dozen other visits since then. My Irish family welcomed me like the prodigal son and I felt embarrassed by their kindness and generosity. I suspect it helped that I could drink a bit, swear, and sing the odd Irish song. Malachy took me fishing on the Corrib,

The son of a Son of Éire returns. Fishing with Uncle Malachy on the Corrib, May 1978, on my first visit to Ireland.

fulfilling a wish of my father's in a letter he sent to me on 3 June 1957, in which he wrote: 'Peter, save up and when you are a young man you must come and do some fishing in Galway. The trout here are just beautiful.'

My trip was really made possible by my mother, who after Dad died continued to correspond with his family and in particular two of my cousins, Geraldine and Marion. But for Mum's diligence and the response from Geraldine and Marion, this trip and others would probably never have taken place.

When I finally left I was crying even on the plane which was taking me to my Bohan cousins, relatives of Dad's mother, in Boston.

The trip to Ireland was life changing. I had finally found my roots. The son of a Son of Éire had come home and found himself.

Te tōrino haere whakamua, whakamuri.

At the same time as the spiral is going forward, it is returning.[12]

Appendix of source material

The appeal board's response to Mick Carr, 6 August 1941.
Courtesy of the Carr family

OUTWARD TELEGRAM.

FROM
2.   The Prime Minister, Wellington.
TO
      The Secretary of State for Dominion Affairs.
DATED   TIME OF DESPATCH
      18th July, 1942.   8.30 p.m.

No. 292.   Your telegram No. 150 of 24th February.
His Majesty's Government in New Zealand have recently been reconsidering
the position of those citizens of Eire resident in New Zealand who have
refused military obligations.   In view of the probability on the one hand
that the shipping space that would be occupied by these people could be
better utilised and on the other hand that the shortage of manpower in
New Zealand affords a strong reason why the services of these people
might well be utilized here in civil employment either at ordinary
award rates or on soldiers' rates, the New Zealand Government are inclined
to feel that there is on the whole little to be gained by repatriation.
Before coming to any final decision on the matter, however, they would
be glad to be advised whether the exemption of these men from military
training and their utilization as proposed above would in any way
embarrass His Majesty's Government in the United Kingdom.

                              (Signed) PRIME MINISTER.

INTERNAL AFFAIRS
HON. MIN. OF INTERNAL AFFAIRS
ARMY
HON. MIN. OF DEFENCE
NATIONAL SERVICE
O.H.S.   For your information   C.A.Berendsen Perm. Head P.M's Dept
                                    19/7/42

A copy of the cable from Prime Minister Peter Fraser asking the
UK Secretary of State for Dominion Affairs (Clement Attlee) for
permission to allow the Citizens of Éire to remain in New Zealand.
Archives New Zealand ACGO 8333, IA1W2271/5, 15/7/301.

INWARD TELEGRAM. REC'D

13 AUG 1942

0. FROM ___ The Secretary of State for Dominion Affairs

TO ___ The Prime Minister, Wellington

DATED ___ 11th August, 1942 — DATE AND TIME OF RECEIPT ___ 12th August, 1942 7:30a.m.

SECRET "T"

No. 586 Your telegram No. 312 of 7th August.
His Majesty's Government in the United Kingdom are most grateful to His Majesty's Government in New Zealand for opportunity of considering possible repercussions of proposals in N.Z. telegram No. 292 of 18th July as to policy as regards treatment of Eire citizens here. In view of differing circumstances here and in N.Z. as explained in latter telegram, United Kingdom have come to conclusion that course of action proposed in New Zealand would not embarrass them.

(Signed) SECRETARY OF STATE FOR DOMINION AFFAIRS.

The U.S. of Internal Affairs.
Referred.

INTERNAL AFFAIRS
HON. MINISTER INTERNAL AFFAIRS
NATIONAL SERVICE DEPT
ARMY
HON. MINISTER DEFENCE
O.N.S.

12.8.42.

FOR INFORMATION.C.A. BERENDSEN PERMANENT HEAD P.M.'S DEPT.
12/8/42

Clement Attlee's response.
Archives New Zealand ACGO 8333, IA1W2271/5, 15/7/301

227

Telegrams: "MAN-POWER."
Telephone: 54-500.

IF ANY FURTHER CORRESPONDENCE
PLEASE QUOTE 13/3/26

NATIONAL SERVICE DEPARTMENT,
HOPE GIBBONS BUILDINGS,
PRIVATE BAG,
WELLINGTON, C.1.

16th January, 1942.

CONFIDENTIAL.

MEMORANDUM for:

    The Under-Secretary,
    Department of Internal Affairs,
    WELLINGTON.

Permits to leave New Zealand – Citizens of Eire.

    I forward herewith one hundred and fifty-five applications for permits to leave New Zealand on behalf of the undermentioned citizens of Eire. These applications have all been perused and permits may now be issued under the terms and conditions which are already known to you.

    In order that we may be enabled to keep a check on each man's departure, I should be pleased if you would let me have a separate notification of each permit which is issued.

Regn. No.	Name	Regn. No.	Name
286623	Allen, Jeremiah	154603	Egan, Patrick
236837	Aylward, Maurice Leo		
052847	Aylward, Walter	428646	Fahey, John Joseph
		429976	Fahey, John
397829	Boyle, Michael	264791	Fahey, James
253151	Boyle, Patrick	489315	Feeney, Patrick
435191	Boyle, Thomas	420531	Finn, Jim
299703	Brosnan, Denis	163293	Fitzsimons, James
422518	Brosnan, Jeremiah (Labourer)	568491	Fitzhenry, Francis
375700	Brosnan, Jeremiah (Porter)	234401	Flahive, Patrick
293862	Brosnan, John	229647	Fleming, John
255455	Brosnan, Martin	432624	Flynn, Michael
376301	Burke, Matthias	299002	Forde, Stephen
454640	Brosnan, Silvester	152219	Foskin, Michael Joseph
		232773	Fox, Thomas
141558	Cahill, Thomas Ignatius		
613670	Carr, Patrick	Over Age	Garvey, James Martin
281907	Carr, Tim	373453	Giles, Charles Vincent
257053	Carr, Michael	247177	Giles, Robert
293861	Casey, Kerry	286384	Goaly, John
409049	Cloherty, Patrick	264728	Grealish, Thomas
236829	Cloonan, Martin	556662	Greally, Darby
270475	Clancy, John	423618	Grogan, John
295591	Collins, Conor	423619	Grogan, Patrick
423314	Coleman, William		
262878	Connolly, Peter	243502	Halligan, Nicholas
306131	Coughlan, Patrick	158885	Hallissey, Michael Joseph
407472	Conway, Hubert	252329	Hackett, Timothy
269205	Connell, Michael	409281	Hannon, Patrick Joseph
408649	Connor, Martin	429020	Heffernan, Owen
253626	Crowley, Daniel	419348	Heffernan, Peter
291937	Crowley, Thomas	089045	Hickey, Patrick
253435	Cullinane, John	293884	Horgan, Denis
383310	Culloty, Daniel	235453	Horan, Con
		431806	Hyland, Thomas
419905	Dirrane, Darra		
272728	Doody, Michael A.	453883	Kearney, Anthony
281810	Duffy, James McFadden	284799	Kelly, Frank
431129	Dunleavy, William	285610	Kelliher, Dennis
145418	Dunne, Richard Joseph	295453	Kerr, James
		259123	Kennedy, Dermot Anthony
		281826	Kennedy, Brian
		Over Age	Kirwan, Percy

Regn. No.	Name.		Regn. No.	Name.
424865	Lally, Thomas		433993	Reidy, William
434586	Lawlee, John Joseph		423931	Riordan, Jeremiah
270146	Lynch, Patrick Joseph		390003	Robinson, John Francis
428334	Loughrey, Joseph		585515	Robinson, Joseph Christopher
277981	Luby, Michael John		427354	Roche, Francis Denis
600035	Lyons, Michael Peter			
			301075	Scannell, Thomas
295857	Mannion, Michael		404096	Scully, Thomas
Not Regd.	Mahony, William		613235	Shanahan, Jeremiah
299004	Maloney, John		145408	Sheehan, John
434378	Mahoney, Edward		257050	Sheridan, Michael
265363	Meehan, Thomas		293413	Sugrue, James Brendan
257023	Melvin, Peter Joseph		235375	Sullivan, Patrick
438100	Molloy, William James			
262892	Mongan, Michael		424768	Tangney, Timothy
314262	Molloy, Michael		410435	Traynor, Sean
415901	Moore, Michael Joseph		422856	Trainor, Hugh
259106	Moriarty, John		611708	Tonrey, Martin
241230	Moriarty, John Joseph			
411013	Moriarty, John James		228974	Walsh, Edward (B. Co. Clare)
406541	Moriarty, Michael		Over Age	Walsh, Edward
415129	Murphy, Patrick James		239492	Walsh, John
314653	Murphy, Edward		264725	Walsh, Michael
143395	Murray, Neil		243042	Walsh, Thomas
			421353	Whooley, Dan
247411	McCarthy, Tim		278585	Whooley, Denis
263316	McCarthy, Thomas Anthony		432272	Whooley, Patrick Joseph
283379	McCullagh, James Francis		375757	Whooley, Michael
604724	McCoy, William Gerald		426122	Wyles, Charles
287841	McDonnell, James Thomas			
232384	McGill, James			
433314	McKenna, John			
284307	McNamara, Joseph			
206187	McPeake, Harry			
279186	McPeake, Charles			
417534	McSweeney, Edmond			
241173	Nally, Joseph			
409284	Nally, John Joseph			
425466	Nee, Peter			
412768	O'Connell, John Joseph			
422262	O'Connell, Laurence			
298837	O'Connell, David			
425134	O'Connor, Denis			
374447	O'Connor, Michael (B.Killarney)			
409844	O'Connor, Michael			
433315	O'Connor, George			
427450	O'Connor, Michael (B. Tralee)			
217267	O'Donnell, Hugh			
454516	O'Donnell, Thomas			
608096	O'Driscoll, James			
432638	O'Shea, John James			
439663	O'Sullivan, Patrick			
293805	O'Sullivan, Patrick Joseph			
285899	Power, Richard			
425376	Purdue, Peter			

The list of 155 Irishmen to be deported from
New Zealand in 1942, showing each individual's
national service number with their name.
Archives New Zealand, ACGO 8333, IA1W2271/5, 15/7/301

J. S. Hunter
Director.

EIRE NATIONAL ASSOCIATION
WELLINGTON.

JULY, 1945

MEMBERS OF EXECUTIVE & COMMITTEE, 1940-1945.

President:	.. ..	P. Feeney, Esq.
Vice-President:	..	E. Walsh, Snr.
Secretary-Delegate:		M. L. Aylward.
Hon. Secretary:	..	M. J. Lafferty.
Hon. Treasurer:	..	T. I. Cahill.
Committee:	.. ..	Messrs. M. Burke, C. Horan, J. Clancy, J. Nally,
		P. Hickey, D. Roche, T. McCarthy.
Legal Adviser:	..	F. W. Ongley, Esq.

FOREWORD.

Fellow Members and Supporters,

Please find attached herewith a complete statement of receipts and payments, together with the amount each member and friend contributed since the formation of the Association over four years ago.

The Executive feel at this stage that as the Association contemplates disbanding in its present form, members should be presented with a complete copy relating to income and expenditure so that you will have first-hand knowledge as to how all finances collected have been disposed of.

You will see from the list of subscribers the very large number of members who failed in their duty to the Association, thereby placing a double burden on their fellow members by the increase in membership fees - to the latter much thanks are due who by their loyalty and generosity gave freely of their support - both moral and financial, a matter that is greatly appreciated by both the Executive and Committee and by all concerned.

OBITUARY:

During the period 1940-1945 a number of members were bereaved of relatives mostly in Eire. To all of these we extend again our sympathy in the loss they have sustained.

The Association suffered a great loss in the death of four of its most active and loyal members - J. Farrell, M. Moore, M. Cloonan and T. Boyle. Letters of condolence have been despatched to their respective relatives in Eire and New Zealand. They were true and loyal sons of Eire. They have left us but their memory lives on. May their souls rest in Peace.

Association members have experienced a very trying time in the past four years. The many difficulties we had to face and the problems to solve were, no doubt, brought about by the outbreak of war in Europe and at a later date in the Pacific. The situation called for the best that was in each and every one of us and we are happy to say that the majority of Irishmen responded nobly and well.

Let us thank a kind providence without which we could never succeed, together with a sympathetic Government, not forgetting our own individual efforts, for the success we have achieved, an achievement which is unparalleled in the history of Irishmen outside of their native land. As a result of the Association's policy in relation to citizenship we have brought our country a long way nearer to its final goal - recognition in the Southern Hemisphere and throughout the world as a free Independent Sovereign State.

We feel grateful also for the success our people have had in Eire during the greatest crisis in its long history and for the wise and prudent leadership of the "Taoiseach", Mr. De Valera, which resulted in our kith and kin at home being saved from the misery and suffering brought about by modern warfare.

2.

In conclusion, by our efforts here we have helped the cause, marching in step with that little green isle and our folk across the ocean. Let us each try to hold fast to the fruits of our country's endeavours and our own efforts here in New Zealand. For that reason we should resolve to carry out all our undertakings and do our duty in accordance with the wishes and in the interest of our native land. Be true to one another and continue to keep warm and living, love and fidelity to the great nation of Ireland.

For and on behalf of the Executive and Committee,

M. L. AYLWARD,   Secretary-Delegate.

T. I. Cahill,   Hon. Treasurer.

Final report to Éire National Association members, July 1945.
Courtesy of Colleen O'Donovan

Name		£	s.	d.
Allen,	J.	27	-	-
Aylward,	M.	27	-	-
Aylward,	M.	23	-	-
Barrett,	J.	5	-	-
Boland,	V.	8	-	-
Bourke,	G.	5	-	-
Bourke,	J.	1	-	-
Boyle,	M.	23	-	-
Boyle,	P.	23	-	-
Boyle,	P.	1	-	-
Boyle,	P.	27	-	-
Boyle,	T.	8	-	-
Bradshaw	Mrs.	5	-	-
Broderick,	J.	1	-	-
Brogan,	J.	27	-	-
Brosnan,	D.	8	-	-
Brosnan,	J.	8	-	-
Brosnan,	J.	13	7	6
Brosnan,	J.	1	-	-
Brosnan,	M.	14	-	-
Brosnan,	S.	23	7	6
Burke,	M.	27	-	-
Cahill,	T.	27	-	-
Carr,	M.	27	-	-
Carr,	P.	13	-	-
Carr,	T.	23	-	-
Carrick,	M.	1	-	-
Carroll,	M.	8	-	-
Carson,	W.	13	-	-
Casey,	K.	13	7	6
Casserley,	W.		10	-
Cassidy,	P.		5	-
Clancy,	J.	32	-	-
Clancy,	R.	1	-	-
Cloherty,	P.	27	-	-
Cloonan,	M.	13	-	-
Cloonan,	P.	13	-	-
Coakley,	T.	15	-	-
Coleman,	W.	8	-	-
Collins,	M.	2	-	-
Cooley,	M.	13	-	-
Concannon,	T.	3	-	-
Connell,	D.	27	-	-
Connell,	L.	23	-	-
Connell,	K.	27	-	-
Connolly,	P.	16	-	-
Connor,	J.		5	-
Connor,	M.	8	-	-
Conway,	K.	27	-	-
Cooney,	J.	23	-	-
Cooney,	T.	23	-	-
Coughlan,	P.	17	-	-
Counihan,	T.		5	-
Crowley,	D.	14	-	-
Crowley,	J.	1	-	-
Crowley,	T.	27	-	-
Coyne,	J.	1	-	-
Coyne,	P.		10	-
Coyne,	P.	8	-	-
Cullinane,	J.	5	-	-
Culloty,	D.	27	-	-
Curtin,	J.	2	-	-
Curtin,	T.	23	-	-
Daley,	E.	13	-	-
Deere,	M.		2	6
Devoy,	Mrs.	5	-	-
Diamond,	E.	21	-	-
Dirrane,	D.	13	-	-
Dolan,	J.	17	-	-
Doody,	L.	2	15	-
Driscoll,	J.	17	-	-
Duffy,	J.	19	-	-
Duffy,	M.	1	-	-
Duffy,	T.	17	10	-
Dunleavy,	W.	13	-	-
Dunne,	R.	18	-	-
Egan,	P.	13	-	-
Egan,	W.	1	-	-
Faherty,	L.	27	-	-
Fahy,	J.	3	-	-
Fahy,	J.	12	-	-
Fahy,	JJ.	34	-	-
Fahy,	S.	15	-	-
Fahy,	T.		10	-
Fanning,	J.	2	-	-
Farrell,	J.	23	-	-
Farrell,	Jn.	20	-	-
Feeney,	P.	17	-	-
Finn,	J.	7	-	-
Fitzhenry,	P.	13	-	-
Fitzpatrick,	J.	2	10	-
Fitzsimmons,	J.	23	-	-
Flaherty,	R.	8	-	-
Flahive,	J.	27	-	-
Fleming,	J.	27	-	-
Flynn,	M.	6	7	6
Forde,	J.	1	-	-
Forde,	S.	27	-	-
Joskin (Napier Area)	M.	48	-	-
Fox,	J.	7	-	-
Fox,	P.	1	-	-
Fox,	T.	2	-	-
Gallagher,	D.	28	-	-
Garvey,	J.	2	-	-
Giles,	C.	23	-	-
Giles,	R.	27	-	-
Goalley,	J.	2	-	-
Grealish,	M.		10	-
Grealish,	T.	27	-	-
Greally,	D.	14	-	-
Greally,	T.	1	-	-
Grogan,	J.	8	-	-
Grogan,	P.	8	-	-
Hackett,	T.	29	-	-
Halligan,	M.	23	-	-
Hallisey,	M.	13	-	-
Hannon,	P.	27	-	-
Hanrahan,	Rev. Fr.	1	-	-
Hardiman,	J.	2	-	-
Hardiman,	J.	2	-	-
Harkin,	P.	1	-	-
Harris,	T.		10	-
Heena,	J.	1	-	-
Heffernan,	O.	23	-	-
Heffernan,	P.	27	-	-
Hickey,	P.	27	-	-
Higgins,	M.	23	-	-
Horan,	C.	8	-	-
Horan,	C.	17	-	-
Horgan,	D.	6	10	-
Hourigan,	P.	8	-	-
Hughes,	J.	13	-	-
Hyland,	T.	27	-	-
Kavanagh,	J.	1	-	-
Kavanagh,	L.	23	-	-
Kearney,	A.	7	-	-
Kearns,	J.	12	-	-
Kelleher,	D.	28	-	-
Kelly,	D.	18	-	-
Kelly,	V.	23	-	-
Kennedy,	B.	13	-	-
Kennedy	D.	23	-	-
Kerr,	J.	27	-	-
Kerwan,	J.	1	-	-
Knox,	B.		10	-
Knox,	R.	10	10	-
Lafferty,	M.	27	-	-
Lally,	T.	13	-	-
Lavin,	E.	7	-	-
Lavin,	J.	8	-	-
Lawlee,	J.	5	-	-
Leen,	T.	15	-	-
Leen,	T.	23	-	-
Loughrey,	J.	27	-	-
Luby,	M.	13	-	-
Lynch,	P.	13	-	-
Lyons,	M.	2	10	-
Maher,	J.	8	-	-
Mahoney,	E.	27	-	-
Mahoney,	E.		10	-
Mahoney,	W.	1	-	-
Maloney,	J.	23	-	-
Mannion,	K.	13	-	-
Martin,	W.	15	10	-
McAuliffe,	T.	5	-	-
McCabe,	T.	3	-	-
McCarthy,	G.	17	10	-
McCarthy,	R.		2	6
McCarthy,	T.	27	-	-
McCarthy,	T.	37	-	-
McConnell,	S.	18	-	-
McCoy,	W.	1	-	-
McCullagh,	J.	23	-	-
McDevitt,	Mrs.		5	-
McDonnell,	J.	8	-	-
McGlynn,	Rev. Fr.	6	-	-
McGrath,	P.	8	-	-
McGrath,	M.	13	-	-
McGrath,	W.	27	-	-
McGill,	J.	2	-	-
McGuire,	J.	2	-	-
McKenna,	J.	13	-	-
McMullen,	J.		10	-
McNamara,	J.	18	-	-
McNeillis,	O.	1	-	-
McPeake,	C.	29	-	-
McPeake,	H.	23	-	-
McSheen,	J.	13	-	-
McSweeney,	E.	6	-	-
Meehan,	T.	23	-	-
Melvin,	P.	23	-	-
Molloy,	W.	14	-	-
Mongan,	M.	13	-	-
Moore,	K.	14	-	-
Moriarty,	Jas.	13	-	-
Moriarty,	J.	27	-	-
Moriarty,	Jos.	19	-	-
Moriarty,	M.	13	7	6
Mulholland,	B.	1	-	-
Mullane,	J.	8	-	-
Murphy,	E.	11	-	-
Murphy,	P.	27	-	-
Murray,	M.	23	-	-
Nally,	J.	27	-	-
Nally,	J.	27	-	-
Nee,	P.	6	-	-
Newell,	P.	5	-	-
Nihil,	J.	27	-	-
O'Brien,	D.	1	-	-
O'Connell,	JJ	23	-	-
O'Connor,	D.	3	-	-
O'Connor,	G.	13	-	-

4.

Name		£	s.	d.	Name		£	s.	d.	Name		£	s.	d.
O'Connor,	M.	13	-	-	Reidy,	D.		10	-	Sullivan,	T.	1	-	-
O'Connor,	M^cnr.	24	-	-	Reidy,	M.	8	-	-	Tangney,	T.	23	-	-
O'Connor,	M.	2	-	-	Reidy,	V.	13	-	-	Tobin,	P.		10	-
O'Donnell,	H.	8	-	-	Riordan,	J.	16	-	-	Towey,	M.	13	-	-
O'Donnell,	J.	13	-	-	Robinson,	Jas.	1	-	-	Toohill,	H.	11	-	-
O'Hagan,	J^as.	13	-	-	Robinson,	J.F.	10	10	-	Trainor,	H.	27	-	-
O'Hagan,	J.	3	-	-	Robinson,	J.C.	5	-	-	Traynor,	S.	18	-	-
O'Hare,	J.	10	10	-	Roche,	D.	29	10	-	Walsh,	D.	1	-	-
O'Leary,	P.	13	-	-	Ronayne,	D.	27	-	-	Walsh,	I.Jun.	23	-	-
O'Neill,	P.		10	-	Ryan,	J.	3	-	-	Walsh,	I.Sen.	16	-	-
O'Rogan,	R.	8	-	-	Ryan,	J.	13	-	-	Walsh,	J.	27	-	-
O'Regan,	T.	16	-	-	Scannell,	T.	13	-	-	Walsh,	M^co.	2	-	-
O'Regan,	L.	17	-	-	Scully,	T.	27	-	-	Walsh,	M.	27	-	-
O'Shea,	J.	13	-	-	Saxton,	P.	1	-	-	Walsh,	T.	17	-	-
O'Sullivan,	P.	9	12	6	Shanahan,	L.	27	-	-	Ward,	C.	15	-	-
O'Sullivan,	P.J.	23	-	-	Shanahan,	J.	14	-	-	Ward,	J.	1	-	-
Perdue,	P.	3	-	-	Sheehan,	J.	27	-	-	Ward,	3.	15	-	-
Power,	R.	8	-	-	Sheehy,	E.	1	-	-	Whooley,	D^a.18	-	-	
Power,	-	1	-	-	Sheridan,	M.	23	-	-	Whooley,	D^a.18	-	-	
Price,	D.	12	-	-	Sugrue,	B.	1	10	-	Whooley,	M.	13	-	-
Purcell,	Rev.Fr.	2	-	-	Sullivan,	D.	23	-	-	Whooley,	P.	28	-	-
Quinn,	J.	1	1	-	Sullivan,	P.	13	-	-	Wilson,	A.	21	8	-
Reasdon,	R.	6	-	-	Sullivan,	P.	23	-	-	Wyles,	C.	15	-	-
Redmond,	P.	5	-	-	Sullivan,	T.	1	-	-					

Members of the Éire National Association as at 30 June 1945, showing how much they contributed financially since the association was formed in early 1940.

Courtesy of Colleen O'Donovan

Final financial report of the ENA, prepared by Maurice Aylward and Tom Cahill. This is a summary of the organisation's financial position and what the subscriptions were spent on.
Courtesy of Colleen O'Donovan

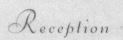

Reception

to

MR. EAMON DE VALERA

AND

MR. FRANK AIKEN

by

The Irish Community

of Wellington

||||

TOWN HALL

TUESDAY, MAY 25th, 1948, at 8 p.m.

||||

.. *Programme* ..

Cover and programme
for the public reception
for Éamon de Valera
and Frank Aiken at the
Wellington Town Hall.
Alexander Turnbull Library,
Eph-A-INTERNATIONAL-1948-01

Musical Items

Solo: (1) "Ireland, Mother Ireland."
(2) Eileen Aroon."

DAN FOLEY

Accompanist: Kathleen Dunne.

Solo: (1) "Gentle Maiden" .... *Irish Melody.*
(2) "Fiddler of Derry" .... *Jeffries.*

ANN CAMPBELL

Accompanist: Mrs. C. McDonald.

||||

Organist: Mr. Clement Howe.

God Save the King.

||||

CHAIRMAN'S ADDRESS—
DR. P. P. LYNCH.

ADDRESS—
THE RT. HON. THE PRIME MINISTER,
Mr. P. Fraser, M.P., P.C

ADDRESS—
HIS GRACE
THE MOST REV. PETER McKEEFREY, D.D.,
Coadjutor-Archbishop of Wellington.

PRESENTATION OF ADDRESS FROM THE IRISH
NATIONAL CLUB—
MR. BRYAN O'BRIEN.

REPLY—
MR. DE VALERA.

||||

" The Soldiers' Song "

The page from Peter Fraser's diary showing his appointments for 20 December 1948, the day he received an honorary doctorate from the National University of Ireland.

Archives New Zealand, C 552 1677, PM10 8, 23

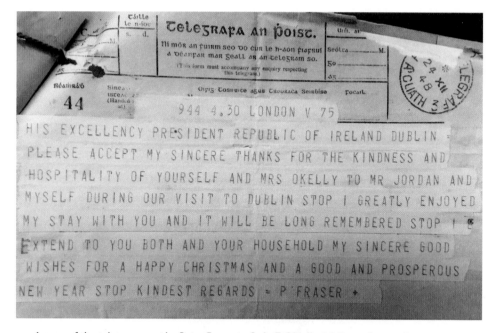

A copy of the telegram sent by Peter Fraser to Seán T. O'Kelly, 24 December 1948.
National Archives of Ireland, Department of the Taoiseach 97/9/477

True to Éire

Written and recorded to celebrate my father's story. Words by Kevin Ikin to a traditional tune: 'Rights of Man'.

1. Born in County Galway in 19 hundred and nine
   Matthias Burke grew up in the troubled times
   He witnessed the atrocities of the Black and Tans
   The torture and the killings at their bloody hands.

2. This Son of Éire was not afraid of work
   And his love for his homeland he would never shirk
   But when he sailed to New Zealand to seek a peaceful life
   Little did he know he was heading for some strife.

CHORUS: They could hound him from the country
        And a banning order sign
        They could threaten retribution if he didn't tow the line
        But when it came to the push a single thing was clear
        He'd be true to Ireland, true to Éire.

3. In 1941 the government made the call
   It said the King and Empire needed them all
   To gather up their guns and march forth to the fray
   To keep Adolf Hitler and the fascist hordes at bay.

4. But the Sons of Éire, they made their stand
   They would not sign up or join the band
   Enlist to fight in a British uniform
   They remembered the terror that Ireland had borne.

CHORUS

5. So Matthias Burke and the Sons of Éire
   Were brought before the army board and ordered to declare
   Why they should escape the fate of those whose blood was spent
   Who answered the call to arms and went where they were sent.

6. In the end, their conscience and their cause won the day
   Fraser and the government said that they could stay
   They would not be deported or forced to join the fight
   In the cause of the power that inflicted Ireland's plight.

CHORUS

Key figures

Aiken, Frank (1898–1983): Joined the Irish Volunteers at the age of 16 and aligned himself with the anti-Treaty side during the Civil War. A close friend of de Valera, he served as Minister for the Co-ordination of Defence Measures during WWII and later as Finance Minister 1945–48, Minister for External Affairs 1957–69 and Tánaiste 1965–69. He accompanied de Valera on his visit to New Zealand in 1948.

Attlee, Clement (1883–1967): British Labour politician who served in Churchill's coalition government in WWII and was Deputy Prime Minister. He had a brief term as Secretary of State for Dominion Affairs in 1942–43. In 1945 he won a landslide victory in the general election which saw Churchill swept from office.

Berendsen, Sir Carl August (1890–1973): Born in Australia, he was one of New Zealand's most influential civil servants in the 1920s, '30s and '40s. He was Head of the Prime Minister's Department from 1932–43 and Secretary of the War Cabinet 1939–43. He served as High Commissioner to Australia and was later Minister to the United Nations. Berendsen accompanied Peter Fraser on several of his wartime journeys to the UK and other parts of the world. He received a knighthood in 1946.

Broadfoot, Sir Walter (1881–1965): Served as a politician for the United and later National parties from November 1928 until October 1954. He was briefly the Minister for National Service in the War Administration in 1942, and a minister in the First National Government in 1949. He was known for his strong opposition to conscientious objectors.

Cranborne, Viscount (1893–1972): Conservative politician and friend of Winston Churchill, he served as Secretary of State for Dominion Affairs from 1940–42 and in the latter part of 1943 until 1945.

Duggan, Eileen (1894–1972): One of New Zealand's foremost poets and writers. Both her parents came from County Kerry and were married in Wellington, New Zealand. She was appointed an OBE in 1937 and made an honorary fellow of the Royal Society of Literature in 1943. Eileen was a close friend of Prime Minister Peter Fraser and highly regarded in literary circles.

Heenan, Sir Joseph (1888–1951): Career public servant and close confidant of Peter Fraser. Heenan was Under-Secretary for the Department of Internal Affairs during WWII and played a major role in dealing with the Sons of Éire. He was of Irish ancestry, describing himself as a 'self-styled liberal', and was popular with both politicians and his peers.

Hunter, J.S. (Stan) (1889–1975): Career public servant who held the position of Director of Mobilisation in the government until 1940. He then became the Director of National Service until 1944 when he was succeeded by his deputy, H.L. Bockett. A key person in the conscription of personnel into the New Zealand armed forces in WWII.

Jordan, William (1879–1959): First Hon Secretary of the New Zealand Labour Party. Fought in France in WWI and later entered Parliament. He was New Zealand High Commissioner in London during WWII.

Rugby, Lord (1887–1967): (Sir John Maffey) British career diplomat who, at Churchill's request, became the first United Kingdom representative to Éire in 1939 and remained in the post until his retirement in 1949.

Savage, Michael Joseph (1872–1940): Born in Australia, Savage was one of the founders of the New Zealand Labour Party and became the first Labour Prime Minister. Remembered as the leader who introduced the country to the welfare state and bought much relief to the poor in the latter stages of the Depression. He was known for his independent view on foreign relations and while other Commonwealth leaders acquiesced when Italy invaded Abyssinia, Savage openly opposed this.

Semple, Robert (Bob) (1873–1955): Labour MP and minister. A colourful character and famous for his public works campaign in New Zealand at the end of the Depression. Served as Minister of National Service in the Labour administration during WWII. In WWI he had opposed conscription but in WWII was a advocate for the concept and drew the first conscription marble.

Shanahan, Foss (1910–1964): Well-known New Zealand public servant who became Assistant Secretary of the War Cabinet in 1943. He served in several high-level roles in the public service, including Secretary for the Cabinet. He was known as 'Foss the boss' for the efficient way he ran any department he was attached to.

Stilwell, Wilfred Fosberry (c.1891–1974): Magistrate and later Judge of the New Zealand Court of Arbitration. Was Chairman of the No.4 Armed Forces Appeal Board during WWII, which heard the case of the Sons of Éire. He served in the New Zealand Army in WWI and was no friend of the Irish or any conscientious objector.

Thorn, James (1882–1956): A former President and National Secretary of the Labour Party. He served as Under-Secretary to Prime Minister Peter Fraser from 1943–46 and wrote an excellent book about Fraser.

Glossary

Irish terms

Auxiliaries: The Auxiliary Division of the Royal Irish Constabulary (ADRIC) was a paramilitary unit during the War of Independence. Set up in July 1920, it comprised former British Army officers, most of whom came from Great Britain.

Black and Tan (the Tans): Officially the Royal Irish Constabulary Special Reserve. This was a force of temporary constables recruited to supplement British forces in Ireland during the War of Independence. Notorious for their brutality, their nickname was derived from the colours of the improvised uniforms they initially wore, composed of mixed khaki British Army and rifle-green RIC uniform parts, resembling a pack of Kerry Beagle hunting dogs.

Civil War: After the Treaty with Britain was signed by Michael Collins and Arthur Griffith, those who still wanted an Irish Republic rallied under the leadership of Éamon de Valera and refused to ratify it, culminating in armed conflict between Free State Forces and the Irish republicans lasting from June 1922 until May 1923. It was a brutal war that in some cases set brother against brother.

Clann na Talmhan: ('Family/Children of the land'; formally known as the National Agricultural Party). An Irish agrarian political party active between 1939 and 1965.

Crown forces: All British forces who occupied Ireland until the signing of the Anglo-Irish Treaty.

Dáil Éireann (Dáil): The Irish Assembly is the lower house of the Oireachtas, the National Parliament of Ireland (see also 'Teachta Dála').

Fianna Fáil: (meaning Soldiers of Destiny or Warriors of Fál). The republican party founded by Éamon de Valera in 1926.

Fine Gael: (meaning Tribe of the Irish). The party's origins are in the pro-Treaty movement but it didn't adopt its present name until 1933.

Flying column: A small group of Irish Volunteers from an IRA unit in the War of Independence, who acted much like a commando unit to carry out special raids against British forces.

Irish Republican Army (IRA): The original Irish Republican Army formed in 1917 from those Irish Volunteers who did not enlist in the British Army during World War I, members of the Irish Citizen Army, and others. It was declared to be the army of the Irish Republic during the War of Independence by the first Dáil Éireann.

Irish Republican Brotherhood (IRB, Bráithreachas Phoblacht na hÉireann): This was a secret oath-bound fraternal organisation, operating between 1858 and 1924, dedicated to the establishment of an independent democratic republic in Ireland. The IRB staged the Easter Rising in 1916, which led to the establishment of the first Dáil Éireann in 1919. All the main participants in the Rising including Éamon de Valera, Michael Collins and Patrick Pearse were members of the IRB.

Irish Volunteers: A military organisation established in 1913 by Irish nationalists. It was ostensibly formed in response to the formation of the Ulster Volunteers in 1912, and its declared aim was 'to secure and maintain the rights and liberties common to the whole people of Ireland'.

The Rising: 1916 Easter Rising.

Royal Irish Constabulary (RIC): The police force in Ireland until 1922. The RIC was often the target for the IRA during the Troubles, despite the majority of its members being Catholic. It was replaced by the Garda Síochána (the Irish Police) in 1922.

Taoiseach: The Irish word for Prime Minister of Ireland.

Tánaiste: Deputy Prime Minister.

Teachta Dála (TD): A member of Dáil Éireann. The equivalent of terms such as 'member of parliament' or 'member of congress' used in other countries. The official translation is 'Deputy to the Dáil', although a more literal translation is 'Assembly Delegate'.

The Emergency: How the Irish Government described WWII.

The Treaty: The 1921 Anglo-Irish Treaty signed by Michael Collins and Arthur Griffith, which gave Ireland its independence but required that it remain as a dominion of the British Empire.

The Troubles: How the Irish refer to the War of Independence.

Townland: The smallest geographical division of land in Ireland with an average size of about 132 hectares. The system is of Gaelic origin and predates the Norman invasion. In 2014 there were 61,098 townlands in Ireland. They are directly linked to a parish, with Ballydotia being part of the Parish of Moycullen.

War of Independence (the Troubles): The fight between Irish Volunteer forces, commonly referred to as the IRA, and various elements of the British forces which took place between 1919 and 1921.

New Zealand terms

Aotearoa: Māori name for New Zealand.

Armed forces appeal boards: These were set up to hear appeals by conscientious objectors to being conscripted to the armed forces in WWII. Specific boards were known by a number – e.g. the board in Wellington was the No.4 Armed Forces Appeal Board.

Citizens of Éire: Refers to the wider group of Irishmen who objected to fighting in WWII – and specifically the list of 155 who were to be deported.

Conscientious objectors (COs, Conchies): Men called up who, for reasons of conscience, refused to fight in a war or join the armed services. They could appeal their call-up as a 'conscientious objector', and their case would be heard and determined by the armed forces appeal boards. Many were sent to camps which were in effect prison camps where they were detained for the duration of the war.

Defaulters: Men who had been called up for National Service but did not turn up – hence defaulting from service. If caught they were sent to defaulters' camps, which were akin to prisons.

Freezing worker/Freezing works: In New Zealand a freezing worker was a person who worked in an abattoir where animals were slaughtered. The term freezing works/worker reflects that at that time all New Zealand meat exported was frozen.

Irish Societies: often referred to as Irish clubs.

Mana: Māori word meaning of high status, prestige and authority.

Ngāi Tahu: Māori tribe in the South Island of New Zealand.

Ngāti: Māori word for tribe or clan.

2nd New Zealand Expeditionary Force (2NZEF): The New Zealand infantry division that fought in the Middle East in WWII, and later served in Italy.

Pipi: a New Zealand shellfish.

Returned and Services Association (RSA): The organisation representing those who have served in the armed forces. Its purpose is to care for veterans and it has clubs scattered around the country where members can socialise. During WWII the RSA strongly supported conscription and was quick to condemn any person who refused to fight, in particular conscientious objectors.

Sons of Éire: Refers specifically to the six Irishmen whose appeals were the basis for the 'test case' against conscription for Irish citizens.

State houses: A system of public housing in New Zealand, offering low-cost rental housing to residents on low to moderate incomes.

Thistle Inn: At 3 Mulgrave Street, it is about 100 yards from where Maurice Aylward lived in a boarding house at 2 Murphy Street, also in the suburb of Thorndon. The Thistle was my father's favourite watering hole and is close to the Wellington Railway Station and also to the Basilica of the Sacred Heart where many of the men in ENA would have gone to church. It's one of the few old hotels in Wellington that has survived the redevelopment of this earthquake prone city. The hotel was built in 1840 and the present structure was erected in 1866 when the original building was destroyed by fire. It's constructed of wood and has been beautifully refurbished retaining its heritage look – and the beer is good!

Abbreviations

CO	Conscientious Objector (New Zealand)
DIA	Department of Internal Affairs
ENA	Éire National Association
EU	European Union
MP	Member of Parliament (New Zealand)
NZ	New Zealand
RAF	Royal Air Force
RIC	Royal Irish Constabulary
RNZAF	Royal New Zealand Air Force
RSA	Returned and Services Association (New Zealand)
TD	Teachta Dála (Deputy to the Dáil)
UK	United Kingdom

Notes

Introduction

1 *Evening Post*, 31/7/1941.

2 ENA Executive (signed by M. Aylward) to ENA members, undated but appears to be mid-1942, referred to as the 'True to Ireland' letter. Archives New Zealand ACIE 8798, EA1/452, 83/3/2.

1 Ireland's risings

1 Matthias Burke affidavit to No.4 Armed Forces Appeal Board, Burke collection.

2 William Henry, *Famine: Galway's Darkest Years*, 2011, pp.36-37.

3 ibid, p.38.

4 ibid, p.113.

5 *Evening Post*, 27/5/1914.

6 Pritchard, David (ed), *Chronology of Irish History*, 2009, p.118.

7 Personal correspondence from St Patrick's College Archives, April 2018.

8 Tomás Kenny, *Galway: Politics & Society 1910–23*, p.9.

9 Darren McDonagh, 'Military Activity in the Peripheral Region of Moycullen from 1916 to 1923', sourced from Moycullen Historical Society, undated.

10 ibid, p.4.

11 Personal Communication from Moycullen Historical Society, September 2017.

12 Bureau of Military History, Witness Statement 374 Mícheál Ó Droighneáin.

13 William Henry, *Pathway to Rebellion*, 2016, p.241.

14 https://nzhistory.govt.nz/people/peter-fraser.

15 J.A. Cole, *Lord Haw-Haw & William Joyce*, 1964, p.21.

16 William Joyce and his family were not connected to the Barna teacher Patrick Joyce, who was executed by the IRA in Galway for allegedly spying for the British in October 1920.

2 A future in New Zealand

1 Sometimes he was called 'Matthew' rather than 'Matthias', as people took 'Matt' as being short for 'Matthew'.

2 *Evening Post*, 25/1/1930. The *Evening Post* was an evening newspaper in Wellington. It has since been merged with the morning paper, the *Dominion*. The combined paper is imaginatively called the *Dominion Post*.

3 Reference for M. Burke from County Engineer, Waitōtara County Council, February 1933, Burke collection.

4 *Hutt News*, 14/4/1937.

5 *Evening Post*, 29/6/1934.

6 Despatch No.1 from É. de Valera, Irish Minister of External Affairs to the New Zealand Prime Minister, George Forbes, 7/2/1934, Archives New Zealand, ACIE 8798, EA1/1075, 159/2/16.

7 New Zealand Prime Minister George Forbes, to É. de Valera, Irish Minister of External Affairs, 27/4/1934, Archives New Zealand, ACIE 8798, EA1/1075, 159/2/16.

8 Despatch No.5 from É. de Valera, Irish Minister of External Affairs, to the New Zealand Prime Minister, George Forbes, 27/8/1934, Archives New Zealand, ACIE 8798, EA1/1075, 159/2/16.

9 *Evening Post*, 9/5/1935.

10 Michael Bassett & Michael King, *Tomorrow Comes the Song*, 2000, p.133.

11 James Thorn, *Peter Fraser*, 1952, p.121.

12 De Valera Speech to League of Nations 2/7/1936 http://www.difp.ie/docs/1936/Failure-of-the-League-of-Nations/1716.htm.

13 Cablegram from Abyssinia Association, London, 13/10/1938, to Prime Minister Michael Savage, www.teara.govt.nz/en/document/38145/telegram-from-the-abyssinia-association.

3 Calm before the war

1 Hugh Templeton (ed), *Mr Ambassador*, 2009, p.125.

2 ibid, p.125.

3 ibid, p.125.

4 Bassett & King, p.168.

5 *Evening Post*, 17/3/1938, p.14.

6 Templeton, p.128.

7 Despatch No.3 from É. de Valera to the Prime Minister of New Zealand, 26/4/1938, Archives New Zealand, AAEG 950/95/A, 207/4/2.

8 M.J. Savage 5/9/1939 https://ngataonga. org.nz/collections/catalogue/catalogue-item?record_id=206464.

9 The official restaurant in Parliament reserved for members of parliament and staff.

10 Templeton, p.131.

11 Ronan Fanning, *Éamon de Valera*, 2015, p.191.

12 Robert Fisk, *In Time of War*, 1983, p.525.

13 *Scotsman*, 12/6/2009, https://www. scotsman.com/news/full-scale-of-irish-wwii-death-toll-revealed-1-1208756.

14 'Pardon for WWII Allies deserters', The *Irish Times*, 12/6/2012.

15 Fisk, p.525.

16 ibid, pp.328-30.

17 ibid, p.101.

18 ibid, p.391.

19 Warren Kimball, 'That Neutral Island', 2009–10, p.54.

20 Richard Holmes, *Churchill's Bunker*, 2009, p.152.

21 R.W. Thompson, *Generalissimo Churchill*, 1973, p.22.

4 The beginning of the battle with Britain

1 ENA Records, Burke collection

2 Pádraic Ó Laoi, *History of Castlegar Parish*, undated, p.133.

3 Patrick Feeney record, Military Service Pensions Collection www.mspesearch. militaryarchives.ie.

4 John Sheenan, 'Gerald Griffin, First PSA 'Organiser',' pp.1-2.

5 *Evening Post*, 7/10/1936. Ironically, this building has been demolished and the British High Commission is on this site.

6 Maurice Leo Aylward is used to distinguish from another Maurice Aylward in New Zealand. All references to Maurice Aylward in this book refer to Maurice Leo Aylward.

7 Author interview with Fr Eamon Aylward, Dublin, September 2016.

8 Author interview with Ann Furneaux, (née Ongley) Fred Ongley's granddaughter, 22/11/2014.

9 Obituary Mr F.J. Ongley, *Evening Post*, 5/6/1944.

10 This ship has been partly restored and is on display at Picton, New Zealand.

11 *Evening Post*, 11/10/1939, 27/4/1940, 12/4/1941, 22/11/1941, 26/2/1944.

12 Author interview with Ann Furneaux (née Ongley).

13 Thorn, p.165.

14 Templeton, p.132.

15 Thorn, p.168.

16 Peter Franks & Jim McAloon, *Labour*, 2016, p.72.

17 Keith Sinclair, *Walter Nash*, 1976, p.190.

18 David Grant, *Field Punishment No.1*, 2008, p.83.

19 Cablegram É. de Valera to New Zealand Prime Minister Michael Savage, 22/1/1940, Archives New Zealand, ACGO 8333, 62/2/5.

20 Telegram from New Zealand Prime Minister Savage to É. de Valera 23/1/1940, Archives New Zealand, ACGO 8333, 62/2/5.

21 Thorn, p.172. Nash was later to become Prime Minister 1957–60 heading the second Labour Government.

22 Templeton, p.133.

23 Thorn, p.172.

24 *The New Zealand Gazette*, 18/6/1940.

25 *The New Zealand Gazette*, 2/10/1940.

26 David Grant, *Out in the Cold*, 1986, pp.120-29.

27 ibid, p.120.

28 *The New Zealand Gazette*, 16/1/1941.

29 Circular A. B. No.1, Director of National Service, J.S. Hunter, to Chairman and members of the Armed Forces Appeal Boards, 17/1/1941, Archives New Zealand, AEJI 18954, NS-DN4/1.

30 ibid, p.3.

31 ibid, p.11.

32 ibid, p.3.

33 ibid, p.5.

34 ibid, p.6.

35 ibid, p.13.

36 ibid, p.4.

37 ibid, p.2.

38 ibid, p.23.

5 Paper war

1 Richard Benson, *Irish Wit & Wisdom*, 2016, p.76.

2 Letter from F. Ongley for ENA to Irish Prime Minister É. de Valera 19/2/1941, Aylward collection.

3 Letter from F. Ongley for ENA to Prime Minister Peter Fraser 26/2/1941, Aylward collection.

4 Letter from New Zealand Prime Minister Peter Fraser to Ongley, O'Donovan & Arndt, 28/2/1941, Aylward collection.

5 *Evening Post*, 31/7/1941.

6 *Evening Post*, 31/7/1941.

7 Murray Horton, 'The secret history of WWII in New Zealand', 1974.

8 Grant, *Out in the Cold*, pp.118-19.

9 Nancy Taylor, *The Home Front: Vol 1*, 1986, p.248.

10 ibid, p.247.

11 ibid, p.247.

12 Sinclair, p.267.

13 *New Zealand Gazette Extraordinary*, 7/5/1941.

14 The bosses at the freezing works where Aylward, Giles & Mahoney worked also lodged a separate and unsuccessful appeal for them to be allowed to remain there because skilled labour was short.

15 *Evening Post*, 4/11/1941.

16 Thorn, pp.190-91.

17 https://nzhistory.govt.nz/war/the-battle-for-crete.

18 Letter from Fred Ongley, lawyer for ENA to Deputy Prime Minister Walter Nash, 9/6/1941, Aylward collection.

19 Grant, *Out in the Cold*, p.121.

20 ibid, p.123.

21 ibid, p.123.

6 Appeal day

1 Matthias Burke Affidavit 'Grounds for appeal' July 1941, Burke collection.

2 *Press*, 30/7/1941.

3 *Evening Post*, 19/5/1974.

4 There is evidence to suggest that he did get a New Zealand passport.

5 Many men from Ireland who did fight for Britain in WWII were effectively treated as traitors when they returned home, and were deprived of privileges such as pensions and work opportunities.

6 His use of 'court' is clearly deliberate to brand the hearings as court cases despite feeble attempts by the New Zealand authorities to refer to them as 'hearings' and thus sanitise the intent of the Appeal Boards.

7 An IRA commander in Moycullen.

8 This appears to be reference to an incident at the Moycullen Co-operative store.

9 This occurred on the Barna Road which links Moycullen with the village of Barna on Galway Bay, and is now marked with a memorial.

10   William Henry, *Blood for Blood*, 2012, pp.110-11.

11   ibid, p.126.

12   Bureau Military History 1913–21, Witness Statement 424, Geraldine Dillon, p.25.

13   All references to Aylward at the Appeal Board are from the *Evening Post* 31/7/1941 unless otherwise stated.

14   *Portland Guardian*, 15/9/1941.

15   No record of a formal response to this letter has been found.

16   Transcript of No.4 Armed Forces Appeal Board Hearing, 31/7/1941, Burke collection.

17   *Evening Post*, 5/8/1941, p.9.

18   ibid.

19   *Portland Guardian*, 15/9/1941.

20   The article does not mention the name of this Irishman.

7   The Troubles in Moycullen

1   Galway Museum, 'Revolution in Galway 1913–23', undated.

2   Bureau of Military History 1913–21 Witness Statement (WS) 1718 & (WS) 374 Mícheál Ó Droighneáin.

3   Bureau of Military History 1913–21 Witness Statement (WS) 374 Mícheál Ó Droighneáin, p.10.

4   WS 1718, p.7.

5   ibid, p.16.

6   WS 1718, p.18.

7   ibid, p.67.

8   Pádraic Ó Laoi, *Fr. Griffin*, 1994, p.67.

9   Henry, *Blood for Blood*, p.148.

10   Ó Laoi, *Fr. Griffin*, p.67.

11   McDonagh, p.17.

12   WS 374, p.13.

13   The location was never revealed and Joyce's remains were only discovered in 1998 when a golf course was being built alongside the Barna–Moycullen Road.

14   Bureau of Military History 1913–21 Witness Statement (WS) 1729, Capt. J. Togher.

15   Bureau of Military History 1913–21 Witness Statement (WS) 424, Geraldine Dillon, p.14.

16   WS 1718 p.21.

17   ibid, p.22.

18   Ó Laoi, *Fr. Griffin*, p.19.

19   ibid, p.22.

20   ibid, p.29.

21   ibid, p.20.

22   ibid, p.21.

23   WS 1718 p.23.

24   Ó Laoi, *Fr. Griffin*, p.29.

25   ibid, p.30.

26   ibid, p.32.

27   WS 1718 p.24.

28   WS 1729, p.8.

29   Ó Laoi, *Fr. Griffin*, p.34.

30   ibid, p.35.

31   ibid, p.37.

32   ibid, p.49.

33   WS 1718, p.28.

34   McDonagh, p.17.

35   David Leeson, *The Black & Tans*, pp.37-38

36   McDonagh, p.18.

37   WS1718, p.29.

38   ibid, p.30.

39   Author interview with Fr Eamon Aylward September 2016.

8   Watching and waiting

1   Paul Bew, *Churchill & Ireland*, 2016, p.59.

2   *Auckland Star*, 8/6/1940.

3   *Evening Post*, 24/10/1940.

4   *New Zealand Herald*, 17/9/1940.

5   Cita Stelzer, *Dinner with Churchill*, 2011, p.197 & p.231.

6   https://nzhistory.govt.nz/war/second-world-war-at-home/in-dissent, p.6.

7   ibid.

8   *Evening Post*, 24/10/1941.

9   https://nzhistory.govt.nz/war/second-world-war-at-home/in-dissent, p.6.

10 *Auckland Star*, 3/3/1943.

11 John Cookson, 'Illiberal New Zealand', in *New Zealand Journal of History*, Vol. 17, No.2, 1983, pp.120-43.

12 Taylor, p.252.

13 *Evening Post*, 17/10/1941.

14 *Evening Post*, 29/2/1944.

15 ibid.

16 Taylor, p.259.

17 ibid, p.259.

18 ibid, p.261.

19 ibid, p.260.

20 *Evening Post*, 23/9/1941.

21 *Auckland Star*, 27/8/1942.

22 *Evening Post*, 2/8/1941.

23 *Evening Post*, 13/1/1943.

24 Christchurch *Press*, 28/5/1941.

25 *Evening Post*, 15/10/1941.

26 Margaret Tate, 'An indeterminate sentence', 2016, pp.35-46.

27 Grant, *Field Punishment No.1*.

28 Tate, p.38.

29 Christchurch *Press*, 7/6/1941.

9 The unknown mates

1   Thomas Scannell, Notice of Appeal against Territorial Service, 11/11/1940, Archives New Zealand, AEJC 18892 NS-A2/18 301075.

2   Thomas Scannell, Letter re. Grounds of Appeal to Manpower Committee received 30/12/1940, Archives New Zealand, AEJC 18892 NS-A2/18 301075.

3   There is the possibility, although there is no evidence, that Ongley helped draft this letter for Scannell as he acted for Scannell and did spend time in Auckland, and that it is a very carefully written letter. It is equally possible that Ongley found Scannell's letter and just copied large sections of it to form the basis of my father's and other Sons of

Éire's statements to the No.4 Appeal Board in Wellington in July 1941.

4   Christchurch *Press*, 10/6/1941.

5   *Evening Post*, 9/8/1939.

6   *Evening Post*, 30/6/1939.

7   Memo from No.2 Armed Forces Appeal Board to District Manpower Officer, Auckland, 17/2/1941, Archives New Zealand, AEJC 18891, NS-A1/1, 15/1/4.

8   Patrick Egan, Notice of Appeal against Territorial Service 16/11/1940, Archives New Zealand, AEJC 18892, NS-A2/7, 154603.

9   *New Zealand Herald*, 5/6/1941.

10 *New Zealand Herald*, 13/6/1941.

11 *Evening Post*, 20/11/1940.

12 ibid.

13 Christchurch *Press*, 21/5/1941.

14 *Bay of Plenty Beacon*, 8/8/1941.

15 Author interview with John Knox November 2014.

16 Author interview with Mike Carr, January 2015.

10 Fight or feck off

1   Telegram No.408 from Prime Minister, New Zealand to Secretary of State for Dominion Affairs, 30/9/1941, Archives New Zealand, ACIE 8798, EA1/1075, 159/2/16.

2   Telegram Secretary of State for Dominion Affairs to Prime Minister, New Zealand, 5/10/1941, Archives New Zealand, ACIE 8798, EA1/1075, 159/2/16.

3   Letter from Ongley, O'Donovan & Arndt on behalf of M.L. Aylward reliability to render service, 2/10/1941, Aylward collection.

4   Decision of No.4 Armed Forces Appeal Board, 9/10/1941, Aylward collection.

5   *Evening Post*, 9/10/1941.

6   Letter from F. Ongley to the Prime Minister of New Zealand re. No.4 Armed Forces Appeal Board decision, 17/10/1941, Aylward collection.

7 Memorandum R.H. Quilliam, Director
of Mobilisation to Area No.5 Army
Office re. Citizens of Éire, 15/10/1941,
Archives New Zealand, AAYS 8638
AD1/1299, 312/5/64.

8 Notice of Michael Carr's Appeal
Dismissed 4/11/1941, provided by the
Carr family, Burke collection.

9 *Evening Post*, 4/11/1941.

10 Memo from J.S. Hunter, Director
National Service Department to R.H.
Quilliam Director Mobilisation re.
war cabinet direction re. Sons of Éire,
5/11/1941, Archives New Zealand, AAYS
8638 AD1/1299, 312/5/64.

11 Memo from J.S. Hunter, Director,
National Service Department to J.
Heenan, Under-Secretary Department
Internal Affairs re. war cabinet direction
and Sons of Éire, 6/11/1941, Archives
New Zealand, ACGO 8333, IA1W2271/5,
15/7/301.

12 Letter from Michael Lafferty to
Department Internal Affairs 29/11/1941,
Archives New Zealand, ACGO 8333,
IA1W2271/5, 15/7/301.

13 Memo from J. Heenan, Under-Secretary,
Department Internal Affairs to J.S.
Hunter, Director of National Service,
5/12/1941 re. Lafferty, Archives New
Zealand, ACGO 8333, IA1W2271/5,
15/7/301.

14 Memo from J.S. Hunter Director
National Service Department to J.
Heenan, Under-Secretary, Department
Internal Affairs 24/12/1941, Archives
New Zealand, ACGO 8333, IA1W2271/5,
15/7/301ANZ.

15 Memo from L. Harris Secretary No.1
Area to Director National Service
25/11/1941 re. Special Tribunal, Archives
New Zealand, AEJC 18892 NS-A2/18
301075.

16 ibid.

11 The 155 to go

1 Speech by Franklin D. Roosevelt, 1941,
https://www.loc.gov/resource/afc1986022.
afc1986022_ms2201/?st=text

2 Gerald Hensley, 'Peter Fraser at War',
Ministry of Culture & Heritage Seminar,
2011, p.5.

3 Frank McCarthy, 'Singapore Harriers',
undated.

4 Tom Barry, *Guerilla Days in Ireland*, 2013,
p.57.

5 Peter Grose, *An Awkward Truth*, 2011, p.193.

6 Kimball, 'That Neutral Island', p.54.

7 Letter from D. Wilson, Associate Minister
of National Service to Ongley, O'Donovan
& Arndt, 9/1/1942, Archives New Zealand,
ACGO 8333, IA1W2271/5, 15/7/301.

8 Memo from J.S. Hunter. Director
National Service to Under-Secretary
Department of Internal Affairs 16/1/1941,
list of 155 names for permits to leave New
Zealand, Archives New Zealand, ACGO
8333, IA1W2271/5, 15/7/301.

9 Memo from J. Heenan Under-Secretary
Department Internal Affairs to Minster
of Internal Affairs, 4/2/1942, Archives
New Zealand, ACGO 8333, IA1W2271/5,
15/7/301.

10 Telegram from Prime Minister, New
Zealand to Secretary of State for
Dominion Affairs UK, 9/2/1942, Archives
New Zealand, ACGO 8333, IA1W2271/5,
15/7/301.

11 Telegram from Secretary of State for
Dominion Affairs UK to Prime Minister,
New Zealand, 25/2/1942, Archives New
Zealand, ACGO 8333, IA1W2271/5,
15/7/301.

12 Letter from F. Ongley to Prime Minister
New Zealand, 26/2/1942, Archives New
Zealand, ACGO 8333, IA1W2271/5,
15/7/301.

13 Letter to F. Ongley from Prime Minister
of New Zealand, 3/3/1942, Archives New
Zealand, ACGO 8333, IA1W2271/5,
15/7/301.

14 Memo from J. Heenan Under-Secretary Department Internal Affairs to J.S. Hunter Director National Service, 11/3/1942, Archives New Zealand, ACGO 8333, IA1W2271/5, 15/7/301.

15 James Belich, *Paradise Reforged*, 2001, pp.280-81.

16 Memo from D. Wilson, Associate Minister of National Service to Prime Minister New Zealand, 30/6/1042, Archives New Zealand, ACIE 8798, EA1/452, 83/3/2.

17 ENA Executive Statement to ENA members, undated, Archives New Zealand, ACIE 8798, EA1/452, 83/3/2.

18 Telegram from New Zealand Prime Minister Peter Fraser to Secretary of State for Dominion Affairs, 18/7/1942, Archives New Zealand, ACGO 8333, IA1W2271/5, 15/7/301.

19 Memo from J.S. Hunter, Director National Service, to Chairmen Armed Forces Appeal Board, 7/8/1942, Archives New Zealand, AEJC 18891, NS-A1/1, 15/1/4.

20 Telegram from Secretary of State for Dominion Affairs to Prime Minister New Zealand, 12/8/1942, Archives New Zealand, ACGO 8333, IA1W2271/5, 15/7/301.

12 A secure future at last

1 Memo from J.S. Hunter Director National Service to Minister National Service, 19/8/942, Archives New Zealand, ACIE 8798, EA1/452, 83/3/2.

2 Letter from W. Broadfoot, Minister of National Service, to Mr Sullivan, acting Prime Minister, 1/9/1942, Archives New Zealand, ACIE 8798, EA1/452, 83/3/2. Sullivan was a member of the war cabinet – Broadfoot was not.

3 *Evening Post*, 15/10/1941.

4 Christchurch *Press*, 15/2/1938.

5 War Cabinet Minute 28/8/1942 re. National Service, Archives New Zealand, ACIE 8798, EA1/452, 83/3/2.

6 Letter from Foss Shanahan to J.S. Hunter Director of National Service, 9/9/1942, Archives New Zealand, ACIE 8798, EA1/452, 83/3/2.

7 Letter from Foss Shanahan to Dan Sullivan, Acting Prime Minister, 11/9/1942, Archives New Zealand, ACIE 8798, EA1/452, 83/3/2.

8 Circular No.AF 66 from National Service Department to Chairmen, Members and Secretaries Armed Forces Appeal Boards, 23/9/1942, Archives New Zealand, AEJI 18954, NS-DN4/1.

9 Memo from J.S. Hunter Director National Service to Director Mobilisation, 29/4/1943, Archives New Zealand, AAYS 8638 AD1/1299, 312/5/64.

10 Letters between Ongley for ENA and Minister of Manpower January–February 1943, Aylward collection.

11 Letters from Minister of Manpower to Ongley for ENA, 3/2/1943, Aylward collection.

12 Letter Minister of Manpower to Ongley for ENA, 2/4/1943, Aylward collection.

13 Memo from Area 3 Commander to Army HQ, 11/11/1942, Archives New Zealand, AAYS 8638 AD1/1299, 312/5/64.

14 Letter from Director of National Service to all men claiming to be Citizens of Éire, 3/2/1943, Aylward collection.

15 Memo from Director National Service to Director of Mobilisation, 12/10/1942, Archives New Zealand, AAYS 8638 AD1/1299, 312/5/64.

16 Correspondence regarding Mitchell, Archives New Zealand, AEJC 18891, NS-A1/1, 15/1/4.

17 F. Ongley to Director of Manpower Auckland, 19/11/1943, Aylward collection.

18 Letter from M. Aylward ENA Secretary to Peter Fraser, Prime Minister New Zealand, 30/10/1945, Archives New Zealand, ACIE 8798, EA1/452, 83/3/2.

19 Letter from Prime Minister of New Zealand to M. Aylward, Secretary of ENA, 14/11/1945, Archives New Zealand, ACIE 8798, EA1/452, 83/3/2.

13 Aylward's Irish Odyssey

1   *Evening Post*, 23/6/1943.

2   Fennell, Jonathan, 'Soldiers and Social Change', 2017.

3   ENA letter to members, 10/9/1943, Aylward collection.

4   List of 195 Irishmen dated 1/1/1942 containing their names and call-up numbers, Aylward collection.

5   Letter from McLagan Minister of National Service to F. Ongley, 4/9/1943. It is clear that the ENA did not write their letter until they got written approval from McLagan. Aylward collection.

6   Letter from McLagan Minister of National Service to F. Ongley, 30/4/1943, Aylward collection.

7   Letter from ENA Executive to 'The Government & People of Éire', 12/10/1943, Aylward collection.

8   Letter from ENA Executive to Éamon de Valera 12/10/1943, Aylward collection.

9   Passenger Arrival List MV *Port Dunedin* 30/12/1943, Aylward collection.

10 William Aylward lived in Australia.

11 From the shipping records it is more likely he arrived in Ireland in early January.

12 National Archives of Ireland, Department of Taoiseach, 97/9/477.

13 Author interview with Éamon Ó Cuív, August 2016.

14 Report to ENA members from M.L. Aylward, 15/5/1945, Aylward collection.

15 Letter from McLagan Minister of National Service to F. Ongley, 30/4/1943, Aylward collection.

14 The Columbans and the family

1   *Evening Post*, 28/8/1942.

2   Maynooth is the main Catholic Seminary, not far from Dublin.

3   *Evening Post*, 13/2/1940.

4   Author interview with Fr Neil Collins, Dalgan Park, August 2017.

5   Brenda Niall, *Mannix*, 2015, p.156.

6   Letter from Fr Jim McGlynn to Matthias Burke, 4/2/1946, Burke collection.

7   The shop was originally called M. Burke but later became Courtenay Casuals. The building is still there but what was Mum's shop is now part of a restaurant.

8   *Evening Post*, 23/2/1944.

15 The Fraser and de Valera connection

1   Letter from M. Aylward to Prime Minister Peter Fraser, 30/8/1945, Archives New Zealand, ACIE 8798, EA1/452, 83/3/2.

2   Bassett & King, p.133.

3   ibid, p.140.

4   Leslie Hobbs, *The Thirty-Year Wonders*, 1967, p.44. This became something of a joke in Wellington with one undertaker saying 'we can't start the funeral, the Prime Minister isn't here'.

5   Edmund Van Esbeck, 'The Rugby Man', p.128-129.

6   Thorn, p.144.

7   ibid, p.248.

8   Bassett & King, pp.74 & 270.

9   *The Patrician*, St Patrick's College magazine, 1938.

10 Bassett & King, p.141.

11 Fanning, p.152.

12 ibid, p.163.

13 Fisk, p.24.

14 ibid, p.24.

15 ibid, p.37.

16 Fanning, p.228.

17 Edward Murrow, *On Winston Churchill*, 1954.

18 Fanning, p.183.

19 ibid, p.185.

20 Tim Pat Coogan, *De Valera, Long Fellow, Long Shadow*, 1995, p.510.

21 Bew, p.155.

22 ibid, p.151.

23 Fanning, pp.193-94.

24 Gerald Hensley, *Beyond the Battlefield*, 2009, p.135.

25 Cita Stelzer, *Dinner with Churchill*, 2011, p.197 & p.231.

26 ibid, pp.177–81.

27 Bassett & King, p.222.

28 Templeton, p.140.

29 Author interview with Éamon Ó Cuív, August 2016.

30 Fanning, p.267.

31 ibid, p.194.

32 Fanning, R, 'Why is Éamon de Valera so unpopular on both sides of the Irish Sea', *Irish Times*, 24/11/2015.

33 Templeton, p.147.

34 ibid, p.131.

35 Hensley, *Beyond the Battlefield*, p.170.

36 Thorn, p.5.

37 Diarmaid Ferriter, 'Churchill Proceedings – The Dev & Mr Churchill', p.48.

38 Kimball, 'That Neutral Island', p.54.

39 Freeman, David, 'Winston Churchill & Éamon de Valera,' 2008.

16 The final meetings

1 Letter from M. Aylward to Prime Minister Peter Fraser, 30/8/1945, Archives New Zealand, ACIE 8798, EA1/452, 83/3/2.

2 *Evening Post*, 9/3/1948.

3 *Evening Post*, 19/4/1948.

4 There is no record of a definitive date as to when the ENA officially went out of existence, but it would seem to be sometime between 1945 and 1947.

5 Letter from Irish National Club, Wellington, to Peter Fraser, Prime Minister of New Zealand, 22/4/1948, Archives New Zealand, AAEG 950/271/A, 207/4/2/1.

6 While there are no records of who held office in the Irish Society in 1947/48, it is assumed that Aylward was signing in his capacity as immediate past president of the society, or that the club simply wanted his name on the paper to give them greater credibility.

7 Letter from Peter Fraser, Prime Minister of New Zealand, to Irish National Club, 26/4/1948, Archives New Zealand, AAEG 950/271/A, 207/4/2/1.

8 Letter from Prime Minister's Office to Irish National Club, 5/5/1948, Archives New Zealand, AAEG 950/271/A, 207/4/2/1.

9 Memo from Frank Corner to Mr Shanahan, Head of Prime Minister's Department, 5/5/1948, Archives New Zealand, ACIE 8798, EA1/251, 59/3/331.

10 https://en.wikipedia.org/wiki/John_Maffey,_1st_Baron_Rugby.

11 Telegram from Fr Murphy from the Auckland Parish of Balmoral to Prime Minister Peter Fraser on 5/5/1948, Archives New Zealand, ACIE 8798, EA1/251, 59/3/331.

12 Telegram from High Commissioner, New Zealand, Canberra, to Minister External Affairs, 13/5/1948, Archives New Zealand, ACIE 8798, EA1/251, 59/3/331.

13 Memo from F. Shanahan, Head of Prime Minister's Department to Under-Secretary of Internal Affairs, 18/5/1948, Archives New Zealand, ACIE 8798, EA1/251, 59/3/331.

14 *Dominion*, 19/5/1948.

15 *Dominion*, 28/4/1948.

16 *Evening Post*, 24/5/1948.

17 *Auckland Star*, 26/5/1948.

18 *Evening Post*, 25/5/1948.

19 Thorn, p.261.

20 Both *Dominion* & *Evening Post*, 26-27/5/1948.

21 *Dominion*, 27/5/1948.

22 *Salient*, Vol 11, No.6, 3/6/1948.

23 *Evening Post*, 27/5/1948.

24 Rory Sweetman, *Bishop in the Dock*, 1997, p.16.

25 Thorn, pp.262-63.

26 Bassett & King, p.307.

27 Fraser's diary, 18-20/12/1948, Archives New Zealand, AECO 18654, PM10/8/23.

28 *Irish Times*, 20/12/1948.

29 *Irish Times*, 21/12/1948, *Irish Independent*, 21/12/1948.

30 Thorn, p.265.

31 Telegram from Fraser to O'Kelly, National Archives of Ireland, Department of Taoiseach, 97/9/477.

32 Thorn, p. 265.

33 Telegram from O'Kelly to Freyberg, National Archives of Ireland, Department of Taoiseach, 97/9/477.

17 Farewells

1 ENA Financial Report July 1945, Burke collection.

2 M. Aylward, 'Achievements in Éire', 7/8/1945, Burke collection.

3 *Evening Post* cutting kept by Mary Burke, c.1978, Burke collection.

4 Personal correspondence from Bernie Gardiner, 10/9/2018.

5 *Evening Post*, 2/7/1969.

6 Max Lambert & Jim Hartley, *The Wahine Disaster*, Wellington, 1969, p.134.

7 ibid, p.196.

8 Author interview with Fr Neil Collins Dalgan Park, August 2017.

9 Author interview with Josie Hogan, January 2015.

10 Material supplied by Josie Hogan and Fr Eamon Aylward, Burke collection.

11 *Taranaki Daily News* c.8/7/1969, clipping provided by Josie Hogan, Burke collection.

12 Proverb sourced from Witi Ihimaera, *Māori Boy*, 2014, p.41.

Bibliography

Primary Sources
New Zealand Gazette

Archives New Zealand
 Government records
 Department of National Service records
 Department of Mobilisation
 Manpower Committees
 Armed Forces Appeal Boards
 Department of Internal Affairs
 Shipping records

National Archives of Ireland
 Department of the Taoiseach

Irish Bureau of Military History
1913–21 Witness Statements (WS)
 WS 374 Mícheál Ó Droighneáin 9 September 1950
 WS 424 Geraldine Dillon (Sister of Joseph Plunkett) 14 September 1950
 WS 674 Capt. J. Togher, Galway Brigade 18 April 1952
 WS 1718 Mícheál Ó Droighneáin 16 December 1959
 WS 1729 Capt. J. Togher, Galway Brigade 25 January 1958
Military Service Pensions Éire: www.mspcsearch.militaryarchives.ie

Burke collection
Burke family papers held by Peter Burke, including Matthias Burke affidavit and transcript of armed forces Appeal Board hearing.
ENA Records
Personal correspondence and interviews:
 Moycullen Historical Society
 St Patrick's College Archives
 Fr Eamon Aylward
 Éamon Ó Cuív
 Ann Furneaux (née Ongley)
 Mike Carr
 John Knox
 Josie Hogan

Aylward collection

Papers, correspondence and photographs collected by Maurice Aylward, now held by
Fr Eamon Aylward, SSC, Dublin.

Newspapers

Auckland Star
Bay of Plenty Beacon
Dominion
Evening Post
Hutt News
Irish Independent
Irish Press
Irish Times
New Zealand Herald
Portland Guardian
Press (Christchurch)
Salient
The Munster Express

Secondary Sources

Books

Barry, Tom, *Guerilla Days in Ireland*, Mercier Press, Cork, 2013.

Bassett, Michael & Michael King, *Tomorrow Comes the Song: A Life of Peter Fraser*, Penguin Books, Auckland, 2000.

Belich, James, *Paradise Reforged: A History of the New Zealanders from the 1880s to the Year 2000*, Allen Lane, Penguin Books, Auckland, 2001.

Bennett, Richard, *The Black and Tans,* Pen & Sword Military, Yorkshire, 1959. Reprinted 2010.

Benson, Richard, *Irish Wit & Wisdom: Quips and Quotes to Suit All Manner of Occasions*, Summersdale Publishers, Chichester, 2016.

Bevan, Denys, *United States Forces in New Zealand 1942–1945*, Macpherson Publishing, Alexandra, 1992.

Bew, Paul, *Churchill & Ireland*, Oxford University Press, Oxford, 2016.

Boyle, Gerry (comp), *Farming and Country Life 1916: History Talks Presented at Teagasc Athenry 10 & 11 June 2016*, Teagasc, Carlow, 2016.

Breen, Dan, *My Fight for Irish Freedom*, Anvil Books, Dublin, 1981.

Brennan, Niall, *Dr Mannix*, Rigby Ltd, Adelaide, 1964.

Clark, Margaret, (ed) *Peter Fraser: Master Politician*, The Dunmore Press, Palmerston North, 1998.

Cole, J.A., *Lord Haw-Haw & William Joyce: The Full Story*, Faber & Faber, London, 1964.

Collins, Neil, *The Splendid Cause: The Missionary Society of St Columban 1916–1954*, The Columba Press, Dublin, 2009.

~ (ed), *Those Who Journeyed With Us: Deceased Columbans 1918–2016*, Missionary Society of St Columban (undated).

Coogan, Tim Pat, *De Valera: Long Fellow, Long Shadow*, Arrow Books, Great Britain, 1995.

Crawford, John (ed) *Kia Kaha: New Zealand in the Second World War*, Oxford University Press, Auckland, 2000.

Faherty, Padhraic, *Barna – A History*, Padhraic Faherty, Galway, 2000.

Fanning, Ronan, *Éamon de Valera: A Will to Power*, Faber & Faber, London, 2015.

Farndale, Nigel, *Haw-Haw: The Tragedy of William and Margaret Joyce*, Macmillan, London, 2005.

Filer, David, *Crete: Death from the Skies – New Zealand's Role in the Loss of Crete*, David Bateman Ltd, Auckland, 2010.

Fisk, Robert, *In Time of War: Ireland, Ulster and the Price of Neutrality 1939–45*, Gill & Macmillan, Dublin, 1983.

Franks, Peter & Jim McAloon, *Labour: The New Zealand Labour Party, 1916–2016*, Victoria University Press, Wellington, 2016.

Grant, David, *Field Punishment No.1: Archibald Baxter, Mark Briggs & New Zealand's Anti-Militarist Tradition*, Steele Roberts, Wellington, 2008.

~ *Out in the Cold: Pacifists and Conscientious Objectors in New Zealand During World War II*, Reed Methuen, Auckland, 1986.

Grose, Peter, *An Awkward Truth: The Bombing of Darwin, February 1942*, Allen & Unwin, Sydney, 2011.

Hanley, Brian, *'None of the Literary Type'. Liam Mellows: His Role in the Galway Easter Rising 1916 and in National Politics 1918–22*, Teagasc, Carlow, 2016.

Henry, William, *Blood for Blood: The Black and Tan War in Galway*, Mercier Press, Cork, 2012.

~ *Coffin Ship: The Wreck of the Brig St. John*, Mercier Press, Cork, 2009.

~ *Famine: Galway's Darkest Years*, Mercier Press, Cork, 2011.

~ *Pathway to Rebellion: Galway 1916*, Mercier Press, Cork, 2016.

Hensley, Gerald, *Beyond the Battlefield: New Zealand and its Allies 1939–45*, Penguin/Viking, Auckland, 2009.

Hobbs, Leslie, *The Thirty-Year Wonders*, Whitcombe & Tombs, Christchurch, 1967.

Holmes, Richard, *Churchill's Bunker: The Cabinet War Rooms and the Culture of Secrecy in Wartime London*, Yale University Press, New Haven & London, 2009.

Ihimaera, Witi, *Māori Boy: A Memoir of Childhood*, Random House, Auckland, 2014.

Jordan, Kevin, *Rebellion in Galway: Easter Rising 1916*, Kevin Jordan, 2016.

Kenny, Tomás, *Galway: Politics and Society, 1910–23*, Maynooth Studies in Local History: Number 95, Four Courts Press, Dublin, 2011.

Kildea, Jeff, *Anzacs and Ireland*, UNSW Press, Sydney, 2007.

Killeen, Richard, *A Short History of Ireland*, Gill & Macmillan, Dublin, 2011.

King, Michael, *God's Farthest Outpost: A History of Catholics in New Zealand*, Viking Penguin Books, Auckland, 1997.

Lambert, Max & Jim Hartley, *The Wahine Disaster*, A.H. & A.W. Reed, Wellington, 1969.

Leary, Peter, *Unapproved Routes: Histories of the Irish Border 1922–1972*, Oxford University Press, Oxford, 2016.

Leeson, David M., *The Black & Tans: British Police and Auxiliaries in the Irish War of Independence 1920–21*, Oxford University Press, Oxford, 2012.

Mannion, Marie (ed), *Centenary Reflections on the 1916 Rising: Galway County Perspectives. Machnamh Céad Bliain ar Éirí Amach 1916: Dearcadh Chontae na Gaillimhe*, Galway County Council, 2016.

McEwan, Watty, *The Salamander's Brood*, Fraser Books, 2007.

McGarry, Fearghal, *The Rising: Ireland: Easter 1916*, Oxford University Press, Oxford, 2010.

Morton, H.V., *Atlantic Meeting*, Methuen & Co Ltd, London, 1943.

Murrow, Edward, 'On Winston Churchill: Introduction to Churchill War Speech Excerpts', CBS broadcast, New York, 1954.

Niall, Brenda, *Mannix*, Text Publishing, Melbourne, 2015.

Ó Laoi, Pádraic, *History of Castlegar Parish*, Connacht Tribune Ltd, Galway, (undated).

-   *Fr. Griffin 1892–1920*, Connacht Tribune Ltd, Galway, 1994.

O'Mahony, Peter Tynan (Ed), *Éamon de Valera 1882–1975: The Controversial Giant of Modern Ireland, a Survey in Text and Pictures of the Life and Influence of a Famous Leader*, The Irish Times, Dublin, 1976.

O'Malley, Cormac K.H. & Cormac Ó Comhraí, *The Men Will Talk To Me: Galway Interviews by Ernie O'Malley*, Mercier Press, Cork, 2013.

O'Shaughnessy, Margaret (ed), *Foynes Flying Boat & Maritime Museum*, Foynes Flying Boat & Maritime Museum, 2015.

Pritchard, David (ed), *Chronology of Irish History*, Geddes & Grosset, Scotland, 2009.

Russell, Andrew (compiler), *The Brendan Behan Quotation Book*, Somerville Press Ltd, Cork, 2015.

Sinclair, Keith, *Walter Nash*, Auckland University Press, Auckland, 1976.

Stelzer, Cita, *Dinner with Churchill: Policy-Making at the Dinner Table*, Short Books, London, 2011.

Sweetman, Rory, *Bishop in the Dock: The Sedition Trial of James Liston*, Auckland University Press, Auckland, 1997.

Taylor, Nancy M., *The Home Front: The Official History of New Zealand in the Second World War 1939–45: Vol 1*, Department of Internal Affairs, Wellington, 1986.

Templeton, Hugh (ed), *Mr Ambassador: Memoirs of Sir Carl Berendsen*, Victoria University Press, Wellington, 2009.

Thompson, R.W., *Generalissimo Churchill*, Hodder & Stoughton, London, 1973.

Thorn, James, *Peter Fraser: New Zealand's Wartime Prime Minister*, Odhams Press, London, 1952.

Wicksteed, Major M.R. (ed), *The New Zealand Army: A History From the 1840s to the 1980s*, Government Printing Office, Wellington, 1983.

Articles and periodicals

Cookson, John, 'Illiberal New Zealand: The Formation of Government Policy on Conscientious Objection, 1940–1', *New Zealand Journal of History*, Vol. 17, No.2, 1983, pp.120–43.

Fanning, R., 'Why is Éamon de Valera so unpopular on both sides of the Irish Sea?', *Irish Times*, Dublin, 24 November 2015, https://www.irishtimes.com/culture/books/ronan-fanning-why-is-éamon-de-valera-so-unpopular-on-both-sides-of-the-irish-sea-1.2441872

Fennell, Jonathan, 'Soldiers and Social Change', 2017, https://defenceindepth.co/2017/05/17/soldiers-and-social-change/

Ferriter, Diarmaid, 'Churchill Proceedings – 'The Dev' and Mr Churchill: An Irish nationalist's view of a complicated relationship', *Finest Hour 145*, Winter 2009–10, p.48.

Freeman, David, 'Winston Churchill and Éamon de Valera: A thirty-year "relationship",' *Finest Hour Extras*, 2008, https://winstonchurchill.org/publications/finest-hour-extras/churchill-and-eamon-de-valera-thirty-year-relationship/

Galway Museum, 'Revolution in Galway: 1913–23', Galway, undated.

Hensley, Gerald, 'Peter Fraser at War', Ministry of Culture & Heritage Seminar, 2011, https://nzhistory.govt.nz/files/documents/peter-fraser-at-war.pdf

Horton, Murray, 'The Secret History of WWII in New Zealand', (first published in *Canta*, 1974) *Redline – Contemporary Marxist Analysis* https://rdln.wordpress.com/2011/07/20/the-secret-history-of-ww2/

Kimball, Warren, F., Churchill Proceedings – 'That Neutral Island', *Finest Hour 145*, Winter 2009–10, p.54.

McCarthy, Frank, 'Singapore Harriers, A Pictorial Record of the R.N.Z.A.F No.1 Aerodrome Construction Squadron, Malaya 1941–1942', Neville Newcomb Ltd, Auckland, undated.

McDonagh, Darren, 'Military Activity in the Peripheral Region of Moycullen from 1916 to 1923', sourced from Moycullen Historical Society, undated.

Roosevelt, Franklin D., *Speech by Franklin D. Roosevelt*, New York Transcript, 1941. https://www.loc.gov/resource/afc1986022.afc1986022_ms2201/?st=text

Sheenan, John, 'Gerald Griffin, First PSA "Organiser"', 2009, www.psa100.org.nz/assets/Uploads/Gerald-Griffin-by-john-Sheenan.pdf

Tate, Margaret, 'An Indeterminate Sentence: The Shannon Objector Camps 1942–1947', *Manawatu Journal of History*, 2016, No.12, pp.35–46.

The Patrician, St Patrick's College, Wellington.

Van Esbeck, Edmund, 'The Rugby Man', in Peter Tynan O'Mahony, (Ed), *Éamon de Valera 1882–1975: The Controversial Giant of Modern Ireland, a Survey in Text and Pictures of the Life and Influence of a Famous Leader*, Irish Times, Dublin, 1976, pp.128–29.

Websites

New Zealand History; https://nzhistory.govt.nz/

Te Ara Encyclopaedia of New Zealand: https://teara.govt.nz/en

Wikipedia: https://en.wikipedia.org/wiki

Index

Peter Burke was born in Wellington and is an old boy of St Francis Xavier School Tawa and St Patrick's College. He has worked for more than 50 years as a journalist in television, radio, print and public relations, travelling widely overseas to cover politics, trade and agriculture. Peter has a small farm on the Kāpiti Coast but Ireland is his second home. His visits to the Emerald Isle have led him to a deep love of Irish and family history.

www.true-to-ireland.com